PELICAN BOOKS

THE HOME OF MAN

Barbara Ward was born in 1914 and took a degree in Politics, Philosophy and Economics at Oxford (1935). She has worked as a university lecturer and for the *Economist*. She was a Governor of Sadler's Wells and the Old Vic (1944–53) as well as a Governor of the BBC (1946–50). She has been awarded honorary doctorates by, among others, Fordham, Columbia and Harvard Universities and Smith and Kenyon Colleges. Her publications include *The West at Bay* (1948), *Policy for the West* (1951, published by Penguins), *India and the West* (1959), *Spaceship Earth* (1966), *The Lopsided World* (1968), and *Only One Earth* (1972, published by Penguins). Barbara Ward was Schweitzer Professor of International Economic Development at Columbia University from 1968 to 1973. She was President of the Conservation Society in 1973 and she was made Dame Commander Order of the British Empire in 1974.

Books by Barbara Ward

THE HOME OF MAN

Barbara Ward

Introduction by Enrique Peñalosa
Secretary-General, United Nations Conference
on Human Settlements

PENGUIN BOOKS

Penguin Books Ltd, Harmondsworth, Middlesex, England
Penguin Books, 625 Madison Avenue, New York, New York 10022, U.S.A.
Penguin Books Australia Ltd, Ringwood, Victoria, Australia
Penguin Books Canada Ltd, 41 Steelcase Road West, Markham, Ontario, Canada
Penguin Books (N.Z.) Ltd, 182–190 Wairau Road, Auckland 10, New Zealand

—

Published simultaneously by Penguin Books and André Deutsch 1976

—

Copyright © The International Institute for Environment and Development, 1976

—

Printed in Great Britain by
Richard Clay (The Chaucer Press) Ltd, Bungay, Suffolk

CONTENTS

Photographs appear between pages 144 and 145

INTRODUCTION

WHAT Barbara Ward is saying in *The Home of Man* is that we are living at a juncture of history in which decisions made or unmade will be crucial not just to the future happiness of one group or another but to all humanity and even to the continuance of life on earth. While I am convinced that this is true, it is also a presumption. In every age men have laid claim to epochal importance, and judgments of relative historical influence are measured quite differently according to vantage points of nation, culture, or religion.

The case for the second half of the twentieth century, and it is set forth brilliantly in the following pages, is not only or even mainly that it is an era of unremitting and inescapable upheaval—in population growth, technology, and political transformation—but that the fact of universality has overtaken us before we are politically and socially able to deal with it.

In recent years the governments of the world have convened a series of extraordinary conferences which have sought to begin a global inquiry into the possibilities of the human future: Stockholm on the environment, Bucharest on population growth, Rome on food supplies, Caracas on the uses of the sea, Mexico City on the role and status of women, and now Vancouver on shelter and the human habitat. Paralleling these conferences have also been the meetings of the United Nations Conference on Trade and Development and the seventh special session of the General Assembly to weigh changes in the world economic order and in the organization of the international community.

Habitat, the United Nations Conference on Human Settlements—to which this book directly relates—is in a sense a synthesis of all these concerns, for it is in human settlements that nearly all people play out their individual lives, benefiting or suffering from a world system which can be judged to be in either a crisis of dissolution or the throes of regeneration.

I also think this book is a synthesis of Barbara Ward's writing, teaching, and lecturing, in which she has so eloquently pleaded for a new understanding of the interdependence of peoples, for planetary management of both the human and the natural environment, and for the moral as well as economic justification and need for a new world order.

In the past two years, as Secretary-General of the Habitat Conference, I have visited nearly one hundred countries to discuss with political and intellectual leaders what is most needed to enhance the quality of life for their peoples. From these discussions I am increasingly convinced that existing technologies are capable of a stupendous improvement in the human condition everywhere on earth if—and only if—they are supported by effective political commitment at both the national and international levels.

This is the issue which is put by *The Home of Man* on the eve of the Habitat conference. Do we have the nerve, vision, and steadiness of purpose to fashion a new relationship within the human community in which men can live together productively and within the natural environment which sustains us?

I do not personally believe that life itself will be extinguished, despite the perils of the nuclear age and the myriad other assaults on our ecological support system. Sooner or later the necessary decisions will be taken. What is at issue now is the degree of human suffering and environmental damage that will be the consequence of unnecessary delay, and also whether the degree of delay will not steadily diminish the chances that change will occur within a context of freedom, human diversity, and tolerance.

Barbara Ward's unique contribution to the analysis and understanding of these issues is more than her skills as economist, social theorist, and writer-advocate. With her dedication and personal energy, and her ability to state her case free of official restraints, she has become the rallying point of a growing movement which demands that the international community reset its priorities and come to grips with the real rather than cosmetic problems of mankind. I would also like to join the author in paying tribute to the memory of the late planner and founder of the Ekistics movement, Constantinos Doxiadis, who must be acknowledged as the modern father of the science of human settlement.

Enrique Peñalosa
Secretary-General, United Nations Conference on Human Settlements

AUTHOR'S NOTE

RARELY CAN an author have reason to be grateful to so many people for so much help. The materials for this book could not have been assembled and sifted without the dedicated work of Stephanie Rice Warren and David Satterthwaite. It would never have emerged from the writer's hieroglyphics without the continuous and invaluable help of Irene Hunter and, in the final stages, of Philippa Barton and Robert Jackson. David Runnalls, Robert Stein, Gerald Leach, Brian Johnson, Christian Halby, Richard Sandbrook, and John Sweeney—all colleagues and friends at the International Institute for Environment and Development—gave admirable advice and searching editorial criticism. They in turn join the author in thanking Mrs. Margaret Rose for all that she has done to sustain their efforts.

An even wider group of helpful and friendly correspondents around the world must be thanked for the patience and care with which they have been ready to contribute papers or answer queries— Mr. David O. Aradeon, Professor Thomas Blair, Mr. Christopher Benninger, Professor Keith Branigan, Miss Coralee Bryant, Mr. Eric Carlson, Dr. George Coelho, Mr. Charles Correa, Professor Jean Gottman, Mr. Frederick Guttheim, Dr. Jorge Hardoy, Professor Chauncy Harris, Professor Jens Hedegaard, Sir James Jones, Professor Otto Koenigsberger, Dr. Appridocio Laquian, Mr. Jack Mundey, Mr. Max Nicholson, Mr. Wilfred Owen, Mrs. Anne Power, Mr. Jonathan Power, Miss Rosemary Righter, Dr. C. A. Shivaramakrishnan, Mrs. Jane Stein, Mr. John Turner, Dr. Luis Unikel, and Mr. Peter Wilsher. Colleagues who have given admirable assistance in various technical tasks include Mr. Tibor Farkas, responsible for the illustrations, and Mr. Philip Quigg, for liaison with the publishers. Thanks are due to the World Bank, the OECD, and other national and international agencies for their unfailing readiness to provide facts and statistics. These official statistics have been used throughout the book, unless exceptions are specified. Thanks are also due New York University Press for permission to use material from the Foreword of *Hunger, Politics and Markets*.

Above all, the Canadian Government, "onlie begetter" of the whole enterprise, must be most warmly thanked for unstinting financial support and encouragement. Their generosity makes it possible to devote all the royalties that may be earned by *The Home of Man* to popular education about the needs of human settlements. Special thanks are also due to the World Bank for a grant that assisted materially in the preparation and distribution of the book.

One debt of gratitude cannot, unhappily, be paid to the living. The author is deeply conscious of the degree to which her own interest—and perhaps that of the world at large—was first stimulated in human settlements by a beloved friend and teacher, now deceased. But at least it is possible to recognize the debt and dedicate this book, gratefully and sadly,

to the memory of

CONSTANTINOS DOXIADIS

PROLOGUE

THERE ARE two reasons why it is exceedingly difficult to get a coherent grip on the issue of the human habitat—the settlement where all the world's peoples, save for dwindling groups of nomads, are born, live out their lives, and go to their death.

The first reason is that this habitat includes everything. A Roman dramatist once said: "Nothing human is alien to me." How much more true is this of the inescapable context within which the whole of existence is carried out. What *can* we leave out when we are talking of the complete life cycle of mankind? Yet to try to grasp everything is to risk grasping nothing. The entirety of the human condition certainly escapes the statistician. It probably escapes the poet. So whatever is written about our habitat must submit to being incomplete. Perhaps, as a result, it will leave out vital clues to coherence and understanding.

The second reason is even more daunting. At no time in human history has the man-made environment of life been in such a state of convulsed and complete crisis. This is not to suggest that great upheavals have not repeatedly overtaken humanity. Great civilizations have perished. Empires have fallen. On the very threshold of the so-called Age of Progress, in the seventeenth century, a perturbed observer like Sir Thomas Browne could observe: "The world's great mutations are ended." Throughout history, in the dark aftermath of plague or war, folk songs and ballads are full of the loss and collapse of human hopes. Compare this Elizabethan verse:

> Brightness falls from the air
> Queens have died young and fair

with the lament made for the destruction of man's earliest city, Ur, about the year 2000 B.C.:

Verily all my birds and winged creatures
                have flown away—
"Alas! for my city" I will say.
My daughters and my sons have been carried off—
"Alas! for my men," I will say.
O my city which exists no longer, my city
                attacked without cause,
O my city attacked and destroyed!

Few lives, indeed, have escaped all echo of the mourning cry in Ecclesiastes: "Man is born to trouble as the spark flyeth upwards."

But if the intensity of crisis is not new, sheer scale undoubtedly is. The figures are becoming so well known that it is hard to remind ourselves how phenomenal they are. Yet they must be repeated. On any recognizable definition of what is a human being, it took at least half a million years for the first 100 million people to appear on the face of the earth—at about the year 1000 B.C. in the wake of improvements in agriculture and increase in food supplies brought about first by Neolithic man and then by the great river valley civilizations in Egypt and Mesopotamia, in North India and China. Farming, handicrafts, and commerce continued to develop irregularly but expansively for the next 2,500 years. By about 1500 A.D., there were perhaps 500 million human beings on earth.

Then the great accelerations began—in knowledge, in power, in resources and technology, in mobility, in conquest. The first thousand million mark for humanity was passed about 1830. The next thousand million took only a hundred years, the next only thirty. Today, with almost four thousand million beings on the planet, the added thousand million has taken only fifteen years. This rate of growth means that in the first decade of the next century, a whole new world, equivalent in numbers to this one, will be piled on top of the present level of population. Further ahead, the predictions become even more fantastic. In fact, unchecked, they could be adding well over 250 million people a year by 2034, the bicentenary of the death of Thomas Malthus—the first man to postulate the theorem that population would always grow to exhaust the available food supplies. But such predictions belong to the world of dream—or rather of nightmare. Before such increases could take place, the old destroyers, hunger, war, plague, "death on a pale horse," would have wiped out the surplus. What we are concerned with today is the imminent doubling of our planetary numbers in less than forty years.

Scale is not the end of the cataclysmic nature of modern change. Once again, the figures are known and repetition can stale their impact. Yet we have to make the effort of imagination needed to realize that after some fifteen to twenty thousand years of organized human existence in recognizable settlements, the whole character of this habitat is being radically transformed in less than a hundred years. If we take "urban" as the adjective to qualify settlements of more than 20,000 inhabitants, throughout most of human history at least ninety percent of the people have lived not in cities but in hamlets, villages, or at most in small towns. At the time of the American Revolution, for instance, this was the percentage of Americans living in centers of no more than 2,500 people.

Now compare with this the sudden explosive acceleration of change in the twentieth century. After a hundred years or so of industrialization, the number of people in urban areas at the end of the nineteenth century was about 250 million in a world population of 1650 million—the urban population accounting for fifteen percent of the world total, a little higher than the earlier urban figure of ten percent but still leaving the world's rural peoples in overwhelming predominance. And now in just a century, this millennial relationship is being overthrown with almost inconceivable speed. By 1960, urban populations had grown to a thousand million in a world of three thousand million—only a two to one rural-urban ratio. Today, urban peoples are racing toward the 1500 million mark out of a total world population of four thousand million. Ten years from now, they will pass the two thousand million level. By the year 2000, there will actually be more urban dwellers than rural people in a world population which will have risen to between six and seven thousand million.

We also have to realize what an astonishingly new phenomenon is the city of a million people. Probably neither Rome nor Byzantium reached that peak even at their greatest extent. True, if Marco Polo's impressions can be trusted, Kinsai in China—on the site of today's Hankow—may have had three million inhabitants in the thirteenth century and Edo—as Tokyo was first called—seems to have reached a million by the eighteenth century. But the concept of a "big city" did not go much beyond 100,000 until the beginnings of the nineteenth century; it is almost comical to recall that at the time of the American Revolution, only two cities, Boston and Philadelphia, had even reached 50,000.

Then with the spread of industrialization and of world-wide trade, the city of a million begins to race ahead. London reached the mark in the 1820s. By 1900, there were eleven "million-cities," six of them in Europe, still the imperial and commercial dominant of the world. But the jump from two to eleven in the nineteenth century has been followed by an infinitely more formidable acceleration in our own time. By 1950, there were seventy-five "million-cities," fifty-one of them in developed regions, twenty-four in the developing world. Today, the developing nations have pulled ahead. They contain 101 such cities, out of a world total of 191. By 1985, the million-city will have jumped from 11 to 273 in less than a century—and 147 of them will be in the less developed lands.

And even this vast multiplication does not fully measure the contemporary upheaval in human settlements. The million-city begins to explode into the ten-million city. There were two of them in 1950—New York and London. By 1970 there were four. But by 1985, there will be at least seventeen of these gigantic agglomerations, ten of them in developing areas—with Mexico City, at nearly eighteen million, only a step behind New York. And at the head of the list Edo's successor, Tokyo, will recover its earlier primacy with the dubious distinction of bringing 25 million people together in a single conurbation.

We may, of course, question whether some of the more surrealist predictions—for instance, Calcutta and Bombay with perhaps 100 million inhabitants—will ever be reached. Various degrees of urban collapse may well have intervened. But the projections are valuable as indicators of the sheer avalanche-like scale with which the world's peoples are increasing, heaving themselves out of the millennial framework of village and small town, and descending in deluges of mixed hope and despair on the world's larger settlements.

To seek analogies for change on this scale, one has the obscure feeling that only the distant billennia of geological time can provide any adequate concept of the scale of upheaval. The Indian subcontinent detaching itself from Antarctica and sweeping across the Indian Ocean to its violent collision with Asia's land mass along the Himalayas, the sea pouring in to change the Caribbean or the South China Seas into a chain of islands, the grinding of continental plates against each other, heaving up the Andes and leaving volcanic chains where Asia and Europe collide—these are surely the images that are appropriate to the scale of the twentieth century's urban deluge. We are in the full tide of this great sweep. Its final consequences lie ahead, but already the ground shakes. We should hear, if we were listening, the mutter of the approaching storm. And the upheaval is not simply a physical upheaval, the largest increase and "wandering of the peoples" in human history. It is taking place within two wider but equally unstable contexts, one social, the other ecological. They, too, are unique in the experience of mankind.

The social context is the deepening conquest of the human imagination by a dimly perceived but passionately longed-for vision of equality and dignity for every human being. This dream has, no doubt, many roots—archetypal memories of the unself-conscious equality of tribal society, the millennial Neolithic experience of shared tasks and modest returns in early agriculture, passionate revulsion against arrogance and greed in the wake of man's first experiments in "high" civilization—in Babylon or Mohenjo-Daro, in Ch'Ang An or Rome. But for modern society, the Biblical strain is unmistakable. The great Hebrew prophets—from Isaiah to Karl Marx—have called on man "to undo the thongs of the yoke, to let the enslaved go free . . . sharing your bread with the hungry and bringing the homeless into your house." * The rights of the downtrodden, the duties of the fortunate, the value and dignity of the poor, the harsh condemnation of irresponsible wealth, these are judgments and energies inherited from Western man's Biblical tradition—inherited even when betrayed—and in our own day this tradition either colors the imagination, troubles the conscience, or at least perturbs the complacency of all mankind. And, as our world prepares to add another world equal in numbers to itself in no more than four decades, the cry for greater justice and dignity for all these thousands of millions will not be stilled. On the contrary, it will be raised all the more insistently as numbers and pressures increase.

But it is one thing to underline the fact that people's growing sense

---

* *Isaiah* 58: 6–7.

of their dignity and equality, both individually and collectively, is a near-universal phenomenon, an "inner limit" to the development of planetary society which can be transgressed only at the risk of the severest social disorder and breakdown. It is quite another to achieve even minimum agreement upon the content of this new perception of the human condition.

As a rough first definition we can start by recognizing that any valid concept of dignity and equality includes a number of nonmaterial "goods"—responsibility, security, and participation, the free exchange of thought and experience, a degree of human respect that is independent of monetary rewards or bureaucratic hierarchies, and a realization that this respect is lacking where rewards and hierarchies are too restrictive or too skewed. All these goods of culture, of man's mind and spirit, need not be costly in terms of material resources. Indeed, they belong to the sphere of life where growth is truly exponential—in knowledge, in beauty, in neighborliness and human concern.

But they require physical underpinning. And here the pressures bring us to a further context of great uncertainty and risk. When we try to establish even the minimum physical conditions of a worthy human existence, we confront the widest possible spectrum of uncertainty. For one thing, there are inescapable differences of climate and culture—Arctic housing tells us nothing about tropical standards, or Mediterranean radiance about the midnight sun. Diet, uses of energy, patterns of worship, work and play partly and rightly reflect a vast and precious variety of cultures and social purposes. But we can perhaps accept an irreducible minimum—another "inner limit," this time the limit of physical well-being, which human society transgresses at its peril and which must include food, energy, shelter, and the training and work required to secure them.

It is all too easy to see that even by this exceedingly modest standard, the task of achieving minimum conditions of human dignity for between six and seven thousand million people by the year 2000 constitutes a tremendous physical task, raises wholly new questions about the use, abuse, and exhaustion of resources, and begins, for the first time in human history, to hint at risks to the integrity of the entire life support systems of the planet's biosphere. These, if you like, are the "outer limits" beyond which the human race cannot march—or stray—without risking its own survival.

To take these high abstractions down to a more homely level, we can note that in the crucial area of food, the average North American eats some 1900 pounds of grain a year, all but 150 pounds of it in high protein food such as the products of cattle and poultry. So does the Soviet Union, though with a higher proportion of bread. It is perfectly possible that, for largely sedentary peoples, this diet is as dangerously overgenerous as the 400 pounds of grain eaten by the South Asian is manifestly too little. A biological norm may lie somewhere between the two—an intake of 1000 to 1200 pounds of grain and grain equivalents, the level general in North America in the 1950s and in parts of Europe today, neither region at either time betraying, it must be admitted, any severe signs of general undernourishment. But to bring up to this level two thousand million or so people in developing lands who are now below a decent norm and to insure that the next two thousand million born there achieve it requires little short of a new agricultural revolution with vast increases in supply—for fertilizer, for improved seed, for farm machinery—and equally vast impacts on the world's reserves of soil and water, both in using and possibly in polluting them.

Nor will the fertilizer and machinery be produced or used without a corresponding leap forward in the demand for energy. Once again, an energy "norm" per person is a difficult concept. In spite of some of the follies of prestigious air conditioning, temperate climates do seem, of their nature, to require less lavish energy-use for man's domestic purposes. Only a really determined rejection of the ideals of thrift can explain why a citizen of the United States uses twice as much energy as an equally prosperous citizen of Sweden. But again there must be some halfway house between extravagance and the direst need. Between 1900 and 1970—another of those giant accelerations—world energy consumption rose from about 650 million metric tons of coal equivalent to 6600 million metric tons, more than a tenfold increase and the bulk of it, from 2560 up to 6600 million, occurred in the halcyon Fifties and Sixties with oil at under two dollars a barrel. Rising costs may, perhaps, check the rate of acceleration but estimates as high as 21,800 million metric tons of consumption for the year 2000 have been made in United Nations' surveys.

We should notice that these extrapolations have been based on present use. Yet today the two-thirds of the world's peoples who live in developing countries consume fifteen times less energy, on the average, than do the citizens of developed societies. Given the vast at-tractiveness of substituting mechanical and muscular energy—the man on the tractor for the man with the hoe, not to speak of the single driver in the four-seater car—future energy use may be grossly un-derestimated unless it assumes at least a doubling and trebling of demand among the present poor. Add that to existing extrapolations and the limit of safe exploitation may be fixed not by the availability, cost, or risk of new energy sources but by the "outer limits" of ther-mal pollution on a planetary scale.

Nor should we forget the part played by energy in a further dimen-sion of basic physical need—the need for shelter. In constructing houses, in using them, in creating in them the warmth for cold win-ters, the coolness for torrid summers, and all the services of the house-hold, from cooking to piped water to sewage, which turn a mere build-ing into a treasured home, energy, usually in its cleanest and apparently most trouble-free form—electricity—has come to dominate the houses of the developed world. In fact, the 4,740,000 sub-standard houses of the United States (1970 figure) are defined by lack of services—plumbing, heating—which require energy to provide them, or dilapidation which needs energy for the repairs. The enor-mous gap between energy use in developed and developing countries is in part explained by the degree to which such services are simply unavailable to the poorest groups. A third of the municipalities of Latin America have neither sewage systems nor piped water. The proportion in the Indian subcontinent and parts of Africa is higher still. The open drain down the main street, the contaminated well at the corner crossing—these can be the ugly symbols of man's habitat in energy-poor societies.

Of course, they are not the only symbols. The degradations con-tinue downward in degrees of squalor, from a family to each room (the figure for eighty percent of the people in Calcutta), to four families to a room, to tarpaper shacks, to shift-sleeping in literally makeshift beds, to no rooms or roofs at all and thousands sleeping on the pave-ment. Various U.N. surveys put the number of houses that need to be built to keep up with growing numbers and repair the worst evils of the past at over forty-seven million units every year. The figure can only be an estimate and tells us not too much about the resources required. Rural housing in reasonable climates makes far less claim on materials or energy than the dense tenements of great urban conglomerations. But if the figures are not absolutely precise, they are precise enough to suggest that perhaps a quarter of mankind has barely attained the dignity of a roof and there are seventy million more humans to accommodate every year.

Add to this trend of inadequate food, energy, and shelter the basic needs of training in a world where illiteracy is actually increasing and of work in areas where half the labor force may be underemployed or completely without employment for part of every year and we can see how near the human race is coming to the point at which the "inner limit" of human dignity is finally transgressed and the most rapidly eroding of all resouces, the patience of the poor, will compound the vast material strains entailed in acting in time, on an adequate scale, and without irreversible environmental disruption, to meet humanity's basic needs. Mankind is in fact engaged in a kind of race for survival between the inner and outer boundaries of social pressure and physical constraint while the doubling of the world's peoples and emergence of a half-urban world takes place in only four decades.

These overlapping contexts of violent demographic, social, and environmental change all meet—one could say collide—in human settlements. These places must carry the vast weight of the migrations—overcrowding at the terminus, decay and blight in the deserted areas. They are also the meeting place of all the aspirations and demands of mankind's enlarged sense of its human dignity. In village or town, in suburb or slum, men and women experience in their daily environment the fulfillment or frustration of all the drives and demands of aspiring modernity. Above all, it is in settlements that the physical consequences of the vast upheavals will reach their climax. Millions upon millions crowded in the exploding cities, all too often without the minimal provisions for urban cleanliness, offer man's most concentrated insult to the support systems of air, water, and soil upon whose integrity the survival of life itself depends. If it seems difficult, almost by definition, to grasp the full scale and implications of the problems raised by the human habitat, it seems virtually impossible to do so if they are caught in these changing contexts, this whirling kaleidoscope of interlocking and contradictory forces, needs, aspirations, and risks.

But, remarkably enough, the vast and uncertain contexts of explosive growth, explosive aspirations, and potential biophysical limits do not compound the problem of devising some sense of meaning and strategy in our approach to human settlements. On the contrary, the three contexts, rightly placed and judged, can provide clues for analysis and priorities for action. The demographic flood is potentially so damaging precisely because it is a flood; in other words, an unmanaged, unintended, disorganized rush, pellmell, into the new urban order. But what this suggests is not further confusion but the opposite intention—a fully human one— to grasp the meaning of the phenomenon and produce urban settlements not by chance but by some measure of design. The first pointer is thus away from building the city by chance and toward the city built for human purposes.

Then the other two contexts fall better into place. For the first purpose of any settlement must be to end inhuman deprivation. There are a great many other needs, no doubt. And some of the aspirations of more fortunate citizens may, consciously or unconsciously, contribute to degradation elsewhere. But this does not change the priority. Before the problem of, say, the highly rewarded but often culturally deprived life-styles of wealthy single-class suburbs is dealt with, families in settlements must be able to satisfy the minimum needs—food, energy, secure shelter, and work. Often there are no contradictions. Nothing, for instance, so reduced the death rate of the nineteenth-century poor as the sewage systems built at the instance of the nineteenth-century rich. But cities must be built not for economics alone—to build up the property market—not for politics alone—to glorify the Prince (in whatever form of government). They must be built for people and for the poorest first.

And in this new intended order, the limits on material resources and on the environment must, for the first time, be recognized as fundamental challenges and constraints. The settlement by design, the settlement for people, the conserving and enhancing settlement—these are the priorities suggested by the convoluted and interdependent revolutions of our time. With these three priorities as strategic guidelines, the tactics of the business—land use, shelter, utilities, traffic, work, recreation, convenience, beauty—can be rationally considered and some decisions for policy arrived at. We do not need to repeat the pessimism of Clemenceau in 1919. As he said, we do indeed have chaos. But, unlike him, we can realize that we have enough "to make a world."

Part One: The Coming of the City

1 SETTLEMENTS AND EMPIRES

WHEN WE LOOK at the explosion of growth and change in the twentieth-century city, the first question must surely be how and why mankind ever came to reach this extraordinary upheaval in all traditional scales and types of settlement. What process of history brought him here? How did he make the quantum jump from settlements of 2,000 to the megacity of twenty million?

But some will deny that this is the real question. It is perfectly possible to argue that what we confront now is so profoundly unlike the experience of any previous generation that the past has nothing to tell us. The balance between towns and villages in, say, medieval Europe or Attic Greece or Bronze Age Sumeria is simply too different from our own problems to be worth considering. A total discontinuity has intervened. History may not be, in Henry Ford's immortal phrase, "bunk." But it *is* irrelevant.

Yet there are two good reasons for dismissing the argument. Human settlements may have changed unrecognizably, but the people inside them have not. Take the joyful song that has come down to us from Sumeria four thousand years ago, of the gods meeting in assembly:

> They smacked their tongues and sat down to feast
> They ate and drank
> Sweet drink dispelled their fears.
> They sang for joy, drinking strong wine
> Carefree they grew, their hearts elated.

One would hardly maintain that this is not a recognizably modern experience.

Or take an example from diplomacy. From early Assyrian history we have recovered the royal archives covering the years between 1810 and 1760 B.C. Since they are inscribed on baked clay tablets, they have been preserved through four thousand years virtually intact. Their mixture of national self-interest, care, shrewdness, and cynical expediency would not have surprised Machiavelli or Metternich—not to speak of the U.N. debaters. At a more personal level, what author—including this author—has not, at times, echoed the weary complaint of an Egyptian writing over two thousand years ago: "Would that I had words that are unknown, utterances and sayings in fresh language that has not been debased . . . an utterance that has not grown stale." At the simplest level, the familiarity is even more unmistakable. The Sumerian wisecrack "into an open mouth goes the fly" can still be a symbol of credulity after four thousand years. In joy and grief, in duplicity and boredom, in love and fear, the voice of individual men and women come to us across the millennia. We recognize them. They are us—*"mon semblable, mon frère."*

Nor is the resemblance simply one of personal experience and shared humanity. One of the remarkable facts about the human record is the length of time during which, for all their cultural differences, their vast varieties of style and taste and worship and art, the world's great civilizations did not seem to differ very much in the actual physical arrangements and civic institutions of their settled life. Village society, which began some 15,000 years ago, with the invention of settled agriculture, could still be found in much the same physical shape in parts of twentieth-century Asia and Africa.

Cities built three thousand years before European cities in the Middle Ages had as often as not better paved streets, more elaborate sewage systems, greater convenience in bathrooms and lavatories, larger monuments, and more elaborate city walls. Mohenjo-daro, built on the Indus River around 3500 B.C. is certainly no less elaborately laid out than, say, sixteenth-century Paris. The "containers" of civic life show extraordinary continuity.

It can be argued that man's activities inside these cities show a similar continuity. They all have their origins in the need to develop large-scale systems of water management in the great river valley—in Egypt, Mesopotamia, North India, China—and this more elaborate economic base brought more people and hence more strangers together in one place, varied their jobs and responsibilities, increased the exchange of goods, and demanded new institutions—such as kingship and civic religion—to replace the old small-scale loyalties of the agricultural village. According to the noted archeologist Gordon Childe, the invention of the city "is the story of accumulating wealth, of increasing specialization of labor and of expanding trade."

And this process of accumulation and expansion had a further consequence. The invention of the city in the fourth millennium B.C. appears to have coincided with the invention of war. From the very first days of the Cities of the Plain in Mesopotamia, Ur and Uruk, Eridu and Lagash fought each other—for territory, for leadership, to control trade routes, to capture slaves. After a half-millennium of perpetual but indeterminate quarreling they fell victim to a larger movement of violence. The earliest imperial adventure of which we have the full record—that of Sargon of Akkad—added a new dimension to military power and armed conflict. It is worth examining in a little more detail.

About 2400 B.C. a son, Sargon, was born, probably to a family of semi-nomadic Semites. He left the countryside, drawn, like so many millions after him, by the magnet of city life and opportunity. He went to Kish and was skilful enough to become cup-bearer to the King. We need guesswork for the next step but, like many courtiers, he may have acquired an estate for himself and, like some of them, built himself a city, the better to secure dependent settlers and to organize the peasants' work—a process we can still follow in medieval Europe, three thousand years later.

Now with a town of his own—Sargon called it Akkad—he joined in the now familiar exercise of defeating other cities and achieving a recognized supremacy. And there the story might have ended. Sargon of Akkad for a time would have ruled the most powerful city state. Uruk, Lagash, Umma, Ur would have lost their preeminence and another bloody dynastic round would have been played out.

But Sargon did not stop. After conquering the cities of the Plain, both in the Akkadian North and the Sumerian South, he simply went on conquering. He pressed on to the Mediterranean through the cedars of Lebanon. He may have crossed the borders into Anatolia. He conquered Assar and its lands (round today's Mosul) which were later to be the ominous realm of the Assyrians. He hastened south and knocked out the Elamites and on down the Persian Gulf to get control of the growing trade with Bahrein, Oman, and India. This vast realm he kept together—rather like the nineteenth-century British— by "indirect rule," leaving the local leaders in charge but keeping them under constant military surveillance.

The fact that he could do so points to a relatively new kind of specialism, no doubt invented during the wars of the cities—the profession of permanent soldier, dedicated to the arts of war. Sargon himself seems to have been his own inspector-general. He had a long reign—the chroniclers speak of fifty-six years—and spent much of it continuously touring and ruling an empire which covered virtually the whole land mass between Turkey and the Gulf.

The movement was necessary because the enormous variety of peoples, the proud independence of the conquered cities and continued resentment at his imperial pretensions caused revolts in his own lifetime and brought the whole experiment to an end in less than two hundred years. But we are left with the problem of why he did it at all. Earlier Sumerian kings had let supremacy shift round and about from city to city but had not then gone on to pursue every additional opening to sovereignty within sight. What had changed?

We can adduce formidable material reasons for the invention of empire and the imperial city. One certainly played a part in the earlier wars—the temptation to secure manpower by capturing prisoners either as slaves or, after due conditioning, as mercenaries for further wars. Another reason lay in the steady increase in international trade that had developed in the half-millennium between the first King of Ur and the emergence of Sargon. In spite of recurrent war, the life of commerce had gone on developing strongly in Sumer and Akkad. Some artisans and merchants had gone beyond traditional trade— which supplied no more than their own city, each with its circle of dependent villages. Soon their markets and quays, their metal-working quarters, their own busy streets and squares served far more than local commerce. We have cuneiform tablets that are the equivalents of bills of exchange. Money had not quite been invented and many payments were still made in barley. The temple grain store, which took the place of a primitive reserve bank, was prepared to lend at interest to merchants needing cash to cover lengthening commercial operations. Payments, however, were also beginning to be made in gold and silver in the form not of coins but of weights—so many shekels (a unit of weight) for so much material. That coins would quickly develop from this system is shown by the use of the word "shekel" for a type of coin, once the convenience of money became clear.

A vital issue in the whole unfolding of Mesopotamian trade—one which contemporary Japanese and British corporations will easily comprehend—was the shortage of local materials. Apart from the unique scale of food supplies maintained by the perennial irrigation of the Twin Rivers, if manufacturers wanted to produce and merchants to trade, they had to have access to foreign materials.

It is therefore not unreasonable to guess that whether the Sumerian traders resembled the East India Company or Soviet state traders, whether they were private commercial interests, or a mixture of both, the ability to trade freely from Harappa on the Indus to Hatussas in Anatolia was a fundamental economic interest and the upstart Sargon may have been encouraged by both public bodies and private interests to make the trade routes "secure" by taking them over, a short-term solution which, throughout history, has usually led to long-term collapse. Thus at the very start of the human city, we find an almost exact playing out of the commercial dramas of Europe's recent colonialism.

There are thus enough material explanations for the emergence of empire—the "protection of trade routes," monopoly control of resources, rounding up captives for manpower. And the reasons are quite sufficient to explain the steady recurrence of the phenomenon and its equally steady collapse. It starts up because a dominant group has these material interests. It is maintained so long as they can contain the resentment of the peoples they exploit. And, at last, they themselves, wealthy but weakened by internal discontent, are picked off by the next rising ruler with sufficient ambition and power to restart the cycle. All the early civilizations are masters and victims of the process. At the beginning of the second millennium B.C. Hammurabi of Babylon reestablished much of Sargon's domain. In the next millennium, after a rough struggle with the Assyrian Empire, Babylon was briefly restored under a Chaldean ruler only to be submerged forever in 539 B.C. by the incoming Medes and Persians.

In Egypt, for millennia the main disputes were concentrated on the internal rivalry. But a determined imperial exercise began under the first Totmes. About 1600 B.C. he carried his kingdom to the Euphrates, hunted elephants in Syria and claimed—like the British some three thousand years later—an empire "as far as the circuit of the sun." The Egyptian experiment, like the Babylonian, was wiped out by the Persians. They in turn received their death blow from Alexander of Macedon and his Hellenic Empire passed largely to the control of Rome. But the power of Rome in Europe was defeated by its internal weakness and by the frontier wars with Northern and Eastern "barbarians." Moving its headquarters to Byzantium, it lost outlying provinces to the rising power of Islam and was finally overwhelmed by the Turks. Meanwhile the Northern raiders continued their ravages—of Europe, of India, of China and when they ceased, in the fifteenth century, a revived Europe took up the tale and its colonial excursions continued to our own day. Up and up, round and round, down and down go the cycles of empire, perhaps providing the image of earthly reality defined by the Lord Buddha as human bondage to "the melancholy wheel."

If this is the record history presents us with—the ever-renewed round of conquest predetermined by an unshakable commitment to material ambition and greed—can it tell us anything new when our own predicaments can be so easily explained in much the same terms? The city-states have become nation-states. The cities themselves have become megalopolises. One round of empire is over. We wait uneasily fearing that another may be about to begin. It is easy to conclude that the melancholy wheel is still spinning and that "there is nothing left remarkable under the visiting moon."

Easy—but false: if the record is more carefully examined, the dominant themes begin to look much less closed and predetermined. No one can deny the influence of material conditioning. No history of any civilization is without its cycles of war and conquest. But these are not the sole forces by which human destiny has been driven forward in the last four millennia of recorded time. What emerges from the record is much more complex, much more perplexing, infinitely more unlikely and, as a result, much more open and promising. For all the rise and fall of empires, the ruined cities, the poisoned wells, the empty fields and roofless villages, another movement is apparent—of mankind reaching out to grasp, intellectually and morally, the meaning of existence and not to conform to the weight of material conditioning but to transfigure and transcend it. And in this search for meaning, it is simply untrue to claim that power and force are the sole determining factors. In addition, there are Wordsworth's "great allies" . . . exultations, agonies and love and man's unconquerable mind."

The sheer destructiveness of the early cycles of conquest brought about a profound moral revulsion. Sargon's story was only the first. Assurbanipal, emperor of the Assyrians, thus describes his method of conquest:

"I cut off their heads. I burned them with fire; a pile of living men as of heads I set up against the city gate. Men I impaled on stakes. The city I destroyed, I turned it into mounds and ruins. The young men and maidens in the fire I burned."

For the mass of the people, the revulsion against such horrors was an ignorant misery. A few of the more enlightened rulers—Hammurabi of Babylon, for instance—tried to redirect destructive energies, codifying laws and producing a recognizable internal order. We hear for the first time of the ruler as "the shepherd of his people," an image of mercy even if it implies a fairly low estimate of the capacities of the ruled. But the deepest challenge comes from a new type of activity—one of moral reflection based upon a certain distance from human affairs, a withdrawal to judge them better. Confucius and Lao-Tsu in China, the writers of the Upanishads and the Lord Buddha in Northern India, Akhetatan, Egypt's only kingly monotheist, Hebrew prophets, Greek philosophers—all these men belong to a new class of saints and sages who look on the works of man and judge their strange admixture of good and evil. And from one end of "civilization" to the other, their judgments, however different the emphasis, fundamentally coincide.

It is the nature of man when exposed to too much power and too much greed to become almost literally deranged. In the village, power could not go far among one's own clansmen. Greed could not much exceed the body's physical limits of consumption. But in the city, with trade stretching across continents and money invented as a medium of exchange, greed could become abstract and hence unlimited. It was the same with power. Controlling distant peoples, exercising mighty decisions, setting in motion vast upheavals—armies, floods, battering rams, conflagrations—arrogance would feed on itself and make leaders all but literally drunk with power.

If the analysis is the same in all great ethical systems, so is the answer. Part of it is personal. Internal restraint must sufficiently command the insistent ego so that it can recognize the equal claims and rights of other selves—the homely wisdom of "do as you would be done by," the sublime command "love thy neighbor as thyself." In part the answer is social. In the community at large, law, not blind interests, must prevail and it reflects in a true if indefinable sense an order of rightness and goodness rooted in the nature of Reality itself. To give a traditional Chinese formulation of this dual rule, the emperor dedicates the whole realm each year to "the way of heaven." He himself by his personal virtue is worthy to carry "the mantle of heaven." His personal righteousness is the guarantee of society's good order.

Of the virtually universal reassessments of human existence in the first millennium B.C., there are two which deserve particular attention. This is partly because they are still potent among us and to this day help to determine what human beings expect and accomplish in their settlements. But there is another reason. They are the supreme illustration of the fact that material power, however elaborately organized, however mightily arrayed, simply is not the final determinant of human destiny. On the contrary, there come moments in history when ideas and experiences, acting almost with the energy of nuclei breaking free in superheated plasma, create a tremendous release of energy and form new ideas, new insights, new expansions of the human imagination which, in their turn, set mankind upon a new route.

The whole world today—even the fifth of it that is Chinese—is in a ferment of change because of a fusion process between intellectual rigor and moral passion in the imagination of the Greeks and the Jews. Yet, two and a half millennia ago, it would have seemed comical to compare the contemporary power of Persia or the glory of Egypt with the material poverty and physical limitations of these two small peoples. The city-states which grew up in Ionia and Attica were poor. Rocky hills and valleys dipping down over short flood plains to a treacherous sea made up the physical background of Greek life. The Israelites, one small community among the vast spread of Semitic peoples in the Fertile Crescent, were never, even under Solomon, more than a minor kingdom compared with their mighty neighbors. Some of their profoundest moral insights were gained when they were actually in exile in other people's empires. If physical power were the determinant of destiny, both Jews and Greeks would have vanished from history without a trace.

Yet it is from the Greeks we inherit the first decisive break with the "civilized" concept of kingship. When the Dorian invaders came down into Greece halfway through the first millennium B.C., they found preexisting Mycenean cities and might easily have gone the way of Sumeria—setting up city-states with city kings and city gods. Instead, in Attica, they brought together the clans in a single council at Athens. Then in the sixth century B.C. when the pressure of farmers on limited land, slavery for debt, and the leaders' extortions seemed to make the whole system ripe for slave-based feudalism, again the Greeks did something different. Under the guidance of Solon, they ended debt-enslavement, redistributed the land, encouraged trade and specialization—the grape, the vine, the potters' art—opened up the franchise to a wider group of citizens, and set Athens on the way to discovering the basis of democracy, the concept of the citizen's right to live under—and be protected by—laws of his own making.

The other vital Greek innovation was also concerned with law—the possibility of natural laws underlying an orderly universe. The Greeks did not invent mathematics or geometry. Chaldeans and Egyptians had systems of numbering, for large-scale irrigation schemes obviously entailed a lot of exact measurement. But the Greeks carried the whole process forward with a growing realization of the astonishing unity of the underlying laws of mathematics and hence with a sense of deepening confidence in the ultimate unity of the universe itself. On the nature of this unity, the guesses were varied—water, flux, air, atoms, archetypal ideas. But the Greeks set mankind for the first time on the path of conceiving a cosmos based on a unified system of law and open to reason. It would take over two thousand years to reach Einstein's equation $E = Mc^2$, and to discover in the mighty pulse of energy the ultimate material unity of the whole universe. But with the Greeks, the journey began.

The other seminal people—the Jews—introduced into the human debate not so much the concept of justice and compassion as an irresistible moral energy in their pursuit. They also added two other visions to mankind—unique visions or releases of energy so strong and haunting that men are driven by them to this day even though their precise meaning is still obscure. The first is the idea of a purpose—for the Jews a divine purpose—working in history, with man as the instrument, toward some final end—Utopia? The classless society? Perfect democracy? The Coming of the Kingdom? The aim may remain vague, the aspiration is political dynamite.

So is the other vision—that of the primordial importance of equal justice in society. All other traditions taught pity and care for the poor and the outcast. The Jewish prophets give them absolute claims and overriding value. The poor are the last who shall come first. The rich are "sent empty away." This is more than a realization that power and greed can corrupt the human spirit. It is an anathema on the corrupted. They have no hope of even approaching "the kingdom" if they have eaten while others starved or were clothed while others went naked or housed when their neighbors had no shelter. Once again, the form of social order which can realize this uncompromising vision is still obscure. But modern man has experienced four major revolutions in less than two centuries trying to find out. No one has detached the fuse from the dynamite. It burns on.

2 THE LAUNCHING PAD

IN THE TWO millennia that have passed since the centuries of moral revulsion and passionate reassessment, we can see a sort of counterpoint in history between the new insights and the old fatalities. In many ways, until the nineteenth century, the physical surface of human existence does not change very much. Busy cities, artisans' quarters, market places, ships at the quayside waiting to sail for the distant Indies—they were a familiar sight in Sumeria. They were not much different in medieval Europe. The scale was increasing. We read of Venice in the fifteenth century with 50,000 workers and seamen employed in the dockyards, stores, and workshops of the arsenal. But there is nothing unfamiliar about the city's pursuits. We are still with Gordon Childe's "story of accumulating wealth, of increasing specialization of labor and of expanding trade."

Yet the shaping ideas are undergoing a steady and fateful change. In the Christian fusion of Greek and Hebrew thought, kingship as the cornerstone of civic order faded before a king crowned with thorns and enthroned on a gibbet. Whatever the attempts of Baroque despotism to revive *le roi soleil,* the British were decapitating their king in the name of government under law, determined, in the last analysis, by the citizens' consent. The tradition of medieval towns with their elected mayors and self-governing charters lived on in the seventeenth- and eighteenth-century struggle against royal prerogatives, monopolies, and tax-gatherers. And this struggle in turn produced the American Revolution which extended the concept of self-determination to whole communities, and, for the first time, four thousand years after Sargon, produced the rationale of ending empire as an acceptable mode of government.

We can see the same fateful intermingling of old and new in the

concepts of wealth and property. Private property became enshrined as
an absolute right in the struggles against Stuart and French absolutism.
Yet its exclusion of the workers and the poor from full economic participation in society did not only contradict many medieval institutions
and traditions—guild self-organization, alms-giving, care and healing—there were no less than ten great hospitals run by religious
orders in Milan in the late thirteenth century. It also ran counter to a
deeper strain of equality and human dignity. Rural rebels in medieval
Britain sang:

> When Adam delved and Eve she span
> Who was then the gentleman?

In every great cathedral that archetypal image of ultimate democracy,
the Last Judgment, sent kings and lords—and even bishops—to the
Everlasting Bonfire while the poor and the suffering and downtrodden
rose to Eternal Bliss. Concentrations of landed wealth, merchant enterprise, the growing fortunes of colonial trade overlaid but could not
extinguish these uncomfortable contradictions.

Perhaps the most fateful counterpoint could be said to exist between the millennial traditions of work and manufacture handed down
from generation to generation, with practical improvements—better
water wheels for the mills, wider yokes for the oxen, lighter alloys for
ships' cannon—and a new and intoxicating realization that the Greek
image of law in nature could be put to work in order to secure, in
Francis Bacon's word, "the relief and benefit of man's estate." Leonardo da Vinci gave the clue—that mathematics would be the key to
mechanics. In other words, what could be measured could be exactly
repeated. Above all, the producer of all "work"—energy itself—
could be measured. The amount needed to push, pull, or raise a given
weight a given distance, once established, would be the basis of repeatable experiments. Fahrenheit's thermometer, exactly measuring
heat for the first time in the eighteenth century, is as great a
breakthrough in man's settled life as the first invention of sowing, not
plucking, the seeds of grain.

The next two centuries are marked above all by the steady expansion of scientific knowledge and, from the middle of the nineteenth
century onward, its increasing application to man's daily work. Steel-
making had started with the Hittites but had been carried on for three

millennia by the processes of trial and error incorporated in practical experience. But in the nineteenth century, accurate scientific knowledge was required before it was possible to "bond" iron's phosphorous impurities with limestone and open up the use of low-grade ores. Science alone made possible the distilleries where exact knowledge separated all the invaluable components of crude oil. Science alone discovered the links between magnetism, electrical flows between positive and negative poles, the existence of similar waves throughout space and hence the beginnings of electricity generation and of universal and instant audio-visual communication.

And, as the twentieth century opened, electricity also provided the clues to the most fateful of all scientific discoveries—the unleashing of the atom. The Greeks had speculated about the ultimate components of matter. But the atoms they envisaged turned out to be minute entities resembling the solar system—with negative electrons circling in well-defined orbits around a central positive nucleus. This nucleus in turn—so tiny that if an atom were blown up to the size of a house, the nucleus would still be no larger than a pinhead—was found to include other minute particles—neutrons, protons—and to be held together by nature's most powerful bond or concentration of energy. And some of the atoms—above all, uranium 235 atoms—were found to be "fissile." Bombarded by neutrons, their nuclei could be ruptured. Break the nucleus or fuse two nuclei and a chain reaction could start, releasing sufficient energy to destroy whole cities. This indeed was the first "work" for which man used atomic power when the bombs fell in 1945 on Hiroshima and Nagasaki. Moreover, the ruptured nuclei would release more than devastating energy. There are other products of the chain reaction, some of them lethal and some as long-lasting as the cancer-producing plutonium 239 whose radioactivity does not die out for half a million years.

While man was establishing his "mastery" of the atom, parallel scientific studies showed him that in doing so he had discovered the fundamental energy of the entire universe. Every second, 657 million tons of hydrogen nuclei at the core of the sun fuse to form 653 million tons of helium and the lost four million tons are flung across our galaxy. The earth receives a two thousand millionth part of it and uses one percent of that. Yet every harvest ripens, every organic being lives by using this fantastic flow.

And the same scientific progress has uncovered something else. In 1974, a remote satellite picked up the primeval explosion of hydrogen ten thousand million years ago which set in motion the universe we are dimly beginning to perceive. Among thousands of millions of galaxies and suns, planet earth in our sun's solar system cooled down to a lump of matter about five thousand million years ago. Thereafter condensing steam turned to rain and poured down for millennia to fill the oceans. The cracking, subsiding earth crumbled its broken rocks into the waters, and although the resulting "chemical soup," including all the carbon compounds, was played on continuously by fierce solar rays and all kinds of mutations were produced, the oceans could shield the first emergence of organic life about three thousand million years ago and as living creatures began over the billennia to "breathe" out oxygen over this planet, this atmospheric shield of oxygen (with a four percent component of ozone) widened to cover the land. Life followed it out of the oceans to produce all the planet's bewildering variety of natural systems and, at last, not more than two million years ago, something near enough to man to be called his ancestor.

And now, after a period which is no more than a blink of an eyelash in billennial time, we have brought the solar fire, the nuclear energy which sustains all nature, down to earth for "the relief and benefit" of man's estate. The power which required billennia of protective action before any life could coexist with it is now among us, stored in arsenals, deployed in power stations, conceivably waiting to become the major servant of man's settlements. Of all the incredible breakthroughs of the technological order, this is, by all odds, the most fateful. And we can remember with awe that those same Greeks who foresaw the unity of the cosmos and first imagined the atom also gave us the myth of Prometheus who stole the fire of the gods and for his sacrilege was chained to lifeless rock. No discussion of man's future, no consideration of his settled life can leave out the possibility that the legend was not so much a myth as the forewarning of a possible reality.

In intellectual terms, the intensity, the virtuosity, the incredible triumphs of experimental science in the last four hundred years are unequaled in human history. Mathematics has proved to be, as Leonardo da Vinci foresaw, the secret of mechanics, and the machines of man can now be powered by energies comparable to those of the sun itself. Nothing detracts from the intellectual splendor of the discoveries nor from the rigorous and unambiguous dedication to truth entailed in scientific method. But in the end, the understanding and the power are available for any use—not necessarily "benefit," not necessarily "relief." And when we look at the human energies that in fact mobilized the whole modernizing process of science and technology and ultimately unleashed the fateful energies of the atom, we find another phrase of Bacon's perhaps more relevant. The outcome did not depend only upon the scientist's passionate search for truth. It was also driven forward by "the idols of the market, and the idols of the tribe."

During the first critical period of industrial development, the Atlantic "tribes," followed as latecomers by Japan and Russia, had as the base of their expansion a world-wide system of markets which on the one hand they fought over but, on the other, they controlled and shared. One of its earliest features was to build up supplies of raw materials in the New World—with the help of slave labor. By the nineteenth century, the goods manufactured from Europe's and North America's own resources, above all coal and iron, had knocked out much of the old luxury handicraft exports from Asia. India and China, too, became exporters of raw materials—tea, jute, cotton—Malaysia of rubber and tin, Latin America of cocoa, coffee, tin, and copper in exchange for Manchester textiles and Pittsburgh ironware. Africa was brought into the system on the same basis. Having long supplied slaves and gold, it began to be developed for new materials. Palm oil for soap became an indispensable commodity amid unspeakable filth in the new industrial order. Cocoa and coffee were added, diamonds and gold simply appropriated. In the twentieth century, the most fateful of all raw materials came into play—petroleum from Arabia and the Caribbean and the East Indies. This underlying pattern of trade—raw materials from the then colonial or near-colonial world in exchange for manufactured products from Europe and North America—provided the larger framework within which Western industrialization took place. The early centuries of trade gave it a higher base of wealth from which to start. Thereafter, since most of the mines and plantations producing the materials were based on Western investment and control, since all the value derived from processing their products was secured for Western factories, and since the final goods were sold back locally at a rate of return controlled by imperial management, the process made no small contribution to "primitive accumulation" in the West. There can be no question but that this wider framework was a prime stimulus to Western industrialization just as control of all Siberia's mineral reserves played a key role in Soviet development.

All in all, the shape of urban and industrial development in the nineteenth century was one of cities being pushed into existence by the growing requirements of thrusting economic growth. The figures bear this out. Almost invariably the percentage of the work force in industry was higher than the proportion of people living in towns of more than 20,000 inhabitants. In France in 1856, twenty-nine percent of the workers were in industry, but only 10.7 percent of the French people lived in urban areas. In 1890, Sweden had 10.8 percent of its people urbanized while twenty-two percent of the work force were in industry; for Austria the percentages were twelve percent and thirty percent. The most remarkable example is Switzerland at the same period. With cantonal decentralization and dispersed settlements, it contrived to have over forty-five percent of its work force in industry and only thirteen percent of its people in towns.

This does not mean that the ups and downs of the trade cycle did not create times of unemployed misery. But jobs and opportunities grew with their cities' expansion. By the time industry required more sophisticated skills, the character of the urban working class had changed. Education, greater experience of urban life, trade union organization, liberal reforms, wider opprtunities for women were encouraging smaller families and a more competent, self-confident, and stable work force. It was not wholly irrational to think of cities as the "quick forge and forcing house" of modern life, preparing their people to take full advantage of all the opportunities—and risks—of the new technological society. Some of the extraordinary exuberance of nineteenth-century civic activities—the Neuschwastein look of St. Pancras Station in London, the multigabled and turreted town halls, even America's tough self-confident breed of big city mayors—of whom Chicago's Mayor Richard Daley may be the last survivor—all spoke of confidence and strength and the feeling that "tomorrow will be better than today."

It would hardly be an exaggeration to say that every historical and local circumstance that has worked to better the condition of developed settlements has had the opposite effect on the developing world.

Take, first of all, the wider setting of international trade. It was precisely designed in colonial times to bring the surpluses back to the metropolitan power. Investment occurred only in those services which underpinned the export sector—routes from mines and plantations in the interior, ports growing into large coastal cities through which materials were dispatched and manufactures returned. These cities gave virtually no wider stimulus to their own hinterlands, and the lines of communication, all running to the coast, with few or no lateral links, gave an almost visual impression of what the great Dominican economist Pere Lebret called "the milch cow economy." In a very real sense, these ports—Buenos Aires, Lagos, Calcutta, Shanghai, with their modern buildings, installations, and services—were as much part of the developed world economy as today's European *bidonvilles* are a projection of the poorer countries.

It was no part of colonial policy to stimulate local manufacture. At the turn of the nineteenth century, India's textile manufacturers still could not secure protection against competition from Lancashire, and by the time the Tata family made their single-minded and determined effort to build an Indian steel industry, such vital stimulants to industrial growth as the building of the railways had already been completed—by British engineering firms and steelmakers. Nor was there much innovating activity in agriculture outside the plantation and export sector. Having introduced feudal tenure into Latin America, the Iberians maintained it. As late as 1960, some ninety percent of the agricultural land was still owned by ten percent of the people. African food production remained in the condition of communal self-sufficiency. In India, save in the large extension of irrigation, there was nothing to compare with Europe's technical revolution in agriculture. It was the great strength of Japan's independent leap into modernization in the late nineteenth century that its leaders were not tied by colonial dependence to Western controls, models, or *laissez faire*. The "Meiji" revolutionaries gave agricultural reform the first priority and built up early industrialism on small-scale enterprise. As late as the 1930s, the great majority of Japanese firms had fewer than thirty employees.

This is the background—of long subservience to an economic system designed for other nations' interests, of an infrastructure still geared to those interests, of relatively stagnant agriculture, little or no industry, and export cities dominating the urban scene—that we must bear in mind when we examine the settlements of the developing world.

Meanwhile, in the heartland of the colonial systems, the stresses of the new system grew more intolerable, the gap widened between what Benjamin Disraeli called "the two nations—the nation of the rich and the nation of the poor." In 1848, revolutions spread all over Europe. In the same year, the Communist Manifesto was published. Two versions of a possible industrial future began to coexist in a conflict of ideology and interest still unresolved a century and a half later. But before we examine this great debate, we should perhaps look more closely at the actual physical reality of the urban order industrialism was beginning to produce. The debate between rival versions of the industrial society—or about the elements lacking in every version—was not about abstract principles but about grievous realities in the life of man. The conflicts and convergences can be better understood if the actual physical context is first sketched in and the system's claims to orderly development, human justice, and an acceptable environment more accurately judged.

3 THE UNINTENDED CITY

OUR FIRST impression must surely be the degree to which the industrial city appears to have been not so much planned for human purposes as simply beaten into some sort of shape by repeated strokes from gigantic hammers—the hammer of technology and applied power, the overwhelming drive of national self-interest, the single-minded pursuit of economic gain. If a few early examples of these violent changes are taken primarily from Britain, it is simply because the industrial system started there and some of its features have been too widely repeated to be due simply to the idiosyncrasies of a single—even if admittedly eccentric—nation.

As the nineteenth century began, the hammer blows of change fell strongly on London, the capital city, the central point of national pride and will. It was not only the seat of government for Britain but also, with the conquests in India, for a widening imperial system. It was the banking center of an increasingly sophisticated and global system of finance and commerce. It was also the world's largest seaport and as the city passed the million mark in the 1820s, the sheer scale of its consumer market, its diversity of trades and skills, its network of suppliers created a "sucking pull" to draw in still more trade, more skill, and more supplies. Even though some industries moved out—Manchester's new textile factories extinguished the artisans' work at Spitalfields—a hundred others took their place. The building of the railways increased the pressure since London was the hub of the entire system. Such self-reinforcing processes went on to produce a metropolis of four and a half million by the end of the century. And this was only the "inner ring" of the city. First carriages and then suburban railways carried the London sprawl rapidly outwards. By the 1860s, there were just under half a million people in this larger area outside the city center. By 1901, the figure was over two million.

Henry James shuddered at London's "horrible numerosity." Even those who were awestruck rather than horrified by the whole process tended to see in it a more than natural phenomenon—something nearer to a great surging ocean than an ordinary concourse of human beings attending to their own affairs.

Every time "improvements" were introduced, largely by private initiative, homes and shops and small businesses were razed to make room for the new miles of docks, the railway tracks and goodsyards and the grandiose railway stations. Since by definition these were the places where new enterprises tended to settle to take full advantage of the easy transport, they were also the gathering places for the city's labor force. Clearing land for industrial and commercial use thus contracted the land available for accessible working class houses and doubled the pressure on already inadequate space.

Admittedly London was fortunate in its inheritance of royal parks and palaces, its churches and open Inns of Court, above all, in the curving grandeur of its great river. Some new city quarters, too, were laid out with formal magnificence by ducal enterprise in Bloomsbury or private initiative in Cubitt's Belgravia. But, in the main, London simply grew as it could, scrambling outwards without layout or amenities or any plan apparently larger than the next set of streets and a new round of profits. As a result of this outward pressure the value of unimproved land in the expanding suburbs increased between ten- and twentyfold between 1840 and 1870.

The records of how all the building was done are not complete. Much of the work seems to have been carried on by quite small speculative builders, packing the sites with terrace houses, to secure the highest rentals. These mean brick terraces crept steadily onwards. When they encountered and surrounded a pre-existent village, some sense of community would be preserved—around Clapham's Common or Streatham's Parish Church. But communities as such were not planned. The only guides were the money to be made by the sale of land and the erection of those premises—whether factories, warehouses, shops or houses—from which the highest returns could be secured. Charles Dickens gives us a vivid description of what this unplanned, expanding, urbanizing sprawl looked like in North London in the 1840s. The city, he wrote, "like the giant in his traveling boots had made a stride . . . and has set his brick and mortar heel a long way in advance; but the intermediate space between the giant's feet, as yet, is only blighted country and not town."

Thereafter in the intermediate "blight" there would shortly be sown a "disorderly crop of beginnings of mean houses, rising out of the rubbish, as if they had been unskillfully sown."

This impression of "disorder" and "unskillful sowing"—in other words, the lack of any shaping idea or intention behind the whole urban enterprise—was not confined to Charles Dickens. A few years earlier Alexis De Tocqueville had noted exactly the same mixture of private purpose and public muddle in the equally rapid expansion of Manchester:

"Everything in the exterior appearance of the city attests the individual powers of man, nothing the directing power of society. At every turn human liberty shows its capricious, creative force. There is no trace of the slow, continuous action of government."

In fact, this is hardly surprising. Even if some shaping idea of urban form had been in the air, who would have put it into effect? Between the 1780s and the 1830s, Manchester grew from about 40,000 to 142,000 inhabitants. During that period it had no instruments of local government larger than its parishes and did not receive the status of an incorporated borough until 1838. There, as in other cities, the really unavoidable nuisances caused by this lack of administrative capacity were offset by setting up, often through separate acts of parliament, special Commissions elected by property holders and empowered to change rates for particular services—paving streets, putting in city lights, even for the police. The work of Commissions should not be underestimated. It drew the rising business classes into some contact with the results of their industrial activities and widened the number of poorer citizens who could feel some sense of influencing their own fate and hence some interest in the possibilities of a democratic society.

The Commissions also showed practical results. Compared with many of the new industrial cities in Europe, British towns acquired a reputation for cleanliness and safety. But a "directing power" was hardly to be expected from so many separate bodies, some of whom had to exercise extreme ingenuity to guide even essential services through the administrative maze. At one point, for instance, the Manchester Police Commission found itself running the gas works.

But even when orderly, elective municipal government had been achieved, the spirit of the age was not friendly to more socially directed growth. The right expansion was the one that paid for itself. Pleas for "improvements" had to fight every step of the way against earnest town councilors convinced that even a penny rate would divert money from the constructive activities of active entrepreneurs. Perhaps no one has expressed this nineteenth-century faith more eloquently than the contemporary British historian, Thomas Macaulay:

"In every human being there is a wish to ameliorate his own condition. . . . It has often been found that profuse expenditure, heavy taxation, absurd commercial restrictions, corrupt tribunals . . . have not been able to destroy capital so fast as the exertions of private citizens have been able to create it."

So with "private exertions" enthroned, without countervailing public institutions or any fully formulated alternative vision, industrialization continued to sweep the cities forward and outward like an undirected force of nature.

Examples of this self-directing urbanization are not confined to Britain. In Western Europe, in the United States, later in Russia and Japan, the human race simply scrambled itself into the cities of the industrial age. Where, as in France, the despotic rule first of the Baroque period and then of the Revolution and its heir, Napoleon, had concentrated most of the nation's energies on the capital city, the contrast between Paris and every other French town was so astonishing that the German poet Goethe exclaimed: "How much happier this beautiful France would be if it had ten centers instead of one all spreading their light and riches." But in the nineteenth century, such critical developments of the industrial era as the building of the railway network only enhanced the primacy of Paris, the hub into which all the spokes of traffic ran.

Next in exuberance to capital cities came the new manufacturing centers growing up in less than fifty years, their siting largely determined by access to materials and energy. This precondition gave ports a headstart in many areas. It was Manchester's proximity to Liverpool and the opening of the Manchester Ship Canal that permitted it to launch Britain's first vast increase in factory production—the textiles woven by steam-driven machines out of imported American cotton. But in terms of general stimulus—to transport, to easy exchange, to the division of labor, to all the machines needed to make still more machines—railways were literally the prime movers of the new economy on both sides of the Atlantic. They turned Chicago from a staging post in the fur trade to an industrial metropolis in little more than a century. They drew Winnipeg from the empty prairies and Vancouver from the virgin coast. They transformed the small metal workers' establishments of a Sheffield or a Solingen into constituent parts in a whole urban region devoted to the products of iron and steel. And behind this stimulus, particularly for such laggards as Germany and Russia, lay the open purse and direct commands of a government determined to fill out its strategic railway network. "Now thrive the armorers" could have been the motto of most of Europe's steel towns as the twentieth century opened to a new round of competitive, aggressive, national self-assertion and preparations for war.

There was little uniformity about the place or timing of emergent manufacturing centers. A new raw material, a new process, even a new set of town councilors could be enough to ignite the spark. Bristol, for instance, watched Liverpool's rapid expansion as a port for nearly half a century before successfully rebuilding and reinvigorating its own once-busy docks. A sister port in France, Bordeaux, almost literally refused to add industry to its commercial activities until the end of the nineteenth century, at which time it had over 2000 unbroken years of urban and searfaring life behind it. And some cities missed the tide entirely, bypassed by the railroads and later by the highways.

Yet, as the nineteenth century advanced, one could observe a change of mood about these unmodernizing places. They were seen to be suffering from economic stagnation and an exodus of youth; but they began to offer a sense of beauty and social scale that could be compared favorably with the confusions of industrial urbanism. Stately cathedrals and quiet cloisters, medieval and Georgian streets and squares in harmonious proximity, a smaller and more intimate scale of community life helped to raise, in the shape of incontrovertible bricks and mortar, the whole question of the degree to which urbanization at breakneck speed with no "directing power of society" could be genuinely reconciled with the fulfillment of human needs. As the century advanced, some of the urban Utopias—the counter-visions of a more human society—began, surprisingly, to recommend the gothic architecture, social guilds, and parish neighborhoods of medieval towns denounced only a century before for brutish superstition and material squalor.

For the counter-visions were beginning to appear. In the midst of all the awestruck acclamations of the new urban order as the latest and most exhilarating stage in mankind's inevitable progress, the actual experience of the first four decades of headlong growth started to stir in life other judgments and other voices. They varied from Charles Dickens denouncing the profit-makers' calculus in *Hard Times* to Friedrich Engels carefully collecting the social realities of poverty in Manchester for his friend Karl Marx. They included devout Christian peers like Lord Shaftesbury and radical secular reformers like Cobden and Bright. But there was an underlying unity—shock and horror at what a government Blue Book in 1842 called the *Sanitary Condition of the Laboring Population of Great Britain*.

The obvious starting point must be the sheer brutal incidence of disease and death. Until the nineteenth century was well advanced, death rates, particularly infant death rates, were higher in the cities than in the countryside. The Report includes the following illuminating table of the effects on mortality according to both class and location:

Type of Person	Average Age at Death (in years)	
	MANCHESTER	RUTLANDSHIRE
Professional people and the gentry	38	52
Tradesmen, farmers, graziers	20	41
Mechanics, laborers	17	38

The desperately low survival rate of the laboring classes reflected in part the appalling mortality of children. They had first to survive infancy where every circumstance of squalid overcrowding and fetid water made infant diarrhea a pandemic fact of death. But by five or six they were packed off to the factories. The plight of pauper children in Manchester's early cotton mills—where they were often sent manacled from the poor houses—had actually led to corrective legislation. In 1802, pauper children's work was limited to daytime and—the figure is hard to swallow—to *twelve* hours a day. There were not many children hardy enough to survive an eighty-four-hour week. And for adolescents' work no limits were set at all until the 1830s when legislation cut back the hours a little for young people, introduced obligatory breaks for meals, and set aside a couple of hours each day for school. It also established a vital precedent—the appointment of inspectors to see that its provisions were carried out. Yet a Ten Hour Day Bill, generally limiting the hours of women and young people, did not pass until 1847.

Meanwhile the wages earned even by an eighty-hour week were often barely enough to keep a family fed on more than water and oatmeal. William Cobbett stoutly declared that no medieval serf had endured the conditions prevailing in the "enlightened North" where "the poor creatures . . . are compelled to work fourteen hours a day, in a heat of eighty-four degrees and are liable to punishment for looking out at a window of the factory."

He could have added the grime, the smoke, the stench of coal from the furnaces, the perpetual deafening noise, the stinking privies—three for 700 people in one part of Manchester—the garbage left in the streets, the inadequate wells, the frequency of waterless days. As for amenities, the Commissioners collecting evidence for the 1842 report were informed that "in all Lancashire there is only one town, Preston, with a public park and only one, Liverpool, with public baths."

These were the "normal" conditions when trade was good and employment steady. But by the 1830s, a new terror had overtaken the urban poor. At the back of the mind of every working class family lurked the nightmare of seeing the mill close and facing the stark alternative—starvation or the workhouse. Private charity, self-help, meager savings, the beginning of Friendly Societies, support from neighbors, begging—all were stretched as far as they would go. But there was always the risk of something very near starvation at the end of the line. It was the children and grandchildren of these wretched families that produced at the end of the century such miserably stunted, undersized, and undernourished recruits for the Boer War that even the most rigidly Conservative opinion was alerted to the need for some alleviation and reform.

The new industrial quarters of busy, dirty factories, shuttling steam trains, high chimneys belching smoke, mean streets, and overcrowded houses inevitably affected the total environment of the city. The sanitary conditions have already been described. Yet in most industrializing countries, the active force that finally provided the major cities with the heroic sewerage and water systems of the late nineteenth century was not human wisdom but repeated onslaughts of typhoid and cholera. It took some time to convince governments of the essential biological link between diarrhea, typhoid, dysentery, cholera, and foul water. That great pioneer of public health in Britain, Edwin Chadwick, made his first efforts to set up effective sanitary commissions in the 1840s. But it was London's renewed cholera epidemic in the 1850s that at last produced decisive action.

Other pollutions had less effect on the public mind. Once drinking water no longer came directly from the rivers into which sewage was released, the rivers were largely left to fend for themselves. And since, in city after city, for reasons of access and easy transport, the river banks were the chosen sites for industry, the weight of pollutants they had to carry away grew with industrial growth and became steadily more complex with industrial diversification. Friedrich Engels had this to say about Manchester's main river in the 1840s: "a narrow, coal-black, foul-smelling stream full of debris and refuse which it deposits on the shallow right bank. In dry weather, a long string of the most disgusting blackish, green slime pools are left standing on the bank, from the depths of which bubbles of miasmatic gas constantly rise and give forth a stench unendurable even on the bridge forty or fifty feet above the surface of the stream."

By the beginning of the twentieth century, the condition of the rivers in the Ruhr valley's industrial area had become so obnoxious that the municipalities introduced Europe's first integrated river valley antipollution scheme in which a basic principle—of which much more would be heard half a century later—was that "the polluter pays."

But such action was exceptional. To a large degree, rivers and seas are natural cleansers in spite of remarkable environmental insult and can carry on their "priestlike tasks of pure ablution" for long periods before their absorptive threshold is passed, their dissolved oxygen exhausted, and they turn into sluggish swamps. Similarly with air pollution, the winds of the earth are in the main reliable spring cleaners. In any case, "progressive thought" in the nineteenth century was not at all sure that it wanted those pristine skies and smogless mornings. In the 1880s, the Mayor of the thrusting new British city of Middlesborough helped to open its grandiose town hall with what one can only call a panegyric in favor of smoke. "Smoke is an indication of plenty of work (applause)—an indication of prosperous times (cheers) that all classes of work people are employed (cheers). Therefore we are proud of our smoke" (prolonged cheers).

The mayor of Middlesborough notwithstanding, the industrial era did bring totally new conditions of noise, dirt, and pressure right into the city and banished from it the refreshment of greenery and natural life. No doubt the blacksmiths' row or the tanneries had never been very salubrious quarters. But small workshops, bakeries, shopping streets, barbers, wine merchants could all coexist with the town gardens and fine buildings of seasonal aristocrats, local magnates, the cathedral chapter, or the foundling hospital. All the people of the neighborhood would have parish links and shared graveyards. This mixture and diversity of living can still be found in older cities. Rich and poor live literally in the next streets to each other in a Chelsea or a Montparnasse or Brooklyn Heights. This is the essence of what Doctor Johnson and James Boswell felt to be the greatest gift of cities—"the whole of human life in all its variety"—the possibility of mixing cultures and experience and even dimly perceiving, under all the quirks and oddities of human behavior, an underlying shared humanity which is enriched, not endangered, by sharing the same community.

One should not romanticize. There were class divisions and class hostilities in cities long before Stephenson patented the steam engine. But from the start purely industrial cities, with no historic quarters, with no old villages embedded in them, tended to exacerbate the differences based on income and opportunity. Almost every Victorian commentator kept coming back to the extraordinary lack of contact between Manchester's mill owners and mill hands and the fierceness of class divisions in the cotton metropolis. Birmingham, starting from much greater diversity of trades and skills, seems to have experienced much less explosive social tensions. Some parts of London—like some parts of Paris or New York—continued a sort of village life within the wider continuum. One such area—Greenwich Village—even clung to the name.

A central symptom of drawing apart was the suburb. The sheer noise and filth of the cities encouraged people to move away and it is important to remember that, whatever the costs of suburbia—in social integration, in transport, in commuting time—they represent a deep and widespread desire for cleanliness, greenery, fresh air, and a back garden. The first departures from Manchester to a Wilmslow or an Alderley Edge seem to have begun as early as the 1790s. By the middle of the nineteenth century, every city was surrounded by rings of suburbia, with the newly enriched middle classes buying themselves mini-versions of the nobleman's country seat. The growth of Greater London from a million to nearly five million in the nineteenth century was accomplished without benefit of motorcar. But it already foreshadowed the social disruptions the automobile would only increase.

With few exceptions, the social classes began to live more segregated lives. The poor stayed close to the squalors and frictions of the industrial sectors or moved into the rundown inner ring of first-generation suburbs from which the genteel had already departed. The well-to-do were either entrenched in particular inner-city districts—the "West End" of London, Upper Fifth and Park Avenues in New York, Passy/Auteuil in Paris, Westmount in Montreal—or they scattered themselves in villas and gardens more widely still. Since, however, the capital city remained the center where most people still earned their daily bread, the commuter pattern of avalanche-like movement morning and evening began to overtake the new urban regions. By increasing mobility, citizens attempted to offset the loss of another of Dr. Johnson's definitions or urban amenity—convenience achieved by concentration. Yet mobility reinforced social divisions and decreased the possibilities of cultural stimulus and variety.

One can perhaps sum up the three contexts of urban living as the new industrial age entered the twentieth century by saying that settlements were more amorphous than ever, many of them more socially and culturally divided and the majority showing a dubious environmental balance sheet. Sanitation had begun to improve. The pollution of air and water was much the same. But the amenities of an acceptable environment in the broadest sense—beauty, spaciousness, variety, natural sights and sounds beyond the roar of traffic and the confining buildings—these amenities were lessened for millions simply by the scale of the new city sprawl. It did not seem a wholly propitious start to a new order of life, and a number of twentieth-century changes have tended to continue many of the earlier evils and even, for a minority in developed countries and a majority in developing lands, to make them worse.

Part Two: Into the Twentieth Century

4 THE UNINTENDED METROPOLIS

IF WE BEGIN with the first of our three contexts—the idea of city-building with some human design, with some trace of a "directing force of society"—it must be said that, for most of this century, the old hammer blows of unintended change have continued to rain down heavily upon developed settlements. In spite of some small shoots of new ideas—Ebenezer Howard's, for instance, of combining work, home, and leisure in small "garden cities" away from the noise and filth of concentrated industrial urbanism—in spite of the beginnings in postwar Britain of a larger effort to construct whole New Towns and in the Soviet Union to plan and construct at breakneck speed the urban infrastructure of an entire industrialized order, the chief forces molding the patterns of settlements have remained wide open to haphazard chance and change.

In mixed economies, distortions of price in the private urban land market have continued to determine much of the cities' location and use. In the twenty-year boom which followed World War II, we read of fortyfold increases in land values within the giant Tokaido conurbation* in Japan, which includes Tokyo's sixteen million and contains about a third of Japan's total population of 109 million. Rates of increase in site values of ten to twenty-five percent a year were registered in Paris and Madrid in the 1950s and 1960s. British cities experi-

* The Tokaido conurbation includes the cities of Tokyo. Yokohama, Osaka, Nagoya, and Kobe.

enced a nearly 220 percent rise between 1970 and 1975. Since by definition land in urban areas is an unexpandable resource, such gains
have done little or nothing to widen its availability, rationalize and
humanize its use, or benefit in any way the poorer groups. It has
largely helped to swell private fortunes and public costs.

The pattern of price increases—highest in central city areas and on
the suburban fringes—points to three other wholly unplanned social
and technological revolutions. One is, of course, the continued movement of workers out of increasingly capital-intensive agriculture into
the urban and suburban belt. By now, over three-quarters of the population in virtually all developed lands live in or around cities.

Within these urban concentrations, some forms of employment
have greatly increased—sophisticated new chemical and electronic industries, the whole tertiary sector of services, from hotels to beauty
parlors to museums, and a new "quaternary" sector of knowledge—
organizing and managerial professions connected by telephone and
telex and space satellite and computer-printouts to a massive flow of
statistics and abstractions upon which decisions, encompassing global
activities, can be elicited by the "beep-beep" of incoming messages
and answered with the flick of a switch. Meanwhile, the old staple industries—iron and steel, textiles, basic engineering—are shedding
manpower as newer machines and higher levels of automation are generally introduced.

All this adds up to a very great increase in the skills and education
needed for the jobs that are rising in number and an uncertain future
for traditional, less-skilled work which is not. Yet the new work tends
to take place in center-cities with a high concentration of business
headquarters or on fresh sites away from the older industrial areas.
This introduces in city after city a mismatch between work and residence, since the more skilled operators are often the children and
grandchildren of those who escaped to nineteenth-century suburbia.
The less skilled workers can find themselves in run down center-city
housing in areas from which the jobs are draining away. In New York
City, for instance, the largest center of employment in the United
States, the percentage of manufacturing employment fell by more than
a quarter between 1962 and 1972. "Quaternary" employment—
finance, real estate, insurance—rose by twelve percent, tertiary jobs in
the services by a remarkable twenty-two percent. The result is a de-

gree of divorce between work and home, between suburban residence and center-city work—or in reverse between city living and work in the suburbs—which is "solved" by one of the most time-consuming and uncomfortable answers ever stumbled into by urban man—the commuting avalanche.

This vast surge has been enormously increased by the third "hammer blow"—the coming of the automobile. It is a strange paradox that a continuous increase in commuting distances with all the endless hours lost in movement, with all the daily wear and tear of rushed and pressured driving is the result of modern man's most treasured possession. The motorcar has encouraged as well as enabled him to put up with the extraordinary discontinuities of his urban life. The image of the motorcar is the very essence of convenience and untrammeled choice. You take it out when you want it. You pile everything into it—from the family to the groceries. It waits uncomplainingly for any hours you choose to keep—no more worry about feeding the horses or keeping the coachman out so late. For many psyches it offers an immense release of pent-up needs for power and even of aggression—how otherwise would one find such astonishing titles as "Jaguar" given to a lump of metal or "Avenger" to a stolid family four-seater? How else can one explain the virtual unconcern with which the European continent accepts a regular annual massacre of 90,000 citizens on the roads when the same number of deaths in any epidemic would have the whole population screaming for effective countermeasures? There clearly has never been a personal possession which satisfies a greater variety of legitimate needs—and more dubious inclinations.

The scale of increase in the use of automobiles is phenomenal. Since the mass car is an American invention, it was the United States, after World War II, that first saw the breakthrough to hyper-motorization. By 1960, there were about 62 million cars in America, roughly one car for every three people. By now, the proportion is nearly one to two and there are 100 million cars. Western Europe was somewhat laggard. In 1960, 250 million people had a mere 22 million cars. But it was nearer 85 million by 1975 and the proportion of cars to people had risen to nearly one in four. Outside the Atlantic group of developed states, Russia delayed motorization as a matter of state policy. However, in the 1960s, under consumer pressure, it began to take off the brakes. Japan showed American exuberance, increasing car ownership thirty-five times over between 1960 and 1975. And the same trends can be seen beginning in the rest of the world, where a three-fold increase in car population was registered between 1960 and 1975.

It is these remarkable figures that have unleashed a deluge of metal upon the world's settlements. Not by intention but by historic drift, the result is even greater incoherence in the urban patterns of home, work, and leisure. Cars first of all reinforce the regular flood of commuting morning and night. Even where, as in London or Paris or New York, the bulk of commuters still use public transport, thousands prefer private movement and cram the approach roads. They continue to do so even when new subway systems are put in to relieve surface pressure. One of the few laws Professor Parkinson did not formulate—that "traffic rises to fill whatever space is made available for it"—has been given all but universal validity in the last couple of decades. In a Dallas or a Los Angeles, over half the city is turned into roads, freeways, and parking lots, yet the congestion does not diminish. Meanwhile, the original dream of the automobile—its gift of freely chosen times and speeds—gives way to the hour-long waits, breathing other peoples' exhausts, in congealed traffic jams. On weekends, when the pleasures of private choice and private enjoyment should reach their peak, three-hour traffic blocks on the roads back from the beaches have to be accepted as part of the "escape" from the urban condition.

It is not only the commuters' daily yo-yo of in and out movement or the weekenders' obstructed comings and goings that are affected. The outward spread into suburbia of shopping centers, light industry, sports areas, stadia, services of all kinds creates an uneven web of potential destinations all around the traditional center. They can be reached by car but not by anything else. Too far for the pedestrian, too dispersed and thinly stretched for regular bus routes, they tie the worker and shopper and the exerciser and the parent and the teacher to private means of movement and, as it were, impose a two-car family. Thus a convoluted pattern of cross-journeys ties up the urban region in a cocoon of movement which few people, starting from scratch, would have chosen but which they now accept—because the private car makes them possible. Yet in doing so they lose the city's main attractions—"concentration" that produces both convenience and high intellectual stimulus. At the same time, they have also lost the green fields, the open space, the fresh air, the sylvan peace which some of them thought they would find in a suburban setting.

This problem of swamping motorization is not simply a matter of passenger cars. True, in the United States, the most highly motorized country, they account for fifty-five percent of all the energy used in transport. But the shift from railway to road for heavy goods haulage has led to a steady increase both in energy consumption and in the possibilities of congestion, of random movement—empty trucks taking "short cuts" through city centers, commercial deliveries timed for hours of high passenger congestion—and of civic decay when older town quarters and ancient villages are almost literally shaken to pieces as the juggernaut trucks roll through. In all this there is only one consistent thread—one cannot call anything so instinctive a "directing power." It is to use mobility to make up for every other inconvenience in the arrangement of human settlements. This in turn becomes a self-reinforcing cause of further disorder.

Were we to project on to the year 2000 the 1970 trends in motorization, many of the results would seem almost literally incredible. Western Europe's cars would increase from about 85 million to 169 million, American cars from 100 to 154 million, Japan's from 19 million to 66 million. But we have, of course, to remember at this point that all future projections have been invalidated for the time being by a single, colossal change—the quintupling in 1973 of the cost of oil. The great bonanza for the automobile occurred at a price of under two dollars a barrel. The last twenty years have shown us how people behave when super-cheap mobility seems within their grasp. But mobility is unlikely to be super-cheap again for some time—if ever. Even if urban mobility did not need to be reconsidered in terms of convenience and concentration, the question of cost cannot be so easily wished away, especially since it radically affects another critical aspect of settlements strategy—their ability, or failure, to offer their citizens a reasonable degree of fairness in the distribution of social goods.

Here we begin to touch on the second of our contexts—the extent to which the needs of citizens are decently and equitably met in modern settlements. There is no reason for not starting with the issue of mobility. Services are of no use if they are not accessible. In the developed world, many of society's necessities and amenities are now geared to the ownership of cars. Yet private cars, even at their cheapest, have already cut off a fair proportion of people from reasonable mobility. The aged, the handicapped, invalids, children, carless workers—all can be penalized by declining public transport, a greater reliance on private driving, and the priority given to policies of road building which consider virtually only the drivers' interests. It should not be forgotten that one of the main reasons for the violent race riots in Watts, California, in 1965 was the lack of public transport and the virtual marooning of the local people who had simply no way of reaching possible areas of employment.

The deprivations which spring from immobility—or indeed from any other aspect of poverty in modern communities—are all the more bitter for the sufferers because they have become exceptional. The most striking thing about developed economies—market and planned—is that, for the first time in "civilized" history, only a minority are really very poor. The twentieth-century reforms—acceptance of "the general welfare," progressive income tax, social insurance, public health, housing and education, Keynesian demand management in the West and Socialist planning in the East—have lifted the mass of the people out of the basements of sordid poverty. The formal level at which deprivation begins—an income of £1,800 for a family of four in Britain for instance or of $5,000 in the United States—is not a very good comparative guide because purchasing power varies considerably and so does the very different subjective value put by people on what they buy. It used to be said that no Frenchman could survive on English cooking and no Englishman in French housing. Today, a comparable divergence might emerge if one asked a West European which he would prefer—Russia's highly subsidized rents or a five-year wait for a motorcar. But if there are differences of definition, poverty itself seems to have many of the same roots.

First come the personal misfortunes—to be old and alone, to be handicapped, to be unskilled, to have a large family in a society where children's allowances are inadequate. Another more general cause has already been mentioned—a rapid change in types of employment combined with barriers to retraining, to new opportunity or to the mobility to secure both. In a recent survey in Britain, it was found that the areas of greatest deprivation—defined as unemployment, overcrowding, and the need to share bathrooms and toilets—tended to coincide with areas in which a decline in employment for manual labor, together with very old housing stock, marked the receding of an earlier industrial tide, flowing strongly, say, up to World War I, then setting toward a steady ebb. Some of the inner boroughs of London are in this category, a condition repeatedly found in the centers of older cities. In Britain, the worst of all areas for overcrowding, lack of facilities, and lack of work is reckoned to be the Glasgow conurbation along the River Clyde from which shipbuilding, ancillary industries, and even shipping itself have all receded in the last forty years, leaving nearly twenty percent of Clydeside's people to live in slums and, even in a prosperous year like 1971, at least twenty-four percent of the labor force out of work.

Broad strategic activities in both the private and the public sector can make the readjustments more difficult. General inflationary pressure on rents (or rent subsidies) are unavoidable when private agencies can buy land at predevelopment prices, hold out for the highest bidder, and pocket the social increment. This speculative element in a booming market can be matched by negative pressures when areas are beginning to sag. Their inhabitants may simply be blacklisted for mortgages or business loans so that their own power to resist the recession of confidence and activity is severely limited. Worse still, as in the celebrated Rachman scandals in London in the 1950s, or in the rundown neighborhoods of New York City—or, indeed, in most older urban quarters in declining areas—property developers can buy up at cheap rates houses that are just barely usable, pack them with very poor and often migrant tenants, and then use fear tactics to hasten the departure of neighboring houseowners, buying the now empty houses and filling up each place with newcomers at the highest densities. Thus they combine maximum returns with minimum standards and transform redeemable neighborhoods into dense, packed, irredeemable slums.

The running down of property can also be accelerated by stringent rent controls, with no element of the kind of flexibility that could be provided by the alternative of giving rent supplements to poorer families. Landlords simply give up on maintenance and as houses begin to crumble around them, tenants move out and neighborhoods start to experience the most destabilizing of pressures—the feeling that no one wants to stay and that the future is simply downhill all the way. In New York, between 1966 and 1970, 90,000 dwelling units were simply abandoned—and this in a town desperate for cheap accommodation.

To get rid of such areas of vile deprivation is a universal aim in developed societies—from the old derelict wooden homes standing at the center of Moscow to the Watts ghettos in Los Angeles. But some of the methods used over the last thirty years have not so much got rid of slums as shifted them onwards while replacing them with a rather different kind of slum on the same spot. In the 1930s, Rexford Tugwell, President Roosevelt's closest advisor on urban affairs, thus defined his ideal American solution: "My idea is to go first outside centers of population, pick up cheap land, build a whole community and tear down whole slums and make parks of them." In essence, this was a latter-day version of Ebenezer Howard's ideal of a garden city and it was indeed one reason why the Federal Housing Administration, set up under the New Deal, became a considerable force in speeding up the American move to the suburbs.

But after World War II, it was usually too late for the Government to look for "cheap land" outside the city. The property developers and wealthier suburbanites were a jump ahead. Until the late 1960s, there was no machinery or public funds for the planning of whole communities. In any case, inner-city land was far too costly to be turned into parks. The ideal of providing space and light and wiping out the old, unsavory rabbit warrens remained but took a different form, one influenced to some extent by the immense impact on modern architecture of Le Corbusier. His solution to the problem of combining high density with space and light was, of course, to build high towers in parklike surroundings. Yet, with some exceptions, for instance, the remarkable high-rise development of Singapore, these tower blocks and massive uniform, barracks-like high-rise apartment buildings have not produced the hoped-for abolition of slum conditions. Entrances and corridors are too anonymous, the distance from the thirtieth floor to the children playing below too great. A general atmosphere of insecurity has all too often plagued permanent family occupants, and this uncertainty and anonymity also draws in tenants of whom any neighbor could have reason to be scared.

One should not exaggerate. Many large apartment blocks certainly work no worse than the old slums. Young people especially can find the view from the thirtieth floor exhilarating. Sanitary arrangements are usually better, though the state of corridors and elevators is not. But the massive blocks have tended to segregate their occupants both by income and by insecurity from the surrounding city, and in this regard a vertical slum can be harder to live in than a horizontal one. At the extreme of disorder is the celebrated Pruitt Igoe complex in St. Louis, Missouri, which experienced such social breakdown that its tower blocks were never fully occupied and it was in fact three-quarters empty when the decision was taken, quite literally, to blow part of it up.

But there are other reasons why the large apartment blocks have not fulfilled the earlier hopes of doing away with conditions of over-crowding and environmental blight. Again and again, the number of dwellings made available in the new buildings does not equal the number destroyed in the razing of the site. The dispossessed have to double up in other already overcrowded accommodations, and as blight is supposedly suppressed, it is actually spreading. A carefully mapped study of slum areas in Detroit in the 1960s showed that with the "cleaning up" of the waterfront, the area of blight in the city had actually increased.

A second drawback is that even with the most generous subsidies to building and even with rent supplements to family incomes, the economic cost of new construction makes it virtually impossible to ar-range rents low enough for the most deprived—the elderly widow, the single-parent family, the invalids and the handicapped, all of whom could still be accommodated in housing stock so old that it had long since been amortized and rents were nominal.

Another difficulty follows from this. The cost of new construction tempts city governments to resell all or part of the razed sites to devel-opers to build not for subsidized tenants but for those who can afford the new apartments. There is, of course, a serious social case to be made for tempting middle class and professional people back from the suburbs, thus increasing the city's tax base and lessening the frequent division of the center city between the super-rich and the super-poor. But if the new blocks are not to rehouse the former inhabitants, where are they to go?

The problem of how to restore mixed communities without increasing the pressures on the poorer citizens can arise even when no houses have been bulldozed and no sites razed. In many older cities, middle class quarters, handsomely and solidly built over a century ago by the new merchant and professional classes, have since been rented in multiple subtenancies, many families to each house in areas of increasing dilapidation. But the housing itself may still have its outward form of Georgian grace or the sturdy structure of a New York brownstone. In the last two decades of rising affluence, these houses have been sought out by enterprising property developers for resale to wealthier families tired of commuting. But existing tenants must first be "persuaded" to leave. This can be done by all manner of unsavory means, including an end to maintenance and visits by alarming gentlemen, known in London as "winklers," who offer "alternative accommodation" in a manner that amounts to a threat. Poor and aged tenants can be scared out by these means. Then the houses are rebuilt and resold at a large profit. The evicted tenants double up where they can.

The ultimate aim—that of recreating mixed neighborhoods where people can coexist and cooperate—must not be thought of as impossible. It is carried on day by day without too much strain in smaller towns, in the older urban villages, and in large cities where savage nineteenth-century segregations, based on intrusive industries or newly built railways—the "beyond the tracks" divisions—have not been followed by equally savage bulldozing for urban renewal or urban motorways. But the property dealer and the unplanned market will not recreate urban communities. This can be achieved only by intent.

Clear intentions and strategy are as necessary for the third of our contexts—the degree of environmental pressure in developed societies. Although the annual rate of population growth is only about one percent a year and indeed has virtually ceased in some developed countries, the absolute number of citizens using up energy, driving about in cars, throwing away mountainous wastes and confidently expecting to continue to do so, has grown from 857 million to 1135 million in the last twenty-five years. These increases are the key to rising pollution. Take first the increase in energy. Consumption has risen from the equivalent of 1150 million metric tons of coal in 1920 to 6600 million metric tons in 1970, over eighty percent of it in the Northern Hemisphere. One of the ways of illustrating the meaning of the link between energy and wealth is simply to calculate the use of energy not in so many ergs or joules but in terms of "human slaves." Early in the fantastic leap in energy-use, Dr. Buckminster Fuller made the estimate that, in terms of energy, each American had 153 slaves working for him. He must have added about sixty since. These "slaves" do what slaves have always done. They take on the back-breaking labor. They help to cook and clean up. They heat, cool, and illuminate the house. They cut hedges and mow lawns. They bring news from distant lands. Above all, they carry their masters about. Even two centuries ago, no feudal lord in Europe enjoyed the degree of convenience and variety at the disposal of a modern middle class household.

But the price that is paid is pollution. Unfortunately, the two most convenient "slaves"—electricity and the motorcar—largely depend upon combustion and are responsible for widespread air pollution. The fullest estimates of their impact have been made in the United States. As the Seventies opened, pollutants in the air equaled about 281 million tons a year—more than one ton for each citizen—composed of sulphur dioxide, soot, fly ash, particulate matter, oxides of carbon and nitrogen, lead, minute shreddings from wear and tear to asbestos and artificial rubber, and, within this chemical broth, the possible combinations between molecules all the way from irritants like photochemical smog to such highly dangerous but happily short-lasting poisons as carbon monoxide. The concentration of motorcar use in big cities—with a large amount of idling time—together with the likely proximity of factories and power stations, gives urban areas a particularly high percentage of the country's heavy air pollution, and if, as in Los Angeles or Tokyo Bay, temperature inversions are possible, the pollutions can be literally lethal. Gas masks—worn in Tokyo in 1971—become a reasonable precaution. In general, however, the effect is not so immediate. There has merely been a marked increase in the death rate from respiratory diseases, especially for those who carry about their own private pollution systems in the shape of cigarette smoking.

If country areas and country towns avoid the concentrated by-products of combustion, they have been the distributing points of other airborne pollutants produced by the new high-energy, high-technology chemical industries which add an even wider range of effluents emitted by the breaking up of various molecular structures and recombining them in new products; fertilizers, for instance, or herbicides. Among such products, pesticides in the group of chlorinated hydrocarbons—of which DDT is the best known and dieldrin and aldrin among the most lethal—have the disadvantage of lasting long enough to build up as they are eaten along the food chains of life, from insect to bird to fish to man, and reach increasingly concentrated and harmful doses. Used repeatedly and indiscriminately, they also create immunities in the pests they are designed to check.

Country districts also contribute to modern man's waterborne pollutions. Here the modern feedlot is a major factor and can easily add to the water courses as much excrement as a full-sized city. In fact, the overall figure for livestock wastes in the U.S.A. is nearly two thousand million tons a year, five times the annual wastes from domestic and commercial sources. To this should be added some runoff from fertilizer. In slow rivers and enclosed waters, a runoff of nitrogen compounds from heavily fertilized fields, added to excessive manure, can cause an overbloom of the rivers' algae, using up dissolved oxygen and killing off fish and plant life.

On the whole, in the developed world, in spite of the number of municipalities and coastal cities which do load the waters with virtually untreated sewage, the defenses against intestinal diseases still hold. But the midcentury's leap forward in energy consumption and in the use of chemicals is making the task steadily more hazardous. Take the Rhine, for instance. In the last four years, the West Germans have spent some three thousand million dollars on various purification and treatment systems. But the result seems to have been no more than to offset further deterioration. The French have not spent so much. Potassium mines in Alsace, coal mines and the soda industry among others in Germany release some 15 million metric tons of waste salts every year into the Rhine and have increased its chloride content at least five times over in the last five decades. The discards of various "bio-industries"—food processing, for example, or brewing—together with untreated municipal wastes make up the equivalent of sewage from 70 million people. Some 50,000 to 75,000 tons of oil seep in from shores and barges. Add 90,000 tons of metals, stir in a pinch of phenol and a touch of phosphate from detergents, mix generously, warm with waste heat from the power stations and what you have is a river in which it is unsafe to swim and the only edible fish left alive is the apparently indestructible eel. Dutch water authorities, literally at the receiving end of the cumulative insults to this vital, international waterway, warn their people that before long, no amount of water treatment can be relied on to offset this mounting misuse. Yet 20 million people still get their tap water from the Rhine.

Since one of the chief aims behind the bounding increase in energy use, the high technology, the astonishing versatility of the new chemical industries—in short, behind all the activities of modern man's "energy slaves"—is to increase his supply of material goods, another severe form of pollution takes the form of disposing of these goods when they are no longer in use. The word "consumption" is itself misleading. Nothing is consumed. It is only used for a time—a can of beer for perhaps half an hour, a bedroom suite for half a lifetime. But at the end of it all, it is still there. Burn it and pollute the air. Put it in the water and risk degradation. Besides, many materials cannot be cleaned up by the action of bacteria—they are not "biodegradable"— and some, mercury, arsenic, or lead, for instance, are too toxic to be put into water or air at all. They have to be safely stowed with other wastes in land-based dumps, carefully compacted without risk of seepage or subsidence. At the beginning of the Seventies, the annual "throw away" component in American garbage included 65 thousand million metal caps, 60 thousand million metal cans, 36 thousand million bottles and over a million junked motorcars.

But, of course, the largest disruptions of land by wastes occurs not at the end but at the beginning of the consumer cycle. Getting one ton of iron ore out of taconite leaves more than three tons of waste behind. It is dumped in Lake Superior. The process also deposits asbestos waste in the lake, in spite of increasing evidence the minute fibers of asbestos can be a cause of cancer. Often the wastes are not moved at all. One thinks of the vast tips that surround Johannesburg with 200-foot pyramids of mine tailings. In the last ten years, over three million acres of land in the United States have been stripped for coal and only a third restored to anything worth the name of reclamation.

And, in a category all by themselves, potential pollutants of air or soil or water are the wastes of nuclear power plants, all toxic, all requiring special safeguards, some with a half-life of 24,000 years. These are wastes of a kind humanity has never had to deal with, and each year, inexorably, they increase.

Let us now think for a moment of all these pollutions together—
heavy, soot-laden skies, water along the beaches too filthy to swim in,
beaches and beauty spots defiled with picnic papers and plastic bottles,
the eyesores of junk yards and dusty noisesome pits for landfill, lakes
darkened with effluent, river estuaries carrying yellow murk miles out
to sea. Add the noise—the steady roar of traffic, life below the flight
path of a busy airport, the grinding up of garbage in the small hours,
steady thuds from the pile drivers, machine gun splutters from pneu-
matic drills, rock and roll—or Bach—at 115 decibels in the next apartment. Remember the incoherence—congested streets, choking with
exhausts, freeways splitting neighborhoods open like broken dolls'
houses, tower blocks out of all proportion with human scale and sensi-
bility, the deserts of concrete and asphalt where vandals cut down the
trees as soon as they are replanted, the "open space" quite empty, full
of blowing rubbish, the areas waiting for demolition with half a sordid
block gutted and wretched elderly remnants of humanity clinging to
what is left of their once habitable homes. It is not the whole picture.
But it is part of it, and it can surely leave one with a sort of horrified
wonder that societies of such wealth should leave themselves with so
many marks of squalor and decay.

5 LIFE AT THE MARGIN

THE FACT has to be recognized that where poverty wears a differently colored face or practices a very different culture, city segregation, injustice, and environmental degradation become infinitely more intractable. The sudden wave of black unskilled American migrants spilled northward by the revolution in Southern agriculture has carried with it an equal wave of segregationist responses. Since the 1950s, for instance, the center-city population in New York has held steady at about 7.8 million. But during these decades about 1.8 million members of the white middle classes left for suburbia and about the same number of poor migrants—black and Puerto Rican—came into the city. Similarly in central Detroit, the total population actually fell after World War II. It was 1.8 million in 1948, down to 1.5 million by 1970. During that time the black percentage grew from twenty to forty-four percent. In metropolis after metropolis, if present trends continue unchanged into the 1980s, the outcome will be a black majority at the center, surrounded by white suburbs—the celebrated doughnut analogy, "A fat white doughnut with a black hole in the middle."

Actually, the certainty of this trend is somewhat offset by the fact that you cannot empty the American South of its agricultural population twice. Some of the pressures are not repeatable. But a mere slowing down in numbers does not of itself reverse the division. On the contrary, the risk is that the strain on inner-city institutions—schools, welfare, police, and services of all sorts—will serve to create all interlocking vicious circles of the poverty trap—poor education and housing leading to diminished performance and diminished performance leading to families destined from the start for bad houses and poor schools. The notorious near-bankruptcy of New York City has some of its roots in these fundamental contradictions, wealth and industry moving out to the suburbs, the problems—and costly services needed to cope with them, such as policemen, firemen, sanitation men—staying and being paid for at the center. The divisions can be socially bankrupting, too. Detroit has the highest murder rate in the United States—one murder for every 1806 of its inhabitants in 1973.

It was easy in the Fifties and Sixties to see these problems as essentially American. The various workers' revolts against intolerable pressure in Eastern Europe—in East Germany in 1952, in Budapest in 1956, in Prague in 1968, in Poland in 1970—were not much exposed to America's type of powerful investigative journalism. In Western Europe, complacent and increasingly affluent people barely observed a fundamental change going on in their own cities. The change is in fact a direct consequence of this affluence. Not only did they absorb into their expanding industries and cities the bulk of their own remaining rural peoples. They had also imported by the early 1970s some ten million "guest workers" from poorer parts of the Mediterranean, from black Africa and from Britain's ex-colonies in Asia and the Caribbean. These migrants, drawn in mainly to undertake work Europeans were no longer prepared to do—sanitation, public transport, the noisier, dirtier industries—tended to find their conditions not wholly dissimilar from the discontents of a Harlem or a Detroit. Where, as in Britain, France, and Holland, many of them are citizens of the defunct empires, they have come to stay and while France and Holland have, on the whole, avoided America's bitter racial confrontations within the working class, the situation in Britain has already many of the hallmarks of the shaping ghetto—the "poverty trap" of an East Harlem or a South Bronx beginning to take tangible form in Wandsworth or Leeds.

But the ghettos are not confined to Britain. In every category of living, Germany's "guest workers" have fewer amenities than the native-born. On the rim of Marseilles, there are settlements where one tap of water may serve two thousand people, where open sewers are never efficiently scoured, and where too much protest would bring in first the bulldozers to level the *bidonville* and then, perhaps the ultimate sanction, the order to quit. These *bidonvilles*—as wretched as the mushrooming shanty towns of the developing world—are in fact the place where the two worlds touch and their connections begin to become explicit. High birthrates, stagnant or mechanizing agriculture, unbalanced industrialization—all the economic pressures that are at work blowing up the swollen metropolises of the poorer nations have pushed a few millions more on and out into Europe.

But these small migrations are nothing compared to the millions upon millions crowding into the exploding cities, trying to escape from the margins of subsistence in the countryside only to find them again in urban life. The degree of urbanization is already a signal that something very unlike Europe's nineteenth-century development is in process. In the late 1950s, the censuses revealed that the proportion of workers in industry to population in cities was almost the reverse of Europe's nineteenth-century pattern. For Venezuela, the figures were 8.8 percent of the labor force in industry and 47.2 of the people in the urban areas; for Brazil, 9.5 and 28.1 percent; for Malaya and Korea, 7 and 20 percent; for Tunisia, 6.5 and 17.5 percent.

The cities were already out of balance but the censuses revealed something else. A virtual halving of the death rate had occurred over recent decades—partly a consequence of better public health, but largely of the new control of epidemics. With birth rates unchanged, population was now growing at more than twice the nineteenth-century rate. This acceleration, by natural increase alone, would have sent the export cities racing on to the one, two, or three million mark. But the inheritance of stagnant agriculture insured that an extra cascade would arrive from the discouraged villages.

Policy decisions have encouraged the imbalance. The first response of most developing governments was a natural and almost exclusive emphasis on infrastructure and industry. Were these not the sectors starved under colonialism? Was it not by their industrial strength that the U.S.A. and the U.S.S.R. had become world powers? In any case, the conventional wisdom prescribed this course. Import substitution, local processing, big investments in power and transport—these would be the means of "take-off" and of absorbing surplus labor from the farms.

But once again history played the game in reverse. Industry had advanced far beyond the Manchester stage of looking for unskilled hands. Most of the new and hence appealing technologies tended to be essentially capital intensive, demanding advanced skills and high managerial competence. In their determination to industrialize under forced draft, governments made every concession to investors, artificially cheapening interest rates, holding down food prices to keep wages in line, offering industry every kind of concession on taxes and import duties. One of the reasons for the remarkably rapid world-wide expansion of the American and European multinational corporations in the last three decades was the very real advantages inherent in comparatively low wage rates, low taxation, and considerable freedom in the movements of capital and profits offered by developing countries determined to industrialize at breakneck speed.

It took a decade to realize that industrialization by this route would depress farming still further, increase the appeal of the cities, yet, with a single new work place demanding anything from $10,000 to $100,000 in capital investment, make sure that a large percentage of the migrants would be unemployed on arrival. If a corporation invests, say, $100,000 in a mechanized plastic sandals factory, it can offer 40 modernized jobs. But it can also knock out 5,000 traditional shoemakers and their suppliers. Some of this kind of displacement occurred in nineteenth-century Europe. One thinks of the despairing weavers who literally starved to death as their operations were mechanized. But then the work force was growing by less than 0.7 percent. The effect of the same processes—at even higher capital costs for each industrial job in countries starved for capital—and with a labor force rising four times as fast—is simply to build rising unemployment into the operations of the formal economy. The whole operation can create a wealthy elite and a small, skilled, and relatively prosperous working class. But the mass of the city population simply remain outside the formal economy. According to World Bank estimates, over half the jobs in Bombay are not in corporate, organized industry or any part of the formal sector. The figure for Jakarta is also above fifty percent, for Belo Horizonte a remarkable sixty-nine percent.

At the same time urban poverty and bare subsistence farming in the countryside can so limit the internal market that industrial growth in general is jeopardized. Export-led expansion is not excluded and a number of countries with a high tradition of skilled, assiduous work—Singapore, South Korea, Taiwan—have thrived. But the world market now hardly offers easy open access when it is already dominated by industrial giants like the Mitsubishis and I.T.T. Thus the rings of shanty towns, the millions of unemployed, the squalor, the lack of services are not simply industrial growing pains, a temporary condition which further "modernization" on traditional lines will put right—just as the nineteenth-century slum dwellers of Europe have been changed to the reasonably well-housed and employed citizenry of today. The settlements in the developing lands are not self-curing or self-restoring by comfortable laws of automatic economic progress. They require not only emergency measures but profound structural changes in both local and international society.

Developed societies are hardly aware yet of the scale and speed of change that is required. They have all but forgotten that such degradation can exist. Yet the facts are irrefutable. Infant mortality can be as high as 150 to 200 per thousand live births, in itself one of the chief reasons why parents in desperation bring more and more children into the world to offset the risk that infant diarrhea or measles or sheer malnutrition will snatch them all away again. Expectation of life is no more than fifty years in South Asia and forty-two in tropical Africa. Protein deficiencies stunt the full growth of children's minds. The average Indian's 400 pounds of grain is no more nourishing than the water and oatmeal of the nineteenth-century Lancashire mill hand. Precarious jobs in the bazaar economy barely pay a living wage and perhaps a quarter of the population hardly even enter the job market. Yet the villages offer so little that still the people come. In the next decade, the number of "million cities" in developing countries will grow from 101 to 147—and ten of them may contain ten million inhabitants. By migration and natural increase, 1300 million new residents will arrive to crowd into the developing cities—the *callampas* (mushroom cities) of Chile, the *bustees* of India, the *favelas* of Brazil, the *gourbevilles* of Tunisia, the *gecekindu* of Turkey (meaning they were built after dusk, before dawn). The names vary but the tarpaper shacks, the unpaved streets and open sewers, the water taken dangerously from local ponds and streams or purchased at monopoly prices from itinerant water carriers—these basic conditions do not much change and it can be argued that they make up the most inhuman environments ever endured by man. Yet in city after city, such settlements make up a third to a half of the urban population and are growing twice as fast as the formal city.

The scale of shanty dwelling does not free the squatters from the added bitterness of knowing what contrasts can be created by other

peoples' wealth and opportunity. Admittedly, the differences vary
from culture to culture. In large Indian cities, a small businessman
does not necessarily leave his old house if his business prospers. He
may simply buy more jewels for his wife. The *bustees* are widely
spread all through Calcutta. There are not many exclusive enclaves of
wealth in Bombay. The leafy villas and spacious avenues of New
Delhi are British, not Indian in style. But in Latin America housing
distinctions are as clear as in ancient Egypt's Aknetatan. The center
cities are also growing the gleaming skyscrapers of steel and glass of
an early quaternary sector in which, by definition, the millions of illit-
erates have no part to play beyond office cleaning and portering. In
Brasilia, the planned and built city appears to be designed almost ex-
clusively for diplomats, civil servants—and motorcars. It is in squatter
settlements round about that the people live—and by all accounts most
of the exuberance and zest of city life are to be found. And with these
geographical divisions between wealth and poverty goes another profound cause of injustice—totally unequal access to the city's services
and jobs.

In transport, the figures speak for themselves. So far, the big export cities have, inevitably, attracted the lion's share of the new industry. Many of them are being reorganized in such a way as to increase a
steady dependence upon the private automobile. One can see why.
The big cars are in the big cities. The proportion of people in the city
and cars in the country tells the tale. Brazil as a whole is not a motorized country. Yet the number of cars per citizen in São Paulo is one
to six, not much different from New York's one to five. Other developing areas show similar trends. In Asia, Bangkok reaches the remarkable proportion of 7.9 percent of the people using 72.8 percent of the
cars. Under such conditions, it is possible to produce highly modernized congestion and pollution in urban areas fully modernized in little
else. But the fundamental issue is, of course, one of justice.

Unjust exclusion extends to other city services—for instance, the
siting of primary schools, the provision of health clinics and the distribution of medical services. But clearly the most dangerous and
debilitating evil of poverty in the world's shanty towns is steady environmental pollution—the nineteenth-century pollution of bad water
and open drains with the twentieth-century pollutions of motor exhausts and chemical effluents thrown in for good measure. Fifty per-

cent of the municipalities in Latin America have no sanitation systems. The figure for Asia and Africa is higher still. Intestinal diseases of every kind are endemic and the chief cause of death among the poorest citizens. Yet in some cities, developed standards of water supply—about 200 liters a day per person—are piped into the wealthier quarters and the shanty towns do not even get communal standpipes. Again and again, local streams and rivers are the source of untreated drinking water and also the outlets for the sewers. In Seoul, for instance, tests of water quality were not even begun until the city had grown to six million. That it is possible to manage with very primitive methods of sewage disposal—latrines or cesspits, cleared by night soil tankers—is shown by the example of Tokyo where, despite all the fabulous growth in GNP, the Central Wards of the city are still cleared by what are known as "honey carts."

But with so little protection and so total an absence of capital to set aside for future improvements, what will be the fate of the four hundred million extra city-dwellers who will arrive to use the rivers and vent their wastes in the next decade? If the rivers of developed Europe are beginning to reach the point where pollution threatens to overtake any form of treatment, what will happen to waters which are still largely unprotected in any way? Of all priorities for action—local and international—this is the highest. And it is not simply developing peoples who need to hope that the necessary sanitary revolution will not be forced through by the old and cruel nineteenth-century goad—outbreaks of waterborne disease—which, carried by all the modern means of transport, could even revive cholera, plague, and dysentery in the homes of the rich.

6 A THOUSAND SCHOOLS

IF WE STOP now and look back over the millennial span of history that has brought mankind from the farming village to the twenty-million metropolis, we may be tempted to say that the last five hundred brilliant, radical, and catastrophic years resemble only one previous period—the age of the original empire-builders, the men who tamed the great rivers, produced the first large agricultural surpluses, invented steel, built the first cities, formed the first civil services, vastly extended managerial and engineering competence, studied the constellations, invented mathematics, grasped the principle of cosmic law, constructed pyramids of unbelievable massiveness, built ziggurats to the skies, and launched terrible armies on an unbroken round of imperial conquest and defeat.

Toward the close of this exhilarating yet death-dealing epoch, one world-wide consequence was a profound and searching debate about the meaning of all this activity, this staggering coincidence of achievement and blind failure, this unbelievable demonstration of man's ability to create and destroy. In every great civilization, ultimate questions about the nature and destiny of man were raised and out of the passion of debate and search came, as we have seen, most of the master-ideas which, far more than bricks and mortar or paving stones and drains, have determined how we live in our settlements.

So we should hardly be surprised if a human epoch of even more staggering creativity and destructiveness—landing men on the moon and annihilating cities with atomic bombs—would not be equally engaged in a profound debate about its nature, its future, the meaning of its enterprises, the fundamental significance of man himself. And this is indeed the case. Humanity is involved in just such a profound journey of discovery and if, as in feudal China in the sixth century B.C. "a thousand schools contend," should we be surprised? Should we even be discouraged? How much less hopeful we should feel about the human enterprise if we had gone from candlelight to atomic power without even asking ourselves what manner of beings we are.

But we need have no fear. Today, once more, a thousand schools contend, their arguments overlapping, dividing, polarizing, crystalizing, and confusing each other at every turn of the controversy. A detailed account of the vast conflicts and convergences of thought is not possible, even though it might tell us more about the possible future of our settlements than all our more humdrum calculations about urban densities and city plans. But possibly a visitor from Mars would be tempted to concentrate on the main lines of the world's greatest ideological division—the claim of the liberal democracies to preserve for the human city the fundamental values of personal freedom and dispersed power, the claim of communist states to have achieved a socially just society for all its members and potentially for all mankind.

These two rival ideologies have already been in confrontation for well over a century. The starting point is, of source, Karl Marx's critique of the new industrial order as he saw it in its earlier stages in the Rhineland, in Fredrich Engels' detailed accounts of Manchester and then in long years of residence in London, at that time capital city of a world-wide imperial system that helped to underpin "the two nations—the nation of the rich and the nation of the poor" both in Victorian England and in the wider empire. His approach was based, we might say in shorthand, on a new fusion of thought, half Greek, half Hebrew. He sought to uncover scientific laws of history, each new phase inevitably and dialectically unfolding within the core of the previous society—slavery to feudalism, feudalism to capitalism, capitalism to the final transformation into the communist, classless society. Much of his analysis was equally concerned with precise socioeconomic laws based on the kind of analysis which would have intrigued the Greeks—and the medieval monks; laws that decreed the sole creation of value to lie with labor, the contradictions that would arise since workers, deprived of this value by bourgeois control of the means of production, would be unable to buy the goods they produced, the consequent crises of so-called "overproduction" which would really represent "underconsumption," the final certainty that these crises would bring bourgeois capitalism to an end and pave the way to the public control of society's productive apparatus and the withering away of the state which, representing no more than the "managing committee of the bourgeoisie" and the policeman protecting domestic and imperial wealth, would vanish, having lost its *raison d'être*.

But if the scientific formulations fitted well into a profound nineteenth-century commitment to objective law and inevitable progress, the furious energy that has informed the doctrine and in a single century turned it into the dominant ideology of a third of the human race has another source—the passion of the Hebrew prophets who, if they could have wandered through Manchester in 1848, would have shared every one of Marx's anathemata on the alienation of the workers, the oppressions of the poor, the death in misery of the children, and the careless indifference and luxury of the new rich. You did not need to be a scientist to analyze such exploitation. Charles Dickens expressed it with as dark a passion in his great novels. Whatever the later developments of early industrialism, its beginning is a tale of almost stupefying injustice and deprivation.

Moreover, in looking forward to the mighty being put down from their seats of power, the rich sent hungry away, and the poor inheriting the kingdom, Marx touched upon one of the profoundest strains of Biblical witness. The prophets could never have been cheated into believing Pope's adage, that God had "bid self-love and social be the same." They knew too well the temptations, the pretensions, and the rapacity of unlimited wealth. They had seen it in Nineveh and Babylon. They would have seen it again in Birmingham and Essen, in the slums of Paris and London, in the pitiful slave plantations of the American South. They would not have been deceived and, like Marx, they would have denounced injustice and looked forward to the future deliverance of the oppressed, the Parousia, the coming of the Kingdom that would wind up history, wipe every tear from the eyes of man and "make all things new."

The industrial West could not listen wholly unmoved to Marx's onslaught. His economics they did not find very troublesome because very few scientific general laws of any kind can be reliably drawn from activities which include the x component, human nature. But Western societies also read the Bible. They could not exclude all the prophetic books. Of course, no one should underestimate the degree to which conscience can be silenced when conscience and self-interest conflict. Nor is there any end to the rationalizations for this silencing. But the miseries and injustices of the nineteenth-century poor were too obtrusive to be wholly ignored. The processes of piecemeal reform—welfare, insurance, progressive taxation, active trade unionism, public housing, sanitation, above all, the extension of the franchise upon which most other reforms depended—were in full swing by the early twentieth century and the process has proliferated into as many compromises between socialism and democracy as there were schools of thought in feudal China.

The processes of change helped to undermine many of the specifics of Marxist economic doctrine—the immiseration of the poor, for instance, or the certainty of inadequate consumption. Instead a vast if fluctuating growth of the middle class and of the consumer market could be seen to be taking place. The Western counterattack has, moreover, drawn on other strains in the Greek and Hebrew tradition. Since 1917, communism has no longer been an abstraction and a future dream but the dominant ideology of a very powerful, traditionally despotic state. The Western critique, applied to this society, underlines the Greek insistence on freedom under law and the Hebrew warnings about the dangers not only of great wealth but of great power. "The mighty" that are to be put down could be not only multinationals but vast state bureaucracies. The powerful and pretentious could base their position not simply on wealth but on undisputed control over the levers of state and police power. In short, over-concentrations of authority are as dangerously heady and dehumanizing as any over-concentrations of wealth. The myth of a vanishing state is a myth indeed. We can take the sober statement of John Stuart Mill to express once and for all the Western argument for dispersed responsibility and "countervailing power":

"If the roads, the railways, the banks, the insurance offices, the great joint stock companies, the universities and the public charities were all of them branches of the government; if, in addition, the municipal corporations and local boards with all that now devolves on them became departments of the central government; if the employees of all of them were appointed and paid by the government and looked to the government for every rise in life; not all the freedom of the press and popular constitution of the legislature would make this or any other country free otherwise than in name."

Perhaps the visitor from Mars, gazing in some bewilderment at the vast ideological divide which keeps modern industrialized societies in perpetual tension and unease, might be tempted to ask a rather simple-minded question. How odd it is, he would say, to see two social orders so steadfastly condemning the mote in its opponent's eye and so calmly disregarding the beam in its own. The fact of continued, desperate, hopeless poverty in a number of super-rich Western countries is an unmistakable, unbearable, and shaming reality. The oppression of freedom, the license of the state police, the despotic power of government are equally facts in planned economies. It is fascinating to see this dialectic of opposite accusations appear not simply between the rivals but within their own ranks. In the week in 1975 that saw the French and Italian Communist Parties declare their fidelity to open institutions and plural power, a distinguished group of Soviet exiles who had sought freedom in the United States wrote to dissident leaders inside the Soviet Union warning them not to overlook the deep injustice, the shaming continuance of poverty in the midst of plenty, the abysmal failure to match recent Soviet achievements in low-cost housing, reliable health services, and equal education, the second-class status of the black citizen, all of which they had discovered within the "home of the brave and the land of the free."

Even more remarkable perhaps is a wider and deeper debate within the world-wide Communist movement. It is not difficult to understand the prophetic appeal of Marxism to Chinese leaders first exposed to Western thought through the imperialist incursions of Western Europe and then of Japan for a century after the 1830s. The exterior attack coincided, as so often before in Chinese history, with a terrible decay in internal order and justice. The virtue and benevolence which should sustain the wise emperor and secure for him "the mantle of heaven" were quite lost by the last Manchus and their Nationalist successors. Between the mid-nineteenth century and World War II there were numberless local famines and peasant revolts. This tragic quotation from a perceptive Western observer, Professor R. A. Tawney, visiting China in the 1930s, gives us the background of what was to Mao Tse-tung the equivalent of the Manchester and London slums for Engels and Marx:

"A large proportion of Chinese peasants are constantly on the brink of actual destitution . . . a propertied proletariat which is saved . . . when it is saved . . . partly by its own admirable ingenuity and fortitude, partly by the communism of the Chinese family. . . . It is, however, true that over a large area of China, the rural population suffers horribly through the insecurity of life and property. It is taxed by one ruffian who calls himself a general, by another, by a third and when it has bought them off, still owes taxes to the government. . . . There are districts in which the position of the rural population is that of a man standing permanently up to the neck in water, so that even a ripple is sufficient to drown him."

Thus the Chinese Communist reaction was not so much to a successful industrial and imperial system as to the terrible consequences of that system breaking the inner cohesion of what would now be called a "developing country" and exposing its largest class, the peasantry (in whom Marx had virtually no interest), to the equivalent of a living death. This difference of vision has developed into a vitally different design of postrevolutionary action, one that has specifically rejected the early industrial predominance in Soviet planning, put major emphasis on agriculture and food production, and with even graver ideological consequences, denounced from inside the Communist movement the tendency of all-powerful states to become the prey of their own bureaucrats and party functionaries.

These inner critiques can serve us as a reminder that both systems have in the last fifty years produced nightmare versions of their own worst evils—a Western market economy degenerating into Nazism, Eastern socialism into Stalinism. Neither appear to have adequate answers to the risks of aggressive and self-centered nationalism. As a result, they are both as far as the Cities of the Plain or the Delian League from the creation of a workable international order. In short, our Martian visitor might be led, however much it may seem a vain hope against a vain hope, to see in the Helsinki Agreement in 1975 some new moral determination to turn the eye of criticism inward, not outward, to discontinue the sterile cries of "You are worse," "No, you are worse," and to begin, instead, the patient internal search for greater justice on the one hand and greater freedom on the other.

We must not, after all, be reduced to an angry choice between what should be compatible and mutually supportive ideals. The human city cannot survive now without freedom of spirit and activity. Man has lived too long with lungs breathing the air of liberty to go back to the gills of despotism. Equally, freedom based on profound, tolerated injustice is not true freedom and will not survive. The chief hope for mankind's continued existence is that the dialectic of abuse can give place to some new synthesis of shared tasks and cooperation. If we dismiss the hope as too Utopian, let us remember the bombs on Hiroshima and Nagasaki. The debate of the nations is literally a matter of planetary life or death and since the path of reform on *both* sides is almost certainly the only way to transcend the threat of mutual destruction, what men and women can do to give their settlements more order, more justice, and a cleaner and more beautiful environment could do more than improve everyday living. It could be a way forward in the search for peace.

7 IS THE FUTURE POSSIBLE?

THERE IS A further reason for trying to lessen the acerbity and self-righteousness of the world's ideological debates. In a profound sense, history has already passed them by. For the last two centuries, first capitalism, then communism have been implicitly based on the idea of an infinity of expanding planetary resources, waiting to be exploited either by the strong and the capable—with ultimate "trickle down" to everyone else—or by the public servants of the community for everybody's benefit—once the apparatus of production is in place. In the last twenty-five years, this material underpinning has been given special force and significance by the application of Keynesian principles of "sustained demand management" to the market economies. This has vastly increased their levels of mass consumption and has added to the determination of communist leaders to catch up and surpass Western standards of life. The result has been, whatever the ideology, an all-out race for growth and consumption.

But suppose the race cannot even be run under the conditions which do not seem likely to prevail much beyond the end of this century? Suppose that the combination of rising numbers—a possible eight thousand million by 2010—the exhaustion of materials—with oil and natural gas on the list during the next four decades—and increasing planetary pollution, especially of our inescapably shared oceans, produce, by some specific date in the twenty-first century, what in *Limits to Growth* is known as "overrun and collapse"? Then by the oldest means of population control—famine, pestilence, fraticidal fighting, and "Death on a pale horse"—a remnant of humanity, or, after nuclear war, perhaps not even that, will struggle to reconstruct some form of terrestrial existence on a planet already mined of most of the materials and sources of energy which at present underpin the existence of market and planned economies alike.

Such an outcome makes present ideologies fairly irrelevant. Whichever of our three contexts we examine—intention, justice, a sustainable environment—an absolute shortage of material resources makes a fundamental difference to the nature and even the possibility of man's rational response. Scarcity will no doubt increase the need for planning, as it does everywhere in time of war. But not all the plans in the world can recreate emptied lodes and mined-out resources. If the national product has ceased to grow, "more for everyone" can no longer cover over acute problems of justice in market economies and of rising aspirations everywhere. And in all economies as scarcities increase and costs rise, open or hidden inflation will steadily undermine the entire social fabric. If, in addition, any of the essential life-support systems of the biosphere—air, water, soil—can be irretrievably corrupted, neither plans nor fair shares nor local environmental safeguards will be much help. The whole nature of man's physical and social relationship will have changed drastically from the world picture evolved during the recent centuries of Baconian progress and headlong expansion. Today the last thing we think about is shortage. We are removed by millennia from such classic summaries of rational human behavior as that given by Lao Tsu:

"Here are my three treasures. Guard and keep them. The first is pity, the second frugality, the third the refusal to be foremost of all things under heaven."

These are almost precisely the treasures our thrusting societies have *not* sought. The temptations lying in wait for kings and emperors, or even in "keeping up with the Joneses," can be said to lie above all in the dangerous belief of there being no limits. At the dawn of the modern world, the myth of the Devil's bargain with Faust was that he should sell his soul in return not only for all knowledge, but for all possessions, pleasure, and power.

Now perhaps there *are* limits. There are material things we cannot have. To this possibility, suggested for the first time only in the last fifteen years, the world's ideological debate is largely irrelevant. In fact, a quite different one has taken its place, at least in Western societies where the new dimensions of difficulty were first recognized and their implications made the object of serious study.

Again in shorthand, we can say that opinion tends in opposite directions. There is an optimistic school for which its opponents have coined the phrase "techno-fixers"; there is a pessimistic school whom the techno-fixers tend to dismiss as "doomsayers." In between lie as many nuances, differences of emphasis, and varying priorities as can be observed in the battle of ideologies. But the broad distinction between hope and despair sets the direction of the debate.

It must be admitted at once that the optimists are more congenial to modern man. Reared on four centuries of deepening faith in material progress, experiencing it exuberantly in the last quarter century, he finds this the most difficult possible moment at which to change gear and change route. So the "techno-fixers" are certain of a ready audience. They begin with the faith that modern science and technology do in fact have the instruments they require for insuring continued growth in the world's material resources. In the first place, reserves are not absolute things. They depend upon constraints of technology, energy-use, and cost. When aluminum, one of industry's most versatile materials, was invented in the early 1920s, it cost $545 a pound. By the Seventies, the same amount was at times being sold for fifteen cents. The reserves of aluminum's parent, bauxite, worth exploiting at one price are totally different at the other, and it is one of the world's most widely distributed resources. This is just one example of the way in which, over the last seventy-five years, the efficiency with which minerals are turned into useful metals has been steadily improving. So has their reuse. For instance, world consumption of pig iron increased ten to eleven times over between 1900 and 1970, but steel output multiplied by a factor of twenty. The difference lies in a steady increase in technical efficiency and the use of scrap. Only ten percent of copper was recycled in the United States in 1900. The U.S. figure in 1970 was thirty-five percent. Lead recycling grew from eight percent in 1910 to the present forty percent. Only recently the energy used in one process of making aluminum fell by thirty percent. Why assume that such economies will not continue?

At the same time, as geological exploration grows in scale and sophistication, the reserves of a fair number of minerals in common use actually grow—bauxite seven times over since 1950, iron ore eleven times, potash twenty-three. Silicon, which is so versatile as a result of "molecular welding" that it can make anything from glass to the nose-cone of a rocket, is literally as plentiful as the sand of the sea since sand is its basic component. Nor should we forget that modern chemical processes can make all-purpose plastics from such renewable resources as cellulose from wood pulp. And over all estimates hangs the uncertainty of what mineral wealth may not be awaiting man's exploitation of the oceans. The World Bank has published an estimate which suggests that if, as some suspect, the nodules of mixed minerals on the ocean bed, which include manganese and copper, are able in some manner to go on growing, there may be a self-sustaining crop to "harvest" and it could provide up to 400 million tons of minerals a year until the sun goes cold or mankind abandons metallurgy for the writing of epic verse. Under these conditions of potential but still unproven abundance, to search for absolute "shortages" is a fruitless exercise.

To those who point out that as the more accessible minerals are exhausted, extra capital and more energy will be required for beneficiation, the answer is again reassuring. Even if, as seems reasonably certain, oil reserves and natural gas at present or increasing consumption rates have little more than four decades ahead of them and coal, for all its trillions of tons, could run out in about a century, the nuclear option offers virtually unlimited supplies of future energy. The fission plants of today depend, it is true, upon an essentially scarce resource—uranium 235. But the breeder reactor is ready to replace them. And if this were not reassuring enough, there is fusion in the middle distance, possibly fueling the planet by the middle of the next century by exploiting the oceans' inexhaustible reserves of deuterium. All this worry about vanishing reserves and declining energy is simply a failure of imagination or a failure of nerve—the equivalent of declaring that the increase in private traffic in London or Paris would bury the city under horse dung just as the motorcar was about to be invented.

And if, the argument continues, exponential material growth is not in question, we can stop worrying about problems of distribution. The increasing availability of materials will offset inflationary tendencies by bringing up supply to match demand. Rising living standards will exercise their customary constraints on family size. If Malthus has been proved wrong about wealthy societies—who invariably stabilize their families at about the two-child level—why suppose he will not be wrong about the next group of countries reaching affluence? In fact, he is already wrong, since many of them—Taiwan, South Korea, China—are in full demographic decline toward stable numbers. And as the world's population spurt ends up in a steady state, there is no reason why science and technology should not preserve the resulting billions in no more misery than is endured today by the average citizen of, say, Atlanta or Zagreb.

Least of all should fears about pollution disturb this trouble-free prospect. The fears betray the same distrust of the powers of technology. What man has messed up, he can clear up again—by Clean Air Acts (which have given London fifty percent more winter sunshine since 1952), by treatment plants that are even cleaning up Cleveland's Cuyahoga River (which used to catch fire), by recycling and sanitizing, by storing atomic wastes in indestructible capsules of clay and glass, and by all the thousands of other processes not yet discovered by the protean invention of *homo scientificus,* including conceivably the ultimate cleanser and transformer, the fusion torch, which breaks all materials down to their original molecules for rewelding into a safe and usable condition.

, It is perhaps this very scale of power and imagination that launches the "doomsayer" on his opposite predictions. Basically, the power is not denied. The terror lies in the possibility of overconfidence and arrogant misuse—or of civil order so undermined by misery and revolt that any form of use becomes either destructive or impossible.

The starting point is the sheer size of population growth. The destitute millions pouring into the cities bear no resemblance to the masses of the nineteenth century, either in numbers or in degree of deprivation. They will breed to the limit of breakdown—of food supplies, of water and sanitation, above all, of frustrated hope. To supply them at all will exercise a continuously upward pressure on scarcer and more expensive materials and hence sustain inflationary pressures of which today's are a mere foretaste. In some of the gloomier forecasts, the survival of a functioning humanity may even demand, in the not too distant future, an agonizing choice. There will only be so much material supplies available to sustain civilized existence. If everyone is assisted, then, as in an overloaded lifeboat, pulling in the survivors will sink the whole boat. Some must be left to drown so that the human enterprise can be carried on.

But this is not the limit of gloom, for it is perfectly easy to point out the falsity of the analogy. It is not a ship that is in question, with the already developed nations in first class, the more successful developing nations traveling steerage, and everyone else in the water. In fact, all human creatures, rich, middling, poor, destitute, are on the same ship and there is no one in the water because there is nothing but ship. And if the millions behind the bulkheads include a few likely lads from the Japanese Red Army with a home-made nuclear device, pieced together from the U.S. Atomic Energy Commission's handbooks, no amount of first-class service above deck will preserve the ship itself from irreparable damage.

And this is where the doomsayers reach their ultimate degree of pessimism. They point out that every argument of the techno-fixers depends upon energy being available in vast and increasing quantities. Yet the means that are being proposed for the near future—increased reliance upon nuclear energy based, as in the first atomic bombs, on the nuclear fission of uranium 235 and, later, as the world's supplies of uranium 235 run out, upon breeder reactors producing plutonium 239 and "conventional" reactors adapted to use plutonium—insure that just as the planetary ship risks being shaken apart by rising despair, misery, and revolt below decks, the holds will be filling up with every kind of long-lasting nuclear waste. In addition, the ship will be increasingly encumbered with the whole array of arsenals, reactors, and reprocessing plants which the plutonium strategy entails. Yet a concentration of plutonium no larger than an orange can irradiate the entire planetary ship's company into the risk of pandemic cancer.

Must we then conclude that we are indeed living at the end of time? That our capacity for destruction now so far surpasses our powers of control and restraint that shipwreck without survivors is to round off the human voyage? When one recalls that no civilization has ever achieved more than half a millennium without widespread political and social breakdown, when one realizes that the bandits and terrorists and guerrillas of the next "interregnum" might carry plutonium bombs, it is indeed easy to foresee little but doom before us. Sir Thomas Browne may simply have got his dates a mere four hundred years wrong. "The world's great mutations" are indeed ended, for we are about to end our world.

Yet, if he was wrong then, our pessimism, too, can lead us astray.

There is at least a chance that the techno-fixers and the doomsayers are both wrong and both right—that the risks are enormous but that answers are possible. It is true that the pressures of escalating population are vast. But, as a world community, we have so far made no concerted effort to extend to the thousand million or so who possess least and grow most rapidly the preconditions of family stability—enough food, clean water, medical services, falling infantile mortality, and education, especially for women. It is certainly not lack of resources that has impeded such an effort. With seventy-five percent of the world's wealth for a quarter of the people, a ten percent reduction in the bill for alcohol alone—over $100 thousand million a year in North America, Europe, and Russia—would provide an ample stimulus to investment in the poor world's basic needs. Whatever may be the position thirty years from now, today absolute scarcity exists only among the poorest nations. And it is the product not of the planet's inadequate endowment but of the present fundamental skew in the distribution of its wealth.

It is true that the risk of malnutrition and recurrent famine is rising. But there is a perfectly coherent world strategy put forward at the 1974 World Food Conference to increase developing countries' output by the needed five percent a year and invest a small but steady part of developed wealth both in this farming effort and in the recreation of an emergency food reserve and of buffer stocks of grain.

It is true that there is an increasing drain on nonrenewable resources and that one of its by-products is world-wide inflationary pressure. But where, in the wealthy world, are genuine policies of restraint and conservation being practiced? In spite of the overdue discipline of higher oil prices, we are slopping around in our gas-guzzlers as unconcernedly as ever, putting up buildings that leak heat like sieves, throwing away as many cans and bottles, triple-packaging our goods, and still loading land, air, and sea with the old pollutions. Where, in developed societies—except perhaps Norway—is a serious national effort engaged to control inflationary pressures not by yet another round of spectacular growth but by more modest and cooperative ways of living, by forms of "consumption" which involve the truly exponential resources of mind and heart, by standards nearer to those of Lao Tsu than of Assurbanipal? In energy, particularly, who cares in the United States that consumption is twice as high, per capita, as in

Sweden, a wealthier and chillier country? Which governments genuinely seek to lessen the most energy-wasting and inflationary of all expenditures—the $250 thousand million spent each year on "defense"?

It is true, appallingly true, that the nuclear economy could, by the accumulation of radioactive wastes and the impossibility of insuring safe millennial guardianship, expose the planet to irreversible contamination, turning the Promethean curse from myth to reality, stealing the sun's nuclear power from the heavens and leaving mankind chained to lifeless, irradiated rock. But energy conservation alone, with no change in styles of life, could already save all—and more than all— the power now provided by nuclear energy. Forty years of oil, and at least a hundred years of coal, give the world's peoples the time to develop other options, chief among them the direct use of the sun's rays streaming safely down through the planet's atmosphere shield to ripen every crop and grow every living thing entirely free of charge. There is no hurry to seize the nuclear option. Indeed, for poorer countries, the one endowment they possess, in total abundance, is the sun's radiance only awaiting the technologies required to develop its direct use. And they are on the way.

These and other possibilities for man's settled life are what we must examine in the pages ahead. But it is vital to recognize from the start that the old counterpoint between new insights and old fatalities is still in process. There is no automatic certainty that the balance between our material power and our human purposes will simply work itself out. Every risk of the doomsayers is a real risk. Many of the technical alternatives of the techno-fixers are real alternatives. But the interplay between risk and response demands full human attention, full human commitment to justice on a planetary scale, and a wholly new realization of the limits to exploitation and degradation the biosphere of air, soil, and water can sustain and still survive. If the forces of growth and expansion could have given us the keys of heaven and earth, it would have been in the last hundred years. Yet in the days when vast temperate supplies of grain were released by the opening of the prairies, people starved on a planet carrying only a thousand million souls. When unlimited energy welled up from the deserts at a cost of fifteen cents a barrel, at least a third of the world's people continued to depend upon back-breaking labor to achieve barely a subsistence diet. If, in short, at the time of maximum cheapness and abundance of resources, we planned so little, shared so meagerly, and did such environmental damage, then we can be sure that drift and stupid optimism and no thought for tomorrow will not provide any better answers in the days of greater stringency ahead.

But is humanity capable of these larger visions and acts of attention? It is all too easy to dismiss this degree of discipline and rationality as much too tall an order. Yet there are two reasons for believing that such pessimism is out of place. The first is the remarkable number of alternative answers that are beginning to be offered to the basic problems of man's life in settlements. Underneath the apparent uniformity of breakneck urbanization, spreading technology, the computer revolution, the homogenization of techniques, communications, and, it is sometimes feared, of man himself, another range of options has started to form, other methods of organization, other ideals which today are perhaps no larger than St. Benedict's first community in the Abruzzi or Mahatma Gandhi's first ashram. But they may have some of the same possibilities for organic growth.

The second reason is simply that the questions of survival are being asked at all. Civilizations are usually ended by sleepwalkers, acting out the nightmare to the end. There are undoubtedly sleepwalkers around. But there has probably never been a time when the risks and evils of society have been admitted and examined with such openness and objectivity. "The sleep of reason produces monsters." Possibly—but reason is now awake and analyzing the monsters down to the last wishbone. This concern, this passionate re-examination, is the best guarantee that, in contradiction to the despairing cry of the prophet, we can rationally hope for delivery "from the wrath to come."

Part Three: The Technological Order

8 ECONOMIC CONSTRAINTS

THE SEARCH for solutions to the problems of the world's unwieldy, unjust, and often unsanitary and degraded settlements must begin in the developed world. This is not a priority of need. The harshest fate, the most urgent priorities for action lie in the villages, towns, and metropolises of the poorest peoples. But it is in the developed world that some of the worst examples of heedless, comfortless urbanization are to be found. If such errors can be committed in spite of relatively ample resources, it is essential that they should not be repeated elsewhere. It is also in the developed world that a number of experiments are being tried out which may assist the developing peoples in the massive tasks of urbanization that lie ahead. In fact, the whole developed scheme of cities—in both its failures and its fresh attempts—is a sort of object lesson or cautionary tale which could, conceivably, help the developing countries not to make quite such a mess of their inescapably approaching urban order.

But before we examine developed settlements in any detail, there are two preliminary issues of policy and direction which concern all societies in whatever stage of development. One turns on the general management of economic resources, particularly in a time of relative overall scarcity—a condition that could be no more than a few decades away. The other is concerned with the best use of what is always scarce—the planet's basic endowment of land. As Mark Twain's father remarked: "Buy land, my son. I notice they are not making any more of it." Once population reaches a certain density—as in and around cities—the unexpandable land base must be carefully managed for optimum use. Essentially scarce, it has only one reaction to a market free-for-all—exploding prices. And this, of course, can be one more element of pressure on a sane and stable use of the country's economic resources. Land prices increasing by ten percent a year, as in much of Europe over the Fifties and Sixties, are a key element in maintaining inflationary pressure.

In fact, probably no section of the economy is so ill-served by inflation as the housing and construction sector or so impeded in the task of mobilizing adequate resources. Inflation is most easily described as "too much money chasing too few goods." It can be created by scarcity of supply—scarce center-city sites, for instance. It can be created by overabundant demand—managers and workers rewarding themselves too highly for the actual work they do, say, in the construction industry. But whatever the cause, the effect is to lower the value of money since everything's price falls if there is too much of it. And this fall hits construction with particular force.

Much of the basic investment needed for decent communities is "lumpy." It is uneconomic for a settlement to subsist with, say, a quarter of a sewage system or half a road system, very few schools, and no hospitals. In any case, the result would hardly be what one would call a community. This kind of investment also takes time and absorbs the savings with which time is "bought." Moreover, the infrastructure of settlements belongs to that part of a nation's expenditure which everyone uses in general and does not pay for in particular. It is basic social expenditure covered by rates and taxes.

If, as building continues, money is losing its value, all the cost calculations for the community's programs for building and infrastructure have to be revised upward. So do the critically important and often overlooked costs of maintenance. The salaries of municipal employees also rise, and here is a field in which it is often excessively difficult to offset rising costs by increasing productiveness. You can hardly have more fires in order to increase the "productivity" of firemen. Nor is it easy to change the fundamentally routine character of a lot of police surveillance. If wages go up to offset inflation, it is difficult, in this area, to devise greater "output" to lessen the load.

While these pressures increase on the side of costs, the means of covering the costs are also in deepening jeopardy. Possible lenders of money take fright at the prospect of the essentially long-term loans required for buildings but to which inflation gives a built-in certainty of declining returns. They demand higher and higher interest rates to attract their money. And since inflation is squeezing the spending plans at all levels of government, the central government is probably in there bidding for itself partly because it needs the funds, partly because it hopes to use high interest rates to check inflation by reducing demand in general. At the same time, hard-pressed citizens, with inflation squeezing their own incomes, are violently opposed to any increase in local or national taxation to cover basic community investment.

Virtually the only pressure in inflationary times working *for* construction is the belief that a "real" asset—a freehold house—could provide cover against an even faster inflation. Since, however, land may be seen as an even better cover in free markets, the search will probably inflate the price of land still further and, in any case, only wealthier citizens can find funds for purchasing land or house. The much larger body of people, whose incomes have not kept pace with inflation, simply drop out of the market and are also unable to meet any rent for new housing which accurately reflects the rising economic costs. But who will then provide the difference? In January 1973, for instance, the Nixon Administration announced a moratorium on *all* federal subsidies for housing—precisely in order to check inflation.

All these pressures can be seen at work in the recent destruction of a strong, indeed flamboyant, strategy to increase housing and community-building in New York State. The Urban Development Corporation was established in 1968, just before inflation began its floodlike surge. The Corporation was designed to fulfill a massive building program for people of lower income to whom the commercial market did not cater. In seven years, it spent over a thousand million dollars and had nearly twice as much committed to new construction. But during the same period, every setback that inflation can inflict caught up with the Corporation. Its schemes began to cost more, its loans had to compete with other borrowers, including the federal government, all paying higher interest rates. In 1973, the federal moratorium knocked out the subsidies the UDC had built into its cost estimates for housing. Meanwhile, its commercial backers—the banks and insurance companies—began to lose faith as the gap between expenditure and income inevitably widened. Finally, in 1975, its ultimate sponsor, the New York State government, ceased to cover its loans, although the

Corporation had received and acted on a "moral obligation" clause inserted in its constitution which appeared to engage the state's good faith. In fact, the clause had been devised to get around the voters' increasing unwillingness to approve state bonds for housing and, without their specific consent, was not legally binding. But the reason did not soften the result—the bankruptcy of UDC and the winding up of its programs.

One could multiply from every market economy these instances of inflation's devastating effect on the orderly and sustained development of communities. In Britain, for instance, the construction programs of local authorities have been virtually halted. And just as the social value of increasing the rate of renovation of older housing had come to be recognized—as is the case all through the European Community—the grants for renovation were more than halved.

But perhaps the most sensational consequences of inflation come from a less humanly tragic but nonetheless critically important sector of construction—the office buildings which represent the living space of the modern economy's most rapidly expanding "quaternary" sector.

At the end of the Sixties, with the prolonged economic growth of the last two decades stretching apparently limitlessly into the future, property developing companies extended their programs to match. In fact, the sheer scale and pressure of their expansion was one of the elements tipping market economies over the edge from orderly growth into what the Japanese beguilingly call a "boomu." The early Seventies brought all the depressing consequences of the reverse process of recession. Costs shot upwards. The rentals people could afford to pay fell in equal degree. Since many companies had borrowed the capital for construction through short-term loans in the expectation of immediate letting or selling, often with a sizable capital gain, they, like the UDC, found their liabilities far exceeding their receipts and as they went into liquidation, they pulled down with them a number of smaller banks which had equally allowed optimism to get the better of judgment.

Nor was there much prospect of a rapid recovery. One of the consequences of the reckless phase of expansion was the legacy, in virtually every metropolitan city, of enough office space to see even the most expansive economy through another half decade. By 1975, in a

list which almost recalls Leporello's record of Don Giovanni's conquests, we read of over a million square feet of office space vacant in
Brussels and Sydney, three million in the Paris region, up to six
million in Frankfurt, ten million in Holland's Randstadt—and (Leporello's climax) in New York City, thirty million. There a single
property corporation has had 1.4 million square feet in 44 stories on a
Manhattan avenue entirely empty since 1974. International hotels
which have also grown like mushrooms to cater to unlimited tourist
expansion—and which require at least a sixty percent level of letting
to break even—are often in equal difficulties.

To sum up, inflation not only helps to disintegrate every reasonably stable economic and hence social relationship. It also exercises a
concentratedly harmful influence on the building and running of settlements. First of all, it condemns the construction industry to a life of
feast and famine in which, in the phase of rapid expansion, prices are
rising too fast for costs to be kept under control while everyone builds;
then, after the crash, the weaker elements go bankrupt and their skilled
work force disperses; then, as the upward rhythm begins again, shortage of contractors and skills makes sure that the price rises will be
even faster next time around and that meanwhile lack of investment
and maintenance in the industry will have materially reduced efficiency and hence increased its costs. As a method of running a sector
responsible for over half the nation's investment in fixed capital and
up to ten percent of its gross national product, it would seem to invite
the signalman's comment when he saw two express trains approaching
each other from opposite directions on the same line: "Hell of a way
to run a railroad."

The next evil is that, especially in larger settlements, all kinds of
municipal services—many of them unimprovable in terms of "output"—become more expensive and if, as a result, industries and commercial undertakings move off in search of cheaper living, the local
tax base shrinks almost in the same measure as the pressures grow—a
classic vicious circle appearing in city after city in the world's mixed
economies.

But the most vicious damage lies in the fact that, of all groups affected by inflation, at every level—county, country, region, planet—
the poorest, weakest citizens, the old, the infirm, the unskilled, the unemployed, suffer the most. No welfare payments anywhere catch up

with their shrinking incomes and opportunities. Migrant workers caught by unemployment in their *bidonvilles,* the unskilled laborer in a declining region or a jobless center city, the widow starving respectably behind lace curtains in a crumbling house, or, particularly in societies whose families no longer care much for their aged, the lonely, elderly pensioner eating dogfood in an unheated apartment— these are the defenseless ones for whom inflation can be the *coup de grâce.*

In market economies in the nineteenth century, the answer to inflation lay simply in allowing recession to work itself out—through falling demand, bankruptcies, and mass unemployment until goods and interest rates were cheap enough to encourage new investment and set the top spinning again. But in the late twentieth century, no such brutal shakeout can be tolerated. The whole battery of social defenses, precisely set up to protect the mass of the people against pauperization, would have to be deliberately dismantled. The level of unemployment needed to produce the old-fashioned ways of deflating excessive demand would become politically intolerable. Yet the phenomenon of "stagflation"—stagnant activity with rising prices— might still continue.

Moreover, of all cures for the particular problems of settlements—the cost of public services, the maintenance of an efficient and stable construction industry, enough houses for the citizens to buy or rent and enough income to allow them to do so—harsh Procrustean cuts in capital spending and high, investment-repelling interest rates are precisely the opposite of what is required. The consequences of just such a solution have in fact appeared in the crisis in New York City. It is, above all, inflationary costs that have driven the city to the brink of bankruptcy. They include, no doubt, a certain amount of unusual bounty—universal free admissions to the University, for instance, and some degree of ransom demanded by powerful municipal unions. But New York City is also still the place which not only took its share of the vast outward movement of rural black migrants from the South after the war but is still the goal of families from Puerto Rico escaping from local deprivation. At the same time, it is the place from which the successful young executive removes himself, his family, and his property tax to a convenient suburb. If the City had more control over its "commutershed"—as is the case, for instance, in

Metropolitan Toronto—and if there were federal policies to meet the problems of poverty and welfare on a national scale—which there should be in a society of free (or fairly free) movement—then a sizable part of New York City's problems could be met from a wider tax base. As it is, the cutbacks proposed to satisfy future lenders—one wonders where they live—must fall most heavily on the poorer groups whose hopes for better housing and services can probably be abandoned for yet another decade. Once again, as an exercise in humane manage- - ment, it must irresistibly recall the signalman's surprise.

If such vicious circles are to be avoided in the future, it may well be that modern governments, having accepted the Keynesian possibilities of managing demand, may now need to look at the side of supply—the supply of purchasing power, the scale of income a nation can allow itself in the light of what it can hope to produce. Such a policy has been tried in an on-again, off-again fashion in market economies, never long enough to see how it works—save in a modified form in Holland and Sweden—and never with enough conviction to meet both its difficulty and its promise. This policy is based on a measure of deliberate public control over incomes and prices, designed to keep a steadier balance between demand and supply. Such a strategy, of course, is anathema to many groups—all the way from theorists of the pure market to the leaders of large and well-organized trade unions. But possibly by the time the next round of inflation and recession has completed its gyration, there may be greater readiness to look at a number of arguments for a moderate but effective incomes policy, possibly on the lines pioneered by the Dutch and the Swedes, an annual "bargain" or "synchro-negotiation" at the national level worked out between government, business, and labor to establish first the prospects for the availability of resources and, in the light of that forecast, to establish a norm which would broadly govern permissible movements of prices and earnings.

Such a bargain would certainly not interfere with the "free market" since it would only apply where concentrations of business power already administer prices and where strong trade unions bargain up their wages, irrespective of productivity or inflation or any consideration extraneous to the size of the paycheck. In these conditions, which prevail over a wide section of industry, farming, and services, control over the market already exists. It simply happens to be private control in the private interest—the king's "overmighty subjects" exercising arbitrary power.

The evolution of such a system by popular consent could be even more vital to mixed economies if, as is not unlikely, the next decades see conditions of greater scarcity built into the world economy. There are already hints of how such a change could be brought about. It would work more smoothly if, as in West Germany, workers were closely associated with the management of enterprises and had acquired a much clearer overall view of the problems and possibilities of the modern economy. It would be helped by really imaginative measures to improve the environment of work places. Sometimes one has the feeling that the world cares more about endangered species than about the noisy, dirty, dangerous factories in which so many in the work-force spend half their lives. In 1971, one in eleven of West Germany's workers were injured—over 6,500 fatally. For France the figure was one in twelve, with over 2,000 fatalities. Experiments to vary boredom, to change jobs and routines, to increase holidays and even encourage part-time work and regular sabbaticals could all lessen the deadening boredom which no increases in pay can really offset. On the contrary, they create human beings incapable of vital enjoyment, whatever their leisure.

But perhaps—given our open and emulative age—restraints on inflationary pressure demand above all a condition one finds in Japan or Sweden, where the gap between the rewards of the best and least paid members of society are not so flagrant as it often seems in, say, the rarified world of the largest banks and corporations, where prestige incomes from 250,000 to a million dollars a year (pre-tax but also pre-loopholes) set standards that make restraint for a garbage collector seem a bad joke. The sheer visibility of modern, highly consumptive life styles—described continuously on television, advocated from every billboard—make the notion of a "national bargain" vain indeed unless there is some agreed scale of reward that does not, by the grandeur of the upper reaches, incite the vast majority of citizens to emulation, which is impossible, and so to envy and anger, which are finally destructive of society itself.

It is in this context of rational reward and of justice seen to be done that we must examine a form of inflationary pressure which has a particularly direct impact upon costs and benefits in human settlements. This is the private market for land in mixed economies and the degree to which distortions of price can not only feed inflation but stand in the way of any really rational patterns of land use.

If we look back over the longest span of ordered human existence in settlements, land has not usually been a marketable commodity. As the single base and source of life for the tribe or the Neolithic village, it seemed no more "private" than water or air. When, in 1855, President Pierce approached the Duwamish tribe with a request that their land should be purchased by the United States Government, their Chief is reported to have said:

"How can you buy or sell the sky—the warmth of the land? The idea is strange to us. Yet we do not own the freshness of the air or the sparkle of the water. How can you buy them from us? . . . Every part of this earth is sacred to my people. . . . For all things share the same breath—the beasts, the trees, the man. . . ."

In theory, this communal base was preserved in the later monarchical systems of more elaborate societies. In medieval Europe, for instance, the revival of the feudal concept, of the "fief" held in trust from the liege-lord, together with widespread monastic settlement, the scale of church lands, foundations for charitable activities and the traditional village commons allowed for a mixed pattern of land-holding and an unmistakable, if ill-defined, sense of community interest. It is instructive that the first recorded payment for "betterment"—in other words, a tax paid by a landowner because action by the community had improved his property—took place in Britain in 1427 when the building of a sea wall at public expense was judged to have increased the value of some newly protected "private" land.

Absolute private property rights are thus quite recent and are grounded, as we have seen, in the particular political events, economic interests, and social preoccupations of the struggle against baroque despotism in the seventeenth century. The absolute right to private property was seen as a defense against absolute government—a right that could be abrogated only for the most overriding and explicit social need, with complete indemnity and through due process of law. The Fifth Amendment to the American Constitution declares: "nor shall private property be taken for public use without just compensation"— which remains a formidable obstacle to forms of social control which the owners of property deem to lessen its economic value. The Civil

Code of Napoleon similarly enshrined "exclusive, absolute, and perpetual" private property rights, and a really startling elaboration of the
theme can be found in Article 2513 of the Civil Code of Argentina in
which the individual owner's right to property is declared to extend as
far as the right to "denaturalize it, degrade it, or destroy it." This apparently perverse extension of property rights is justified in a footnote
to the Code where it is argued that "all restrictions would bring more
dangers than advantages. If the State becomes a judge of abuse, it
would not be long before it becomes a judge of use and all real ideas
of property and liberty would be lost." The community's needs are
thus confounded with the arbitrary inroads of absolute rule.

Add the liberal economy's belief in the market as the most rational
means of deciding between alternative uses. Add the enormous increase in the range of uses introduced by industrialization. Add the
social adage that "everybody's business is nobody's business" and it
is easy to arrive at the formula that private choices in a free land
market will insure optimal results.

But no formula so deceptively simple, for all its elements of truth,
would be able to deal with the problems of an industrializing society.
Perhaps its central problem is precisely the number of different uses to
which most parcels of land can be put and the totally new mobility of
people wanting to use them. Whether a society is a mixed market
economy or a totally planned economy, dogmatically reliable answers
have not yet emerged. We can remark trends and register limited successes. But there are no magic wands.

If we begin with the market formula, it has a number of disadvantages, some of which have reappeared in planned economies as well.
What concerns us first of all—because it contributes directly to inflation—is the question of "unearned increment"; in other words, the
ability of landowners in areas where "improvements" such as roads or
factory sites or whole cities are being planned to secure for themselves
vast fortunes simply by engrossing all the value added to their land,
although the value itself stems either from the community's need for
the land or from its public improvements. The owners' constructive
role is about equal to that of the winner in a lottery—or the gentleman
behind the sea wall in 1427. And it encourages the lottery spirit of
speculation—people buying into land on all the routes of the advancing city and selling it, unimproved, at profits derived not from their

own work but from other people's needs. These speculative windfalls enriched the dukes owning farms in eighteenth-century London's Bloomsbury and Belgravia as comfortably as the twentieth-century developers in New York's Westchester County or on the outskirts of Paris.

Private gains have various other unsatisfactory results. Public improvements cannot be financed out of the growing value of the land. Increased costs are imposed on poorer citizens. Above all, there is considerable distortion in the use of prices as a reliable mechanism of allocation. For there is no guarantee that the highest price offered for the site does insure the best use. A property developer in Los Angeles can buy up a hillside, clear it of trees, layer it almost flat, put up a maximum number of ticky-tacky houses, and reap the largest financial return. But the "best" use for the hill might well have been to leave it as a community park or the site for a school. A city governed entirely by the "cash nexus" will end up, like most of Manhattan or nineteenth-century Lancashire, with virtually only one park. Amenities which cannot be privately costed, bought, and sold will simply be left out—whether they are open space, public gardens, repertory theatres, civic opera houses, or all the other essential amenities of an urbane community. Nearly all of London's great parks are royal inheritances. All of its present attainments in acting, music, and opera and ballet are subsidized. The city based on buying and selling is the typical industrial city which no tourists visit and from which, to recall the words of Patrick Geddes, getting drunk may be the quickest way out. In short, the failure of the undiluted price mechanism is obvious in the whole structure of the modern metropolis. If a free land market could be relied on to produce the proper balance between urbanity, mobility, access, work, and residence, we should not have the cities we have now.

How then can these distortions of the market be set right? Planned economies, returning to the millennial tradition of community ownership of the land, have no problems. The "increment" that is created by changing land use reverts automatically to the public authorities. The difficulties lie between different community institutions, not between individuals and the state. The commonest, as we shall see, has been the tendency of central economic ministries, under the leadership of the state plan, to concentrate so singlemindedly on industrial growth that too little of the gains spill over to the social needs of the citizen.

Market economies have made a variety of attempts to recoup unearned gains for the community. Since Britain's efforts go back to the fifteenth century, it is perhaps not surprising that it has tried a greater variety of expedients than any other Western country. Unhappily, since successive governments have systematically thrown out the experiments of their predecessors and since 1910 no system has been in operation for a full ten years, conclusions are difficult to draw. The 1947 Town and Country Planning Act created a framework for country-wide planning of land use and laid down the basic principle that simply to own land in an area scheduled for a profitable change of use—say, from a field of turnips to a suburban housing development—did not entitle the owners to anything more than the return they would have obtained by the sale of agricultural land. The entire "betterment" or unearned increment would go to the public authority. But the Act recognized, with perfect consistency, that some changes in land use would lessen the value of citizen's land. In that case, a "worsement" would occur and they would be entitled to an indemnity. We do not know whether, over a longer period, this approach might not have developed into a very useful and widely adoptable principle—that citizens have the right to own property but not to combine that ownership with full control of what could be called "development rights." After all, many market economies no longer extend ownership of the land's surface to underlying mineral rights. Transferring development rights to the community—either to local authorities or the central government—would simply mean that owners could gain only from the improvements they had made themselves. If they wished to develop their own land further, they would have to buy back the "development rights" which would equal the entire increase in the land's value. This system, coupled with a period of self-liquidating indemnification (while everyone with a possible grievance was paid off) might have proved consistent and workable. But the reasons given for ending the experiment in the early 1950s point to the difficulties which other countries have experienced in making similar attempts to capture unearned increment.

The first is the technical difficulty of determining its scale. Many landowners have undertaken some improvements. Their claims—as well as the claims of those who think they are losing out—must be objectively assessed and determined. This demands a very large and well trained technical staff—one reason, incidentally, for the difficulty of introducing such procedures into developing countries. It also requires a clearly understood and obviously impartial system to allow citizens to contest their assessments. This need for a large administrative apparatus seems to insure that the costs of collecting such taxes—which, as in France, can be very small—often do not justify the return. Add the overhang of claims for compensation (which grew to $350 million in Britain between 1947 and 1953) and it is easy to conclude that the exercise is hardly worthwhile. This conclusion may be wrong. Land prices rose steadily by seven to ten percent a year in Britain after the abolition of the experiment. And the experiment's length was in any case much too short to allow for the casting of a genuine balance sheet. But the complexity and expense of the system were made the excuse for ending it.

A second problem is that a very high development tax discourages people's readiness to sell their land. True, governments have inherited from the distant past the ultimate right of expropriation in the public good—the right of "eminent domain." But it can be a very large blunt instrument in market societies and implies involved issues of legal rights and agreed compensation. The scale of compensation to be paid for turning land over to public use weighs heavily on modern land use planning in the United States. Happily for the Americans, the vast continent was still empty enough in the nineteenth century to permit such men of enlightenment as Frederic Olmsted to persuade the Congress to establish federal ownership over large areas of unoccupied land, much of it of incomparable beauty and grandeur. About one-third of the United States is thus publicly owned and has the world's largest variety and scale of preserved wildernesses, nature sanctuaries, and national and state parks.

A third problem can rise from conflicts of jurisdiction between the central government and the local authorities in the assessment and distribution of the gain from development levies. In Holland, for instance, the municipalities can compete with each other for the use—or misuse—of very scarce land in one of the world's most densely populated countries and the central government is not always a welcome arbiter. One strand in Britain's yo-yo of experiments has been the unwillingness of local authorities to cede powers to a central Land

Commission. In the present round, the Labor Government has arranged for local authorities to receive all the development rights. The Opposition has duly promised to repeal the Act.

Perhaps the most infuriating difficulty from the point of view of the public authorities is the degree to which, as they begin to map out specific areas for new types of land use—particularly for new urban growth—the maps become what one cynic called "the speculators' guide." Since 1958, the French have tried to fix a date for the land's value and hence its selling price. In their *Zones d'urbanisme en priorité*—the ZUPS—the public authorities have the first right to purchase the land for a period of up to six years and may then pay for it at no more than the market value prevailing a year before it was assigned to the zone. In the *Zones d'aménagement différés*—the ZADS—the government's option to buy lasts fourteen years and the selling price is fixed at the market value at the time of ZAD designation—but adjustments are allowed for inflation. It is hard to say whether this array of controls and regulations has in fact reduced speculative gains. In most areas, landowners have not been willing to sell. The zones also attracted speculators to the land lying on their fringes. Land prices for unimproved but potential building sites tripled between 1950 and 1958, before the regulations were introduced. But then they tripled again in the next five years. Prices in Paris were still rising by ten percent a year in the late Sixties. But we must remember that this was a decade of very rapid urbanization in France which, among industrialized states, still had an exceptional percentage of its people in rural areas after World War II. Compared with, say, the fortyfold increase in land prices which took place in Japan's cities between 1947 and 1968, the constraints may be said to have had some effect.

Other more traditional taxes can be tried. "Unearned increment" can be reflected, as in France, in an individual's annual income tax. Local rates on the value of property can be adjusted, through regular reassessment, to reflect both betterment and "worsement." But it does seem that in Western Europe, at least, outright purchase by municipalities—or New Towns—in advance of need is one of the most workable ways of keeping some brakes on market prices. The Swedes were pioneers here. Gothenburg began buying land for its future as early as 1878, Stockholm in 1904. The city of Stockholm now owns three-quarters of itself and also areas outside for overspill. So do other

Swedish municipalities. Canadian cities such as Edmonton and Saskatoon have large land reserves, partly as a result of tax defaults in the past. Amsterdam is largely self-owned and municipalities in the Netherlands can receive loans from the central government for land acquisition. The prices are negotiated on an agreed basis, as are Britain's purchases for land for New Towns, at a level which does not exclude an element of market value. Appeals are also possible to contest the assessment. In the background is the tool of direct expropriation.

The advantage of these procedures is that the public authority can usually cover the cost of any improvements it makes by selling the improved land later at a higher price to commercial concerns or private interests or—as in Sweden—leasing its properties with periodic reassessments of the rent. Similar policies have helped those of Britain's New Towns that were built in the Fifties to cover their capital costs and begin to earn a reasonable return on the investment. Although these procedures do not directly separate land and development rights, advance buying has some of the same effects. The concept itself may be one of the most creative concepts for more general use in the decades ahead, particularly in developing lands where the next thirty to forty years may see as much building as in the whole previous history of mankind.

9 A GREEN AND PLEASANT LAND

THE QUESTION of who gains from development, important as it is for general principles of justice and particular effects of inflation, is not as vital as the much more complicated problem of insuring both that the right kind of development takes place and that the more intolerable results of past development begin to be erased. Few countries now would not recognize that the whole process implies some form and degree of planning. Even those who, in principle, proclaim most vehemently their dedication to the allocative superiority of the pure price mechanism often take advantage of the kinds of "zoning" for densities and types of housing which effectively exclude unwelcome neighbors. This, too, is "planning" and one of the perplexities of the process is to insure that the kind of preservation needed to safeguard communities whose inhabitants are well balanced and well content does not become a restrictive and selfish exclusivism.

For, clearly, the whole reason for extending the concept of planning in human society is precisely that reliance on price and chance, indifference to the needs of the poorest, and neglect of beauty and cleanliness have given us the plethora of unbalanced, unjust, and unattractive communities we endure today. The control of land use is a basic modern tool for redressing and avoiding traditional and encrusted evils. If it is used simply to perpetuate them, then its moral purpose is lost. So are the chances of creating a genuine community.

Given the mobility and the protean desires of modern man, land use planning cannot be less than nationwide. Resources, farm land, areas for recreation, patterns of mobility—all these help to determine the kind of life citizens can lead in their settlements, and they need to be entered into a careful national inventory. In densely populated and developed countries the careless preemption that has already taken place and the waste of much that is valuable or irreplaceable makes it all the more urgent to make better use of what is left.

In most developed countries, one part of the needed land survey has been more or less completed. Mineral resources and types of soil have been mapped. It would proably be unusual now to confront the dilemma of a town like Yallourn in Australia, which discovered that it has been built on top of the richest seams of opencast coal which the town had been built to secure in the first place. Even so, in Rumania, a country with a highly developed and successful strategy for the distribution of settlements, planners complain that some of their richest farmland has been inadvertently assigned to factories and towns.

The kind of resource planning that is almost certainly not complete is the impact of increased use on a number of "resources"—weather systems, watersheds, estuarine life—which in the past have been taken very much for granted as casual gifts of nature upon which men could draw indefinitely without strain or loss. To give just one instance of the kind of reappraising survey that is still needed, the antipollution measures taken early in this century in the densely industrialized Ruhr valley were long a prototype of what careful water management could achieve in preventing dangerous pollution. But recently it has been discovered that the degree to which the Ruhr has since been built up and paved over has undermined some of the efficiency of the careful earlier drainage systems. The soil no longer acts as a sponge for industrially polluted rain or escaping effluents. A good deal of pollution washes off the concrete surfaces straight into the rivers, bypassing the treatment plants altogether. This in turn increases the general pollution of the very much less carefully managed Rhine. The price of cleanliness is perpetual vigilance.

Many of the most vulnerable areas are also the most beautiful—the headwaters of river valleys, for instance, or the beaches of their estuaries. They, too, become prime targets for mobile man and require protection. Since World War II, more and more countries have followed the lead of the United States in establishing state parks and in trying to safeguard areas of great beauty from too much human intrusion. The Russians have done a Union-wide survey to determine the major areas for recreation and holiday-making for the more affluent days they see ahead. But not even the most farsighted government could have guessed what sustained high employment, three-to-four weeks' holidays with pay, the motorcar and the airplane would do to the number of travelers and to their appetite for sun and sea and mountains, with Baroque palaces, Gothic cathedrals, and Roman remains added, if possible, to the itinerary. Where all can be enjoyed together, as in Mediterranean countries, tourists increased from 24 million to 72 million between 1960 and 1973. Spain alone had to deal with 34.5 million visitors in 1973.

Internal movements can be as vast. In the United States, visitors to state parks increased from just over a hundred million to nearly five hundred million between 1950 and 1970. The increase for the great national parks was from about 40 million to 175 million. To accommodate this avalanche, acreages increased by a modest 700,000 acres in national parks and from 460 million acres to 860 million in state parks. Even so, the new densities were so overwhelming that in many parks, numbers have to be limited and the gates closed to would-be visitors when the quota is full.

Nor is the press of visitors the only problem. The Music Corporation of America was only barely prevented from building a vast convention center in the midst of Yosemite National Park's great peaks, cascading waterfalls, and millennial trees. The Sequoia National Park is threatened with a Disneyland alpine ski village costing $35 million and precisely designed to extend the flood of visitors to the entire year. Unless more areas of park are designated and some control imposed on annual numbers, the visitors will destroy what they come to see.

The pressures are also increasing in a number of areas because mountainsides and wood-ringed lakes and golden beaches are the favorite places for a new and growing phenomenon—the second home. Half of Sweden retires into modest cabins in the forests. Florida, California, the mountain states are the chief targets in America. Clearly, there is no way in which these pressures can be accommodated without some forms of planning and environmental control. Wall-to-wall hotels along the Costa Brava, alpine slopes covered with dinky little chalets straight out of Grimm's fairy tales spoil the view and the fun and the refreshment for everyone—visitors, second homers, residents alike.

One of the most spectacular ways of *not* exercising control acquired deserved notoriety in the United States in the booming Sixties. High-pressure salesmen went around selling speculative lots of unimproved land in such favorite retirement areas as Florida or the West

Coast. It is reported that prices of up to $8,000 an acre were being
charged for "choice sites" in California. Yet, nearby, land for $100
an acre could well be available. The effect of such boom prices—even
if they are also bust prices which lost their customers' shirts—means
that serious development planning for open space and for the preservation of natural beauty has to contend with a network of property claims
which may impede proper conservation for years and even, depending
upon court decision, forever.

It is estimated that a high percentage of the American customers
were really only taking a speculative ride. Again in California, at the
beginning of the Seventies, between 50,000 and 100,000 acres of rural
land were being subdivided every year. Yet in 1971, houses had been
built on only three percent of them. But the difficulties can be as great
with bona fide home builders. If every lot that has been sold in two
counties in the Pocono Mountains were to be built on, the population
would leap from 25,000 to 118,400 and change the character of the
area from mountain beauty to the beginnings of suburban sprawl.

Sound land use and environmental protection do not mean that
there should be no second homes, no centers for built-up recreation in
parks, no retreats for the elderly where the climate is kinder to aching
old bones. It simply implies that some areas should be preserved as
wilderness without intrusive human construction and that the second
homes and retirement communities should be grouped in pleasing settlements which respect the environment and mold themselves into the
scenery as comfortably and modestly as a Swiss mountain village or a
Cretan fishing port. There is also place for clearly defined, well-con-
tained, and unsprawling "recreation cities" which provide all the
commercial entertainment, pizza parlors, discotheques, beauty shows,
water skiing, and motor boating which a large number of tourists
prefer. The point is that only with firm land use planning, unimpeded
by rocketing land prices, can such variety be provided and the citizens' precious rights of choice maintained.

The principle of using land use regulations to construct workable
and attractive settlements poses a problem which goes far beyond recreation centers or second homes. The citizens' own choice of the kind
of community they want can be debated in cities, towns, villages, in
fact wherever residents begin to feel that growth and change are not
opportunities but threats.

In the Fifties and Sixties an almost unanimous pursuit of economic expansion swept across the United States, communities competing with each other to tempt industrial and commercial enterprise (admittedly even then the preference was for the highest, newest technology innoxiously run by white-coated PhDs). But in many areas the mood has changed. Oregon has taken away the welcoming mat not only to settlers but even to visitors. It had discovered that by the late Seventies it might have to accommodate ten million tourists in a state of only two million people. Denver refused to play host to the Winter Olympic Games, reckoning the increase in needed facilities and boost to further growth to be exactly what the city did not require. A California community—Petaluma—may find itself turned into a constitutional precedent on the issue of whether a community has the right to preserve its present integrity against uncontrollable pressures for growth coming from outside. This small town, about forty miles north of San Francisco and to a degree part of its "magnetic field," grew from 10,300 in 1950 to 24,000 in 1969. In two years it grew to over 30,000. With the concurrence of the community, the city fathers said: stop.

In June 1973, the citizens approved, by four to one, an ordinance instituted in August 1972 rationing growth to 500 dwelling units a year for the ensuing five years. This law does not affect single-family homes or four-unit apartments so long as they are not part of a larger project. But at this point, the issue of controlling land use through community decision raised an extremely complicated set of legal issues. We have already noted the fact that land use planning, far from being a newcomer to the American scene, has long been used to preserve the quality of high and middle income settlements. The instrument is zoning. If the ratio of land to houses and of rooms to houses is high enough, poorer people—who are often black—are effectively excluded.

However, the decision to slow down growth as a general community interest is perceived by some landowners and most construction companies as a possible threat to their interest. In Petaluma, the builders took the city to court to have the limitation on growth overturned on the grounds that it denied people their constitutional right to move and settle at will anywhere in the United States. In the first round, they won. But the town appealed and in the summer of 1975 the federal appeals court upheld the legality of the city's right to regulate its own pace of growth. The building industry, which is reported to have set up a $500 million war chest to fight this and similar decisions, says it will go to the Supreme Court. The degree to which, for generations, exclusive zoning has not raised a flicker of protest somewhat undermines an outside observer's faith in the pure constitutional ardor of the construction industry. Yet the risk that setting limits to a community's growth can even further reduce the mobility of the poor is a serious issue and there is point in the argument that if every community took to exclusive provisions, a certain proportion of the people—the majority of them poor, handicapped, and powerless—could almost literally have nowhere to go.

Are there any positive answers to these dilemmas? Possible social responses designed to lessen the strains inside urban communities will be discussed on a later page. In terms of land use planning, the difficulties point to two conclusions; one is to hasten, in market economies, the separation of development and property rights so that vested interests in higher land prices do not even arise. The second is to recognize that a rational policy for enhancing human settlements cannot be built up simply community by community. A *national* plan is required to secure reasonable balance and to see that both the gains and burdens of growth and change are more equitably shared.

The problems of small, balanced communities bring us to another category of land use—land devoted to agriculture and the communities occupied by rural people. The first requirement is clearly to map and protect the usable soils. And where, for a time, alternative uses unavoidably conflict with each other—for instance, coal that can be strip-mined lying under very fertile soil—the restoration of the land once mined to agricultural quality and the avoidance of slopes or watersheds where the mining does irretrievable damage should be written into the preconditions for the mining project. What can be achieved is well illustrated by the Rheinische Braunkohlenwerke of Cologne. This firm takes 42 million tons of brown coal out of their Fortuna Garsdorf pit each year—the largest output in the world from a single brown coal mine. Yet to the South and East of the twelve-square-mile mine, sugarbeet and wheat are already growing lushly on restored land which has been given a gentle southern slope to improve growing conditions. Since twelve tons of water has to be pumped out with every ton of coal, this too is being "reprocessed" for water supplies in nearby Düsseldorf and for creation of lakes. This example of scrupulous conservation and land use has the added advantage of making a profit.

Land does not farm itself. The human communities responsible for production may also need protection. The actual number of agricultural workers—managers or laborers—has shrunk or is still shrinking in every developed land. But there is an irreducible minimum and on these workers the impact of outsiders and would-be settlers can be positive or negative. In every developed country, there are a certain number of citizens who long for the country as passionately as Marie Antoinette loved playing shepherdess in the Petit Trianon away from the incredible boredom and stupidity of the Versailles routine. These town dwellers do not want to be farmers. But they love gardening and the small scale and profound quiet of the countryside renew jangled nerves and weary minds after weeks in the highly pressured and often inhumanly abstract urban world of the "transactional society." Nor is the country cottage always a weekend retreat. If a train journey of fifty miles takes not much longer than the five-mile trip from the suburbs, why not commute? New York's "commutershed" spreads over parts of three states and half of Long Island.

This longing for the rural is not simply an odd Anglo-Saxon attitude. The Trianon mood has not faded in France either. In the Sixties, at a time when the number of working agriculturalists was continuing to decline rapidly, rural population actually increased in a quarter of France's communes, particularly in those near large industrial or urban agglomerations. The positive aspect of this occupation of rural settlements by urban people is quite simply that all too often there simply is not the local money to restore rural homes to decent standards. The gleaming new thatch, the fresh white stucco, those genuinely "Tudor" beams would all have been a jumble of sagging roofs and broken walls without the injection of outside money. The negative aspect is an urban invasion which pushes land costs and the cost of everything else beyond the reach of rural purses and gives the farming community the sense of being compelled to live beyond its means in order to provide a stage-setting for urban actors. (An interesting parallel can be found in the mountainous parts of New England, where local residents discovered that the free selling of subdivisions for summer homes and winter skiing was driving taxes and prices beyond the modest local income level and as a result literally forcing the resident population to leave.) Once again, control of land prices and careful community planning are part of the answer.

It may be that the plight of Europe's farmers raises a new and more fundamental question. What scale of agricultural community do developed nations require in new conditions of possible world scarcity? If one thing is certain in the next quarter century, it is that the world's need for food will inexorably increase. In developed countries, in the last fifty years, the sheer availability of supplies made glut, not shortage, the main problem. This led to notable casualness in the transfer of even prime agricultural land to other purposes—roads, airports, suburbs. Yet countries like Britain or Japan provide less than half their own food and have long lived on the assumption of cheap world supplies of grain. So have the Dutch. However, the emergence of the Soviet Union and possibly, later, of China as major competitors for what could be fairly static grain reserves must surely compel some drastic rethinking of the role of land use planning in preserving or releasing land for the farmers. But a relative lack of attention to the needs and priorities of rural settlements has not reflected simply the easy availability of food. It is also a function of the overwhelming urbanization of developed societies. With virtually three-quarters of the people living in built-up areas in the market economies and the percentage steadily rising in Eastern Europe and the U.S.S.R., town dwellers have enjoyed a kind of natural, unnoticed priority.

They have also produced the most intractable problems all around the modern urban conurbations. In many developed countries, careful land use planning has not developed any further than in the days of Dickens' giant concrete footsteps. City after city is surrounded by a no-man's land of areas lapsing from farming, waiting for redevelopment, held in speculative lots and suffering all the ugliness of purposelessness and neglect. When such zones stretch twenty or thirty miles out from the center-city, they impose an added deprivation on the poorest citizens who cannot afford to travel further in the search for natural beauty and refreshment. When one remembers that an average car outing is not much above twenty-five miles away from home, even well-to-do families may go out to see cows and fields and greenery and come back having seen privately barred suburban gates, abandoned fields, decaying poultry sheds, second-hand car lots, and all the paraphernalia of declining use and care—hardly a refreshment to the weary urban spirit. The poor citizens barely get out of their impacted slums and in many areas do not even have access to a public park because there is no park. If they try bathing in the local river they may, as was once said of the chemically polluted Hudson River, "not drown but dissolve."

A restoration of use and beauty to the land within and around the conurbations should therefore be given a much higher priority for reasons both of justice and of environmental decency. Part of the answer lies in the designation and clearing of areas for public recreation with the provision of woodlands, bathing areas, and picnic places. (It is remarkable how often a careful restoration of lands emptied of gravel can be restored to graceful parks with lakes for fishing and boating). Another answer is for suburban citizens to take into their own hands a measure of local "spring cleaning." Especially if it proves possible to develop, in the gray sprawl of undifferentiated suburban areas, more tightly-knit and well-provided communities—an issue discussed on a later page—one of the means of differentiation could lie in the systematic planting of trees and groves to establish borderlines, emphasize communities, and at the same time create pleasant walks and sights within easy reach. The use of intercity land for food production is also likely to need a quite new emphasis. It is significant that that most frugal of people, the Chinese, have brought their horticulture and their market gardens into the inner rings of land surrounding the older cities. It is significant, too, that in many developed countries there are queues of eager urban citizens who would gladly cultivate their own patch of soil, their "allotment," if more land were available and procedures simplified.

Wasted, polluted, corrupted earth, filled with junked cars and old iron, is more than just sloppy and ugly. It spells indifference to human need, a wanton neglect of fundamental decencies. As one of Britain's most distinguished town planners, Sir Colin Buchanan, once put it: "I hate squalor. It subtly suggests violence." How can we hope that a whole generation of young people, growing up with nothing but roads to play on, with slagheaps as a background and dirty rubbish lying all around, will learn to be anything but rough and careless themselves? And it takes so little human effort for the community itself to turn the neglected places into sports fields, adventure playgrounds, or public parks that no one can blame the children if vandalism and violence take over as a result of the adults' culpable failure to care and act. When one remembers that Britain's public bill for vandalism and mindless destruction amounted to a thousand million dollars in 1974, one sees it is a very expensive neglect that communities can inflict upon themselves.

10 RESHAPING THE NATION

THE MOST complicated questions of land use arise in the developed countries' cities for the simple reason that so much has been built and so many mistakes have already been firmly encased in steel and concrete. But perhaps three problems are emerging as most troublesome and most likely to counter the basic aims we are trying to examine—coherence in policy, justice in execution, and a sound environmental balance sheet.

The first concerns the relationship between the center-city, its surrounding conurbation, and the increasing evidence that a mismatch of jobs and residence is wasting untold hours of time and uncounted units of petroleum in trying to offset the effects by universal mobility. The second is the problem of keeping a regional balance of vitality and wealth so that no areas drift into the atmosphere of stagnation and decay to be found in parts of Northern France or Scotland's Clydeside or much of Southern Italy. The third is in effect a particular part of this wider problem. Every country has a very large number of smaller towns, often inherited from a more agricultural past, which combine a valuable inheritance with a steadily declining economic base. This may not be a priority issue compared with the "grandeurs and miseries" of the big metropolis. But in any adding up of all the nation's debits and credits, it can determine the life of at least a third of the citizens.

What have developed countries to tell us about these problems? What solutions are beginning to emerge? We must look first at the Soviet Union since it is, by all odds, the "master builder" of our time. With 1400 new towns constructed over the last half century, it has displayed an élan of urban growth equal to the most booming periods of early industrialism and, in theory at least, it has done so without the sometimes irrational consequences of relying solely on price signals.

There were no obstacles to a planned development since all the levers of power were under government control.

But planning in the sense of a careful balancing of better and worse, of economic and social priorities, and of special problems and interests was hardly the kind of planning the Soviet Union could afford first in the gigantic Stalinist effort of the 1930s to catch up with the industrial power of Western Europe (including that of Nazi Germany) and then in the equally herculean task of making good the ravages of war. Planning in fact was concentrated on virtually one objective, massive industrial growth and, within it, priority for resource development and heavy industry. The cities were built as appendages to this drive, rather as Manchester followed the cotton industry or Pittsburgh the growth of steel. And some of the same evils followed—neglect of social costs and civic amenities and a tendency for industrial cities to grow and sprawl beyond the ideal limits of theoretical plans. Indeed, as late as the 1960s, some of the largest centers—Kiev, Sverdlovsk, Kharkov, Odessa—had no city plans at all. And in most settlements, dominant power has tended to remain with the industrial sector, supplying direct links to the all-Union economic ministries and the final arbiter, the Gosplan.

What effect has this overwhelming drive of industrialization had on the main problems of spatial planning? The largest cities have grown beyond communist planners' optimum size—which is a city of between half a million and a million inhabitants. Moscow, as capital city, has broken every restraint. In 1932, all further industrialization was banned to keep the people at about three million. In 1935, five million was fixed for the upper limit and a rough system of work permits introduced to block all immigration. The devastations and disorganizations of war slowed growth a little but also dismantled the controls. By the 1950s, the population had risen to five million and another million were added when in 1960 outlying settlements were included in the city's jurisdiction. United Nations forecasts speak of eight million by the 1980s. Leningrad, too, was supposed to have reached its permissible limit in the 1930s but has since doubled to over four million. Other traditional cities have passed the million mark, in spite of long-standing efforts to concentrate growth in nearby satellite settlements and a more recent ban on any further industrialization in all major cities this side of the Urals.

Yet, on any international scale, with or without effective planning,

Soviet urban growth has been more compact and more regionally balanced than in many Western countries. Moscow may be heading for eight million but it only contains just under three percent of Russia's total population. The Paris region contains about seventeen percent of all French people, Greater London some twenty percent of Britain's inhabitants. Again, as a federal system, Russia devolves to provincial capitals a level of tertiary and "quaternary" functions which the country's machinery of centralized economic planning does not entirely override. Another factor in city concentration is the absence of motorcars until very recently and the need to keep jobs and homes within the capacity of a workable if, in Moscow, a somewhat dispersed system of public transport. In fact, the chief criticisms made of Soviet planning have been leveled not at spatial distribution but at conditions *inside* the cities and at the overwhelming economic and industrial preoccupations of central governments which are held to be responsible for gaps in urban amenities. And this shortcoming is probably most keenly felt in smaller towns which make their comparisons with the relative well-being of provincial capitals; they in turn envy the prestige accorded to Moscow's city government and civic institutions. "If only we could go to Moscow"—the cry of Chekhov's three sisters is still heard (especially perhaps in Siberia) and is one reason why it is difficult to stop the city's steady, stealthy expansion.

That a functioning federal system can exercise some pressure for regionalism and decentralization is confirmed by the experience of West Germany and Switzerland. Both are intensely industrialized and highly involved in the world's "transactional" society. Yet the provincial capitals in Germany are either about or not much above the million mark. They preserve a degree of separate identity even within the densely populated urban region of the Ruhr (helped no doubt by its configuration of hills and valleys). Sturdy memories of historical independence have also helped to reinforce local demands for genuine autonomy in planning. Switzerland's cantonal government gives it the most decentralized structure in the developed world, and with the usual eighty percent of the population in industrial, tertiary, and transactional activities, only thirty-five percent of the Swiss live in cities larger than 200,000 inhabitants. But, once again, mountains and valleys help.

One of the paradoxes of Britain's position is that it produced the first "urban region," has tried out probably the greatest variety of policies to offset its disadvantages, but still cannot be said to have found a satisfactory pattern. One answer may be simply historical. The reason why in the nineteenth century London pulled so far ahead of other centers—first Manchester, then Birmingham—was its status as a world city, head of a vast empire, financial center for the whole globe, and keeping in Westminister all the sovereign powers of an administratively very united kingdom. These were also the political magnets bringing twenty percent of the population to Greater London and an even larger share to Southeast England.

Since World War II, a number of strategies for spatial planning have been pursued to counter imbalances in the distribution of the country's wealth and population. They have undoubtedly had considerable impact on world thinking about town planning. But they do not seem to have produced all the answers that were hoped for on the spot. The first strategy is to take the strain off big center cities by building completely New Towns around them—rather on the Ebenezer Howard principle of enjoying home, work, and recreation within walking distance of each other in green and open surroundings. These new communities are designed to remove excess urban population and thus lessen congestion in the inner city. To encourage regional balance the policy has also been applied not only to London with its ten New Towns but to other such overcrowded and aging centers as Manchester and Glasgow. All in all, thirty-one New Towns have been designated or built since 1945. To counter the magnetic attraction of the whole Southeast, a more ambitious "New City" in the shape of Milton Keynes is being built for 400,000 inhabitants well to the north of London. In addition, the larger towns have been encouraged to make "overspill" arrangements with smaller neighbors, again to lessen pressure and spread economic activity and purchasing power. To this we should add strong economic incentives to industries to set themselves up in the older conurbations and the dispersal to regional centers of some of Central London's large bureaucracies such as those for social insurance and the licensing of motor vehicles.

But, quite apart from the general malaise and uncertain economic and social climate in a country learning not to be at the center of a world system, some of the calculations and balances seem to have gone wrong. In moving people and services and light industries to New Towns, the plans, often inadvertently, seem to have left too many unskilled people behind without jobs at the center. For them, no increase in transactional or bureaucratic opportunity can help. They lack the training. Too many needed occupations have moved out. Too many commuters still come in. Would a part of the New Town invest-ment—some $4,000 million over the years—have worked better in a plan for, say, new "cities-within-cities" in London or Liverpool or Glasgow? The Greater London Council thinks so. It is also the opinion of a distinguished and experienced urbanist, Dr. Laughlin Currie. He believes that "in some cases, the New Towns appear to have gone too far, as in the Liverpool region where they have shared responsibility for the decline of the population of Liverpool itself from 800,000 to 600,000 and, worse, have drained off much of the more remunerative employment, leaving a desolate city unable to provide adequate ser-vices." New York and Detroit have tried few of Britain's bold decen-tralizing policies. But is the result very different if, by private or public decision, the match between jobs and homes falls equally away?

At another level, does the construction of completely New Towns in the regions lessen the chances of traditional smaller cities—a Pres-ton or a Hereford or a Gloucester—to maintain an economic base strong enough to prevent the departure of skilled people and an exodus of the young? Would it have been wiser to have directed the new in-dustrial and service opportunities to them?

The fact that these questions are raised makes all the more lively and searching the interest in France's urban plans. Those who have watched New York teeter on the edge of bankruptcy and Glasgow turn into the most deprived of British cities follow with profound attention and hope what is by far the boldest experiment yet made in mixed market economies to achieve better national balance by spatial plan-ning. The French experiment, conceived in the late 1950s, aims at reshaping the whole of France's urban environment. It is now gather-ing momentum all over the country and is precisely designed to counter over-concentration, achieve better regional balance, and insure that smaller communities are not left behind. The starting point is, of course, the overwhelming predominance of Paris. In 1960, the Pari-sian conurbation had almost reached eight million. In the whole of the rest of France only two cities had more than half a million inhabitants, not one a million. True, forty cities added together reached eight million. But the point is that they were scattered and isolated. If market and industrial expansion in the postwar years had been allowed to remain combined with traditional centralized administration, the whole of France's future growth might well have ended up as part of one vast, all-embracing region of Paris.

To prevent this gargantuan possibility, the French Government in the last two decades has employed virtually every known instrument of positive land use planning. Within Paris itself, to offset the risk of urban decline, it has three projects for renewed "cities-within-cities"—Défense, Italie, and, more dubiously, Les Halles. At the same time, a part of the population is being encouraged to move out. One means of persuasion is heavy taxation on business enterprises which seek to establish themselves in Paris, another is equally heavy taxes on those who stay—the proceeds are destined to improve public transport, which includes modernizing the subway system, renewing the entire rolling stock used on subways and commuter lines, and building road systems to bypass Paris completely. Moreover, the number of houses eligible for state money in the Sixth Plan (1971–1975) was fixed at 500,000. Estimates suggest that in 1973, for the first time in Paris' centuries-old history, more people left the city than came into it.

But at the same time, care is to be taken to see that Paris can still exercise its world role as a center of business, investment, scholarship, research, tourism—the "quaternary" sector which truly designates the great international city. The University of Paris has been given ten new campuses, spread over the whole city, new large hotels are being built, and convention centers are in construction. However, one of the proposed districts—a new financial center on the old site of the historic wholesale market, Les Halles—has run into difficulties. They resemble a similar impasse in London, also over an old market district, Covent Garden. It, too, had a fine-sounding plan with, no doubt, five multistory car parks, four business blocks, three international hotels, two convention centers, and conceivably one remaining partridge in a rather discouraged pear tree. But at this point, in both cities, the scale and impersonality of what was proposed, the intense life and human scale of what was to be destroyed called a halt. It is part of a wider questioning of the tactic of "clear felling" for urban renewal which we must examine on a later page.

To prevent the exodus from Paris from simply turning into sprawling undifferentiated rings of suburbia around the center city—with only very limited curbs on commuting—a further strategy was introduced. The whole basin of the River Seine round Paris is being reorganized on the basis of five new clustered communities much influenced in plans and financing by the British New Towns concept but on a larger scale and with more intention of organizing direct links with the center city. Cergy-Pontoise, St. Quentin-en-Yvelines, Évry, Melun-Sénart, and Marne-La-Vallée all combine local employment, experiments in housing, layout and traffic, and quick rapid transit into Paris. But, as in Britain, there still seems to be some problem in organizing green space, parks, and areas for recreation in the interstices of the new system.

Yet Paris is held to exercise so heroic a pull on the whole country that local reorganization is not enough. The plans include two further instruments of decentralization. One corresponds to some extent to the Milton Keynes concept—counter-magnets just beyond the present Parisian field of force. Eight cities, all with over 100,000 inhabitants and all between 110 and 220 kilometers distant from Paris, are being strengthened and diversified so that they can take more of the industry diverted from Paris and also gain a larger share of transactional activities and the office buildings and specialized institutions they require. Amiens, Rouen, Caen, Le Mans, Tours and Orléans, Rheims and Troyes, all cities with a proud tradition and a solid civic infrastructure, have been chosen and are being developed in a variety of ways. Universities have been founded at Rheims, Orléans, and Tours. Caen has had its office space expanded. Rouen was given a new town, Le Vaudreuil, within its metropolitan area and this town is being built to entirely new specifications for recycling materials and countering pollution. Tours and Orléans are seen as twinned cities, defining between them a new "metropolitan region."

Yet given the past history of overwhelming concentration, the French authorities have gone still further toward the kind of regional development West Germany and Switzerland appear to have achieved more by federation than by planning. From among the forty cities with a combined population of eight million, the authorities chose eight of the largest to become *métropoles d'équilibre*—"balancing metropolitan centers"—capable of entering the magic new modern world of international contacts and transactional activities and thus offer Paris the genuine challenge of comparable influence, attraction, excitement, and skill.

Lille, Strasbourg, Nancy and Metz as twinned cities, Nantes and St. Nazaire—twinned again—Lyon (with St. Etienne and Grenoble as cooperating triplets), Bordeaux, Toulouse, and Marseilles (with Aix as a linked city) were selected and work started on a whole variety of balancing strategies. Bordeaux and Nantes-St. Nazaire are to receive heavy industry and Nantes, a new university. Industrial renewal and extension are planned for Metz-Nancy. Lille, too, is a triplet with two old industrial centers, Tourcoing and Roubaix, and has in addition a new town in Lille-Est. Lyon gets an international airport as well as a new town—at L'Isle d'Abeau—while Marseilles acquires not only a new port complex but a series of "new towns" round Etang de Berre which, with 700,000 inhabitants, will create a new urban region.

With so much activity concentrated on the immediate Paris basin, in the wider Paris region and in the eight "balancing metropolitan centers," it would be pardonable to guess that the limit of resources and organizing skill had been reached and that, as a result, a whole range of valuable, historical, and somewhat vulnerable medium cities would fall into neglect and decay. But this is not the case. The French plan is, after all, a full national plan with a dedication to the highest degree of creative integration for all the people. The chief instrument of French planning, DATAR (*Direction d'Aménagement Territorial et Régional*) is certainly not skimped for either funds or talents and has decided on one further element in the program, one which bears some resemblance to the special arrangements worked out between Britain's urban regions and the smaller towns nearby.

In the late Sixties, there were 193 French cities with populations of between 20,000 and 200,000. They were showing some of the weaknesses demonstrated in Britain—a decline in the number of younger inhabitants, an exodus of professions and skills. Moreover, one element in their recent rapid growth had ceased. Migration out of farming was all but complete. Yet they were and are basically endowed with real advantages. Their costs per citizen for urban infrastructure and services are lower than in the larger metropolises and this advantage does not seem to be offset by relatively less output per worker until the half million mark is passed. All these calculations are, in any case, what President Roosevelt used to like to call "iffy." Lower urban costs simply reflect lower investment *if* local services are less adequate. Higher productivity in larger centers is fictitious *if* the so-called economies of scale leave out heavy social and environmental costs. It is uncertainties of this sort that tend to discourage the search for an "optimum" size. It can vary with costs, endowments, geography, and tradition. What is certain is that medium cities are perfectly viable entities. Economically, they do not offer acute difficulty. In terms of community, of access to nature, of pace of life they clearly offer considerable attractions, especially if they are within reach of the cultural and intellectual stimulus that a citizen looks for (sometimes vainly) in a larger urban complex. It is these smaller cities which have continued to grow, even after the slowing down of the agricultural exodus. Strategies for a more balanced population can hardly afford to disregard such a balance sheet and the French planners are now at work, negotiating conventions, city by city, to tailor the aid and stimulus they can give to the precise needs of the local community.

At one place, it may be the restoration of an historic town center, at another a renewal program for durable but rundown housing, at yet another, help with pedestrian areas and parking space or the addition of an institution of higher education. It is more like constructing a mosaic than a map. But the aim in each place is to discover the exact sliver of stone that pulls the pattern into place—or perhaps the more appropriate analogy would be the right enzyme to speed up the desired processes of change. In addition, the medium cities are being more closely linked to the national road network. Another general measure, designed to safeguard their historic character and medium scale, was introduced recently. If a town has fewer than 50,000 inhabitants, no single housing plan can have more than 1000 units. In cities above 50,000, the limit is 2000. In this way, it is hoped to preserve the nonmetropolitan character of smaller places and avoid the spread of uniform, anonymous, styleless factory-type architecture across the fair face of France.

No developed society has evolved so complete and sophisticated a land use plan as the French. It includes every feature by which planners have tried since the Second World War to lessen the combination of over-concentration and sprawl that has marked the "unintended city." We shall encounter particular aspects of the effort later on. Here it need only be repeated that in literally every postwar plan we discover an effort to take the load off center-cities, to snatch back identity and community from the vast gray areas of suburban sprawl, to check unwieldy urban growth by countergrowth in other areas, and at the same time to safeguard the continued vitality of a whole spectrum of sizes and traditions in human communities. The plans do not all succeed. But their direction is remarkably similar.

11 HOUSE AND HOME

LET US BEGIN with the issue of intention—do affluent societies seriously mean to house all their people? It is important to state from the outset with the strongest possible emphasis that if a wealthy nation does leave any of its citizens in poor, unhealthy, substandard housing, the issue is one of choice, not necessity. It means that government and people alike have not given the provision of homes the attention and priority which, in justice, in humanity, in dignity and compassion, they require. As we shall see, there are all kinds of hurdles and obstacles to overcome in achieving such a program. Nor should anyone suppose that all social problems—violence, delinquency, broken homes, infirm and lonely old age—will automatically vanish if decent housing is provided. Social processes and pressures are far too complicated for any "one-shot" solution to be relied on to work automatic miracles. But we can say that every social problem is made worse by what the French call "insalubrious housing," and that in wealthy lands this aggravation is a matter of choice, not necessity. To give the example of Britain, the official estimate in 1974 was that some 393,000 more houses a year would be needed in the quinquennium 1972 to 1977. The shortfall between 1972 and 1975 was 300,000. In spite of all Britain's problems of inflationary pressure and high public spending, no one could maintain that 100,000 more houses a year would have ruined a country whose spending, for instance, on cars and roads during that period reach $22,000 million.* The shortfall was political, not economic.

The example of West Germany is a decisive proof of this. Ger-

* This figure covers public spending on roads and private spending on cars.

many's record in housing until the Second World War was probably as unsatisfactory as any in the then industrializing world. In 1939, only ten and a half million houses, many of them substandard, served a population of nearly 69 million. Then came the deluge—the battering of Germany's cities under wartime bombardment and the irreparable loss in Western Germany of over two million homes, with another two and a quarter million heavily damaged. War losses of population were amply compensated by the arrival of some ten million migrants from East Germany and other parts of Eastern Europe. The rough estimate for West Germany's housing deficit in the late 1940s was from four to five and a half million homes.

The federal government then gave the highest priority to rebuilding. Incentives and subsidies encouraged private builders. Cooperatives and nonprofit institutions—the equivalent of Britain's Building Societies—undertook subsidized building for poorer families. The target of two million new houses was met by 1956 (nearly 600,000 homes were completed in that year alone). By 1970, another eight million houses had been built for a population that had reached sixty million people. Thus, the number in each "dwelling unit" had fallen by nearly half—from 4.6 persons to 2.7. The ideal of one person to each room had been achieved, indeed rather more than achieved since the "statistical inhabitant" per room had fallen to a strange, rather Picasso-like abstract figure of 0.79 of a person.

Of these 20 million houses, about forty percent are subsidized and nearly a third of those put up since the war have been built by the nonprofit sector. Not all the houses are up to standard. Among the older and often rural stock, nineteen percent have no indoor lavatory, thirty percent no bathroom. But given the scale of the destruction and the prewar record of shabby neglect, the Germans have proved that if a resourceful and hard-working people devote a steady five to six percent of their gross national product to housing, a vast transformation can be achieved in only two decades. Nor can anyone, following the growth of the German economy through the same period, argue that the priority for housing has acted as much of a drag on other sectors. On the contrary, the very steadiness and comprehensiveness of the program has been an important stimulus to the rest of the economy. It is unfortunate for the "image" of a number of other market economies that the Germans should have inconveniently removed so many respectable fig leaves and alibis in the matter of providing ample housing. If wealthy industrialized countries want to give their citizens decent homes, they can. If they do not, the will is absent and the first need is not new building codes or new industrialized construction systems or yet another redistribution of responsibility or that ever rotating, ever passing, high speed buck. It is a political conversion, a change of heart.

And in case the German lesson is dismissed as special or untypical or explicable only in terms of German industriousness, one can point out that the Dutch, the most densely populated of all developed peoples, have managed to achieve virtually the same record. Heavy war damage and a shortfall of over a quarter of a million dwellings after the war has been turned into a near-surplus. The housing stock has more than doubled since 1945 and 130,000 new units are being added every year. In fact, if the postwar years had not seen a rapid increase in small "nuclear" families and single occupiers, there would now be a genuine surplus of homes in Holland.

In the planned economies where, as we have seen, the first postwar need was the reconstruction of the economy's productive base, housing has enjoyed a steadily increasing priority since the mid-Fifties. The Soviet Union, for instance, had to contend not only with vast war damage but with a rate of urbanization more typical of a developing country than of an already industrialized power. At a time when Britain experienced very little change in its percentage of rural people—around twenty-two percent of the national total—the rural percentage in Russia fell by at least nine percent and urban construction had to make good the houses lost through war, cope with a natural urban increase of over 14 million souls, and absorb the rural increment. Between 1959 and 1965, the aim was to double urban dwelling units—to some 30 million—a target that was eighty-five percent fulfilled. Between 1966 and 1970 there was a further eighteen percent increase in the volume of housing. All in all, over the two postwar decades, the number of houses tripled while population only doubled.

There is no claim that the housing problem is "solved." Indeed, the 1971–75 Plan included a further increase, as well as new attention to emerging criticisms of architectural poverty of design and poor maintenance. But the sheer bulk of housing construction is yet another proof that the decisive element in developed countries' housing policy is political will.

We can, therefore, conclude that every developed country is perfectly able to meet the first need in the provision of shelter—a stock of housing with at least one room for each member of the family, together with the usual services. Such a sustained national strategy, with clearly defined goals and a commitment which is not left to the mercy of recurrent fluctuations in economic activity not only helps the citizen; it makes a vital contribution to a large labor-intensive economic sector, stimulates private savings for home-ownership, and thus becomes a steadying factor in the maintenance of a more stable economy and level of employment. Until the onslaught of inflation in 1972, developed societies in general had shown a considerable improvement both in the priority given to housing and in the numbers of dwellings built each year. In both market and planned economies, the number of houses completed for each group of 1,000 citizens tended to lie within the six to ten range at the beginning of the Seventies. Britain, Italy, and East Germany were among the few with a rather lower level. Sweden providing nearly thirteen houses and Japan nearly seventeen were exceptionally high—but the backlog in Japan was correspondingly large. For the next decade, a steady target of eight to ten houses per 1,000 people would be perfectly manageable, and given Europe's more or less stable population, would tend to produce a comfortable margin there by, say, 1985.

The existence of a near-surplus is in itself one of the most straightforward ways of insuring that every citizen, including the poorest—and preferably, the poorest first—will be housed in decency. Obviously, if the housing stock is deficient, the pressure on rents or prices will move upward in market economies, and favors and under-the-counter arrangements are likely to increase in planned ones. Much of Belgium's housing is over half a century old and perhaps thirty percent of it is below acceptable standards. But just because the stock is very large—it is said that every Belgian is born with a brick in his belly—there are in fact more homes than families and accommodation is easily available for renting.

But the intention to secure a statistically satisfactory provision of houses does not necessarily satisfy our second precondition for acceptable settlements—the achievement of elementary justice. In developed countries the large and usually growing middle classes can house themselves. The critical, and difficult, question is whether the poorest citizens are being steadily removed from squalid houses and communities and here the answer is much less certain.

There are a number of ways in which the people who cannot afford the full economic cost of a house can find shelter. One is to subsidize housing from the public purse. In Holland, eighty percent of the houses built since the war—some two million of them—have received subsidies.

About forty percent of West Germany's housing is termed "social" because some public support has been given to its construction. In some countries, Britain for instance, the public authorities are the owners of thirty-one percent of the housing stock. The subsidy is, as it were, attached to the building and the tenant receives the benefit in a rent that does not cover full economic costs. One of the miseries of inflation is that the widening gap between the cost of new homes and the level of rent that an increasing number of poor tenants can pay implies ever larger subsidies, higher public spending, and further inflationary pressure.

There is another difficulty. Many families, especially families with more than one earner, have long since ceased to be hard-pressed. They could comfortably afford higher rents. But they are not about to move themselves out of a subsidized house simply to oblige the local borough council. So the authorities lack the flexibility that would come from being able to spread their costs over the whole spectrum of their housing—from the oldest that have long since been fully amortized to the new, often much more expensive construction. In this way, they could manage with uniformly lower rents.

This problem of economic rent can complicate the provision of new housing in another way. Since so many cities are already covered with dense housing on the verge of sliding into slums—or already there—it can be argued, with Rex Tugwell, that the first job is to get rid of the decrepit building and build new shining edifices in their place. But the old buildings, long since amortized, allowed very low rents. Knock them down and their former residents may find that the new buildings, however well equipped, are entirely beyond their means, even with a measure of subsidy. They have to move on, doubling up where they can—and the blight spreads. This helps to explain the paradox we encounter in some countries—that the number of houses is increasing and homelessness growing at the same time. Even in a country with as fine a housing record as that of the Netherlands, 35,000 households are reckoned to be technically "homeless."

Some governments find it more flexible and workable to subsidize the tenant rather than the house. In West Germany, for instance, rent supplements (*wohngeld*) are issued, without any bureaucratic fuss—or any annoying official prying into private lives and habits—simply on the production of a certificate stating the applicant's income. Countries which permit mortgage payment to be deducted from gross income—the United States, for instance, or Britain—also subsidize the citizen, not the house, in this case, for ownership. Such a procedure can be used as a tool for helping the poorer groups, although tax deductions allowable on expensive houses represent a very considerable transfer of public funds to wealthier members of society. It has been estimated, for instance, that if the cost of the mortgage for which British tax deductions are permissible were reduced from $50,000 to $20,000, the British government would gain between $600 and $800 million a year in extra taxation. This would be a not inconsiderable sum to devote to rent or mortgage subsidies for the poorest citizens. In fact, in 1975, $200 million was cut from the annual sum of $500 million that had been set aside for the renovation of old housing stock. It would be no small thing in Britain's present condition of stringency to be able to double and treble the funds for rehabilitating really poor homes.

These two issues, mortgages and rehabilitation, have a relevance to housing problems that goes far beyond the British experience. In a highly mobile population, rented accommodation will always be necessary and have an important part to play, provided reasonable safeguards can be arranged against gouging landlords on the one hand and slovenly and immovable tenants on the other—for instance, by the kind of negotiation and supervision of rentals carried out by the Netherlands authorities. But if one fact more than any other has emerged from the whole range of postwar experiments in rehousing the people, it is a steady growth in the desire for personal ownership, for "a home of one's own," for the dignity and autonomy of being in secure possession of the family roof. One finds evidence of this trend throughout the developed world.

The proportion of houses that are privately owned has gone up from five percent to thirty-six percent in Holland since 1945. Grants and tax incentives have brought the proportion of home owners up to about the same percentage in Germany. In Belgium the percentage is as high as sixty. There are comparable figures for the planned economies. Twenty-five percent of the urban homes in the Soviet Union are privately owned and a much higher proportion still in rural areas. In Hungary, seventy-three percent of the housing is private, in Yugoslavia, over eighty percent. Hungary, Rumania, and Czechoslovakia all give government grants to citizens who want to build their own homes.

Government surveys in France have shown that eighty percent of the citizenry wish to live in individual homes of their own. A recent report from Britain's New Towns revealed the fact that 70 percent of the inhabitants wanted to own their houses. For this reason, a number of experts and some political leaders in Britain are beginning to ask why the rent paid for public housing might not be transformed into a mortgage. Families who had paid their rents over the whole period required to cover interest payments and amortization might now receive the freehold of their home. Rents would become the equivalent of interest on a loan, and as income rose, the family could either continue a slow process of purchase or increase the "rent" and hasten full ownership. To those who fear that such a policy would make the provision of housing for a mobile population even more inflexible— and hence exacerbate the nation's general problems of redeploying workers and changing jobs—a partial answer is to take steps to bring more private accommodation back into the rental market. Another would be to equal Germany's record in providing some degree of surplus in housing, still another to transfer the freehold to the tenant on condition that the public authority has the first right to repurchase it and thus replenish its housing stock.

The "home of one's own" that people apparently want most to buy is the detached, semidetached or terrace house with that blessing for all inventive children and industrious parents—the back yard where anything from dahlias to pet rabbits to amateur carpentry can make up the rich content of "puttering about." But the goal of home ownership can be achieved in apartment housing and city blocks. Cooperative ownership is widely encouraged in planned economies and it can sometimes come about, spontaneously, on the lines suggested by British planners for the transformation of rents into mortgage payments. In a number of rundown apartment blocks in New York where the cruel cycle of landlord neglect and city demolition was beginning to roll closer, tenants formed their own self-improvement associations, put in "sweat equity" in cleaning up and fixing up their own near-derelict premises, and then—almost as an afterthought—negotiated at a realistic price for the transfer of the freehold upon which the original owner had simply given up.

This American experience is a reminder that the policy of encouraging home ownership can be used effectively to help poorer citizens. It does more than simply provide them with secure shelter. Even deeper needs are at issue here. It has been said of the poorest citizens, sadly but with too much truth, that they are "the people whose plans never work out." Between exploiting landlords, ominous "winklers," efficient but officious welfare workers, and a bewildering bureaucracy, overmanning and overmanaging so much of public housing, the citizens with no clout—the aged pensioner, the single-parent family, the workless, the handicapped—can easily feel utterly powerless in the face of a system which, private or public, seems simply to push them around. To this helplessness, the natural reaction is a sort of despairing apathy. "The plan will not work out." "They will not allow it." "What's the use?" Perhaps the fundamental point in tenants organizing themselves for action is not simply to get themselves their own homes. It is the very act of organization. So often the better off and more powerful groups reserve their deepest indignation for the "fecklessness" of those whose margins are so small that getting through today is all that can be managed. This contempt, this impatience are as old as recorded time. Even in the supposedly compassionate Middle Ages, no poet has expressed it better than Piers Plowman:

> But beggars about midsummer go breadless to supper,
> And winter is worse, for they are wet-shod wanderers
> Frozen and famished and foully challenged
> And berated by rich men so that it is rueful to listen.

This is the ultimate indignity—in slum or *bidonvilles,* in shabby boarding houses or overnight shelters—to be "foully challenged" and "berated" by those with authority and fortune. To this contempt, self-organization can be the creative answer. It turns the flow of authority back to the citizen, however impoverished. It can be the beginning of a plan that actually works out and by mobilizing unused energies, can even convince public authorities that resources are being saved, houses restored to use, families taken off the streets. On both sides this is the step back from the dying slum and forward to the possibility of a living community.

As a result, there can be further advantages. People take more care of what is their own and do a fair amount of the maintenance work themselves. If maintenance is, by definition, someone else's responsibility, it tends to be more neglected, to cost more and to be less well done. The commonest complaint of a Soviet citizen, for instance, is no longer the waiting list for housing. The chief criticisms now tend to center on stopped pipes, faulty boilers, peeling paint, and poor masonry. Citizens have been known to carry their protest against long-standing leaks in the roof to the point of threatening not to take part in the next election and thus reduce the voting record of their street. It also happens that the tactic works.

In discussing good maintenance as a by-product of home ownership, we are not dealing with a side issue. In too many rented public housing developments, a large bureaucracy has grown up to do repairs which tenants have no personal interest in undertaking. As the manager of one British New Town put it: "It surely is not necessary to bring along three plumbers and a housing official every time Mrs. Brown's sink is stopped up." Multiply Mrs. Brown by a million and the costs become mountainous.

In any case the issue is much more than one of care and repair. Successful cities are, in obscure ways that are hard to define, organisms with collective memories, a shaping influence, a civilizing—or uncivilizing—impact. For these subconscious but powerful forces to be creative, it seems that they must suggest continuity, inherited experience, the glory and wonder of having withstood the ravages of destroying time. But poor maintenance is precisely time left to do its destruction. The profoundest significance of the Polish people's decision to rebuild, stone for stone, the historic center of Warsaw after its total destruction in war was its statement, in visual terms, of the Polish nation's unconquerable continuity. So was the loving restoration of beleaguered Leningrad. Even at the level of the single house, good maintenance is more than a matter of convenience. There is in it an element of *pietas,* of love for the family hearth and for the wider life of the community.

12 THE SEARCH FOR COMMUNITY

ALL THESE ELEMENTS—the preference for home ownership, the rising problem of maintenance, the feeling for continuity and familiarity in one's neighborhood—are at the root of another profound psychological reaction brought to the surface by the postwar experience in housing. This is the widespread revulsion against large, what one might almost call cataclysmic housing—the tower blocks and high-rise barracks built up in areas razed clean of any past buildings or even associations. In its place is growing up a preference for more modest arrangements within a community that can be shared.

One root of this revulsion is simply sheer scale. It can induce a great sense of helplessness. Maintenance, in high-rise buildings, must be a largely professional job. It takes a brave man, however handy, to fix a broken window on the thirtieth floor. It simply is beyond the tenants' means to resupply the corridors' steadily stolen light bulbs. It takes difficult efforts of collective imagination and organization to see how the large empty surrounding area, possibly grassed over, possibly not, can be turned into anything useful. It could be "puttering" space. But how can the division be devised?

Another failure can be a sense of profound social segregation. In too many cities, the fortresslike buildings, dwarfing the surrounding terraces or standing in isolated and identical boredom among the tarmac parking lots, seem to have stamped all over them: "This is public housing. Here live the poor. Here live the people on welfare. Here live the ones who didn't make it." And, given the tendency of citizens in all societies, but especially, perhaps, in competitive ones, to despise the less fortunate—"I thank Thee, Lord, that I am not as other men"—the children of these skyscraping ghettos face the risk of growing up either with the sense of being losers or with a fierce determination to "get even," neither of them a generally desirable prelude to the long art of becoming human. The dangers are obviously all the greater if the children are of different racial or cultural background.

This mixture of a sense of failure and of helplessness adds an extra edge to what has become the greatest anxiety—the increasing connection made between large scale public housing and the rise in public disorder. Rationally or not, more and more citizens see in their city blocks and towers an urban environment in which fear is a dominant element.

A city, by its very nature, is a place where strangers meet. It exists for a wide variety of purposes. Its attraction and vitality depend upon diverse uses which transcend the sometimes inbred quality of smaller communilies. But a lot of different people doing a lot of different things will include some people doing highly undesirable things and how is there to be a civilized surveillance to see that their activities—"crime in the streets"—do not undermine good order for the mass of citizens? An honest, reliable police force known to the community and cooperating closely with it—"the cop on the beat" even more than the swiftly moving police car—is part of the answer. But the policeman's effectiveness is profoundly affected by community attitudes and support. In busy city quarters where the pavements are full of people coming and going about their infinite variety of purposes and the streets are lined with shops, cafes, markets—many of them owned and served by well-established local figures—the mix of strangers and familiar people makes, as Jane Jacobs has so cogently described, an informal network of security. Enough people know the pattern of coming and going—what she calls "the ballet" of the street—for unusual events to be observed and marked before they can become sinister.

But it is precisely this diversity, movement, and mix of familiar and strange that is lacking in most of the vast blocks of high-rise apartment buildings which, in most developed countries, were the public authorities' first response to the destruction of war or the need to replace increasingly decrepit housing or the combination of both. The aim, undoubtedly, was well-intentioned. Slum dwellers would be rescued from overcrowding, bad air, bad light, dirt, noise, and the absence of domestic services by receiving modern apartments in fine new tower blocks, all air and light, with wide open spaces round them and a measure of insulation from the traffic, noise, and disturbance of the streets. But it is precisely this anonymity and insulation that feed the fears. Over those wide, windy spaces, into those entrances serving over a hundred families, up those deserted elevators and along the connecting corridors, anybody can roam and no one can be certain whether it is neighbor or enemy—particularly if vandals have removed the house lights and broken the elevator.

All these reactions taken together—the sense of being dwarfed, helplessness, segregation, anonymity, and fear—make one thing clear. From London to New York to St. Louis to Holland's Bjilmereer to the *Grands Ensembles* in Paris, a massive commitment to high-rise housing for poorer citizens is a failure, an expensive, corrosive, tragic failure, too costly to be solved now by the most direct means—the Pruitt Igoe method—but at least a sufficient warning of "clear and present danger" for the practice to be stopped, at once, for any but exceptional uses and cases. It is significant that it is, in effect, being phased out in London and Holland and pressure for reversal is growing generally in Western Europe.

What can be done now that so much has been ill-done? What are the clues to better policy? Ending anonymity is probably the highest priority and this can be sought by external and internal measures. Externally, public authorities can attempt to relink the monster blocks with the surrounding community by cutting new streets through the unused space, lining them with row housing (which should first be offered to local families with small children), setting up shops, launderettes, beauty parlors, and cafes, turning the smaller remaining space into play areas allotted to particular housing blocks, encouraging variety in wall painting and tree planting, creating a number of community centers where legal, civic, and medical advice is available, encouraging local clubs and drawing the local police force into a sustained dialogue with the tenants. It is sometimes forgotten that by far the greatest number of victims of big-city violence are themselves poor.

Evidence that external authority cares enough to sponsor change—and not simply lecture, blame, and pry—will in itself encourage internal change, the creation of tenant associations who, with support but not too much paternalist prodding, can first organize themselves for safety, then think out ways of satisfying communal needs—say, a whole floor of apartments converted into a day-care center or an old peoples' club—and, as confidence grows, move on to cooperative ownership. And in case the reader pauses at this point and wonders whether an angelic choir may not be about to strike up, complete with electronic harps, it is relevant to recall that in a large rundown block of public housing precisely in St. Louis—the Darst project—which seemed all set for the Pruitt Igoe route to ruin, the formation of a tenants' association did in fact have many of these consequences, including the extremely popular transformation of one bit of empty space into a skating rink, and all who studied the process agreed that a critical breakthrough occurred when, as a result of regular tenants' meetings, neighbors began to recognize and know each other. The fatal trap of anonymity was avoided. It is not irrelevant to point to the general belief in the Soviet Union that a less apparent distaste for massive housing blocks springs from the speed with which Russians, traditionally, make friends with their neighbors and establish networks of mutual support and conviviality.

The ending of anonymity and its twin, isolation, can be the beginning of the tenants' genuine identification of their interests not simply with their own apartment but with the whole complex in which they live. Part of the overwhelming case for abandoning the tower block or fortress high-rise is that it is much easier to arrange for personal responsibility and interest in apartments that are no more than a few stories high, where each entrance is used by perhaps a dozen families who know each other well by sight and the internal corridors serve only three or four families. Marked-out garden and play areas fill up the communal space which is easily supervised from overlooking windows and quickly reached by any resident who spies trouble. In one significant study made by Mr. Oscar Newman in New York, two housing projects were examined, facing each other across the same street, in a much disturbed area with high crime rates and delinquency. One of the projects, Van Dyke, is a typical high-rise development with some hundred and twenty families sharing the single entrance and the towers set in a large open-paved space. Opposite, in Brownsville, the same number of families live at the same density but in three- to six-story "walk-up" apartments. They have no more than nine to thirteen families served by each entrance and do in fact use the communal space regularly and usefully. It hardly needs to be added that Van Dyke has a high crime rate and Brownsville has not.

It is not quite clear why, after the Second World War, so many public authorities chose the high-rise design. It is no cheaper to build. Its maintenance costs are higher. It does not in most cases provide higher density and hence more accommodation than two- to three-story apartments. Above all, it all too often proclaims itself for what it is—public housing, where people live "at the taxpayers' expense." Lower apartment buildings, row housing in terraces, separate or semi-detached houses tend to merge imperceptibly into the urban environment, and at this point we can perhaps begin to see a way out of the dilemmas created by the highly visible, mammoth blocks of flats—a way out which also responds to the clear preference of so many citizens for their own homes, for smaller, more intimate buildings, and for access to space which is usable and in some sense their own. This route concentrates upon creating what can perhaps best be called a "continuum" of housing types, rents, costs, tenants, occupiers, and owners so that, little by little, sharp and brutal contrasts based on income and occupation—of which the urban ghetto is the ultimate archetype—are lessened and the mixed communities which still exist in every developed country, in the main in the smaller centers, gradually return to being the norm.

The interweaving of different styles, incomes, and employment is not an impossibly Utopian dream. It was the pattern of the traditional market town or merchant city. One overriding aim of all socially stable and civically constructive housing policy in the next quarter century should be to attempt to recreate the old mix—the Chelseas, the Trasteveres, the Greenwich Villages—the myriad examples of older communities where people of different background, interest, and income live in reasonable proximity and mutual respect.

The concept of phasing out cataclysmic housing schemes is perhaps most advanced in Britain. The first decisive step in the direction of conservation, rehabilitation, and building to a human scale must be dated from the late 1960s when the Commission set up to inquire into the future development of Covent Garden (after the closing and relocating of its wholesale product market) could not agree on the expected conventional plan for a cluster of high-rise office blocks and tourist attractions. Careful surveys had uncovered a vivid social community within the area with tiny businesses serving the surrounding network of theaters, with cheap, relatively renewable housing and a fierce sense of local loyalty.

In the early Seventies the new mood began to spread across the boroughs. In Clapham in 1971, for instance, the residents learned that the local borough council intended to raze a part of their area for wholesale redevelopment. They set up a community group to rally public support behind their campaign for preservation. This group was able to work closely with the official inspector designated to survey the plan; and one reason why, in his report, he strongly recommended rehabilitation, together with piecemeal infilling where houses were irretrievably run down, was the evidence he found of a "well integrated community living happily and neighborly." Moreover, this survey confirmed that razing and redeveloping would not in fact provide any more housing and, given the council's less than satisfactory record in the matter of clearing first and building later—much later—the intervening years of blight and desertion would have run the whole neighborhood into the ground.

Rehabilitation as a preferred technique is spreading. In France the new public concern for medium-sized cities specifically underlines its respect for their architectural inheritance and for the historic form of the community. This is encouraging since it only takes one or two really ill-placed glass or concrete high-rises to destroy the entire balance of a city, in even a city as wave-lapped and island-studded as Stockholm, "Venice of the North." In fact, the style and quality of the buildings with which earlier French governments proposed to modernize Paris itself—the brooding darkness of the Montparnasse "fortress," the brutal indentations of the towers of La Défense jutting into the city's peaceful skyline—induce in any incurable devotee of French culture the profound hope that the recent presidential gestures which have saved Les Halles and banned the monstrous proposal for a Left Bank motorway point toward France's future orientation. There is now an official commitment to an annual renovation of a quarter of a million houses and its potential popularity can be gauged by the fact that public opinion has gone on record to disapprove, by a commanding sixty-eight percent, the vast *Grands Ensembles* which, as at Sarcelles, brought as many as 50,000 people together in blocks of 12,000 apartments on the outskirts of the city with virtually no local amenities or employment—a pattern followed, on a smaller scale, in other areas. Nor is it unimportant that, according to all present calculations, renovation is considerably less expensive than razing and rebuilding.

In West Germany, too, public opinion is swinging decisively away from massive urban renewal projects. New regulations are in preparation to provide, as in Britain, grants for renovation to owner-occupiers of old buildings. In the Netherlands, the number of houses renovated is beginning to accelerate. In Belgium, spectacular unpopularity was achieved by the urban renewal project which razed all the buildings in Brussels' Quartier Nord to make way for a futurist agglomeration of tower blocks, hotels, and conference centers while providing literally no alternative accommodation for the families—all very poor—who were evicted. As a result, directions changed. Five experimental areas for renovation have been established, one of them, Les Marolles, precisely on a site formerly designated for total razing and renewal and now spared in order to preserve all the housing that can be repaired for the local inhabitants.

Les Marolles is a reminder of a wider issue. It is not enough to get away from the bulldozing mentality. It is not enough to insure the survival of usable stock. There remains the equally vital problem of who is to occupy them. If the whole operation of renovating old (and often beautiful) houses is conducted on a strictly commercial basis, there is only one result—the ousting of the poor and the return of the well-to-do. And the fact must be repeated. If no alternative provision for excluded tenants, many of them old, infirm, or with large families, is built into such schemes, they contribute directly to increased overcrowding and accelerating decay in other housing areas and, at the end of the line, to complete homelessness. They also contribute nothing to one of the fundamental aims of a socially acceptable housing strategy—the recreation of mixed neighborhoods, the "continuum" of houses, incomes, tenancies, and amenities which is at the root of a lively, satisfying urban environment. With the poor and the unskilled excluded, with prices also exceeding, especially in central-city locations, anything that skilled or clerical workers can afford to pay, the social outcome can finally be about as varied, mixed, and truly urbane as a single-class, high-income suburb.

Thus it is not enough to have a policy of renovation. It is not enough simply to abandon the high-rise habit. The recreation of mixed, lively urban communities is a compound strategy of many parts. In fact, only one element is a precondition of all the rest—national commitment on the part of governments and citizens alike to the building and preservation of the urban "continuum."

13 LIVING AS NEIGHBORS

ONE OF THE bravest—and saddest—sights in an old city is a single house or a small row of houses, painted, swept and garnished, scrupulously clean with plants in window boxes and flowers at the gate and all around the unmistakable evidence of disorder, vandalism, and decline. It is a visual image of a social fact—that housing exists within a community and its effectiveness as an element of family support and social stability must be profoundly affected by what is going on round about. If the right to shelter is a basic human right, it cannot be fully enjoyed unless there are corresponding rights to community, or rather to those human benefits which can only be provided by a community.

Some of them are social—health, literacy, employment, personal security. Some of them are physical—pure water, good drains, clean air, access, and mobility. Some are cultural—freedom of expression and choice, continuity, responsibility, effective influence, beauty, great art, the right to visions and dreams. They are all, given the inescapable nature of reality, inextricably bound up with each other. What awaits a child whose full development is permanently stunted by malnutrition? What is the use of unspoiled nature to the urban dweller with no means of reaching it? What is civic responsibility if all decisions are made by remote bureaucracies? What is the impact of all the visions ever written by poets and philosophers if citizens have never learned to read or are not allowed to give their free opinions if they have? Yet these are all essential aspects of the "safe and happy life." These are what man, against most experience and almost all the lessons of history, goes on doggedly hoping to achieve.

The chief obstacles to the achievement of these aims of community in planned societies lies precisely in their being too planned and allowing too little for free creativity and inventiveness of individual citizens. The physical and social goals are more easily attained than cultural ones. Well-fed, reasonably housed, healthy and literate populations may yet produce few contributions to creative—as opposed to performing—art and make their largest intellectual achievements in natural science rather than human philosophy. Even in applied science, some lack of creativity seems to encourage a certain dependence upon the technological inventiveness of more open societies. And even if medical care increases life expectancy, it can hardly escape criticism if it is used to stupefy political dissidents in psychiatric institutions.

Some of the basic difficulties in open societies stem from the over-concentration on personal interest and self-advancement which, carried beyond a certain point, makes it all but impossible to achieve a proper and general balance of justice and sharing. It is the nature of a large number of the basic services to become available to all citizens only if they are provided through public expenditure. Even such rewarding if less essential services as the performing arts cannot flourish without patronage. But the citizen in developed societies tends to believe that what he spends on the public good through taxation—the "tax bite"—is less valuable than what he can choose for himself. It may be that the choice lies between help for someone else's handicapped child or one's own holiday in Bermuda. But this is not how the comparison strikes average taxpayers and they are the first to point to any failure, any disappointment in public spending as proof that the "tax bite" is not doing its job and should be suitably reduced.

But there are a number of reasons for looking with a little skepticism at this demand for quickly identifiable results. What would critics say of public housing if 90,000 people were burned to death in their homes every year? What would they say of public education if 63,000 young people were beaten to death and fifty times as many injured in each scholastic year? Yet virtually without a murmur of protest, 90,000 people are killed every year on Europe's roads, 63,000 on North America's. The injuries rise toward the 10 million mark. But where are the critics of massive public spending on roads? Which government is not ready to prop up at least part of its probably over-manned and possibly obsolete car industry? Indignation which explodes about the failures of public education and does not even remark the consequences of public road building is selective indeed.

A second reason for skepticism is that if critics were really concerned about the mistakes and errors, they would not be advocating cutting the funds but reexamining the programs. If it is true that throwing a dollar after a problem is no solution, the reason is, again and again, that the problem needed more than a thrown dollar—often appropriated by an unintended recipient. But this does not mean fewer dollars would have given better results. If, after the most scrupulous inquiry, it is found that better results could be achieved by other methods, then a case for reduced spending can be made. But where is the inquiry? Where is the careful research? Where are the alternative answers? The deathly silence suggests that the critic really resents not the mistakes but the spending itself.

But the third reason for challenging the "tax bite" theory and its usually unresearched complaint about poor results raises profounder issues. It can normally be expected that better education, better health, and better housing give a higher chance of shaping a responsible and self-reliant citizenry. True, if as in the summer of 1975, wealthy young Italians can rape and murder poor and uneducated girls lured to drinking parties for the purpose, we cannot hope for automatic salvation by material means alone. America has its Manson family, Britain its Moors murders, and, on a larger scale, Stalin his purges, the Nazis their "final solution." The participants were not notably undernourished or ill-housed.

But the essence of the issue of providing good shelter, education, and health is not to make the poor more virtuous or at least less troublesome. It is that justice should be done. To send any citizen out into society handicapped by wretched shelter, poor health, and illiteracy when the means to do better are available contradicts the fundamental ideals of a just and civilized society. To reduce the goal is a sort of manipulative justice—do this or we may get too many bad guys—and will probably insure that even this narrower purpose fails. The deprivation of citizens in affluent societies is not to be seen primarily as a possible threat to social order. It is the social order itself failing to work and debasing its claim to be called a functioning civilization. This is, incidentally, one reason why the profoundest impact made on Western visitors to contemporary China seems to be the evidence of a community not yet affluent in the developed sense, yet able to secure a decent minimum existence for everyone—no small achievement when "everyone" makes up a fifth of the human race.

A general strategy for recovering a sense of neighborhood in the urban region has been broadly outlined in the pages dealing with the control of land use. Its central point, as we have seen, is to recreate workable communities both in the city center and in the surrounding suburban sprawl. However discouraging some of the names invented for this strategy—for instance, the "polynucleated mega-region"—the underlying purpose is a precondition of restoring true communities.

The next question, given the strategy, is, What elements do or should make up these sometimes new, sometimes revised communities? One fact should be repeated at this point. Given the length of life of most buildings, no more than a quarter of any built-up area can easily be changed before the year 2000, especially since the days of heroic bulldozing may, mercifully, be over. Existing settlements have the fundamental social value of experienced continuity. Carefully renovated houses reinforce it. But they put some limits, in brick and concrete and asphalt, to the rearrangement of space. Planners will have to know how to "think small" and be ingenious in pursuit of larger aims. "Thinking small" in fact means a deep respect for all existing evidences of community and close cooperation with its members to find out what they feel to be chiefly missing. Too many recent noncommunities have sprung fully shaped from the architects' and planners' drawing boards. Given the neo-brutalism of some of them, one is tempted to say "fully armed." The hallmarks of good design are now seen to lie with the ungrandiose and the unimposed. As with the St. Paul's area in the London Borough of Clapham, a church with its churchyard and perhaps a cluster of older houses may well be the central point of self-recognition and orientation for the whole neighborhood. To see it half sliced through by an access road is to see the community itself in danger. It was the local reaction of Canadian citizens in a threatened community in Toronto that began the process of putting a sensational end to the Spadina Expressway when it had already reached the city's outskirts. Residents especially need to be consulted over the development of open space and recreation. If not, they will not help with running them later on and keeping them safe for themselves and their children. A play area can develop into a much-used, much-loved "adventure playground" with local volunteers lending a hand and a community of help coming into existence round it. Equally, it can stay empty—and dangerous.

This kind of creative planning with its acceptance of citizen participation gives added effect to the effort to build urban communities with a "continuum" not too deeply divided by income or culture. As we have seen, this means drawing the middle classes back to live in city centers near their tertiary and "quaternary" work and seeing to it that surrounding suburban communities accept the jobs and provide the housing which less skilled people can do and afford. The switch cannot be undertaken "catastrophically." A sudden vast barracks of public housing plumped down in a conservative community of bungalows and commuting clerks is *the* recipe for social malaise. Add ethnic differences and the malaise can turn to violence. Ideally, the strategy evolved in Chicago's Hyde Park is the technique to strive for—a balance achieved not by exterior compulsion (or stealth) but by the district's own discussion, cooperation, persuasion, and commitment to the basic value of an open community.

General rules of balance are not possible. Each country must work out its own. In New York City, a proportion of seventy percent well-to-do citizens to thirty percent poor has been proposed as a rough guide to "balance." But the percentage of really poor people in developed societies is much lower than this percentage. If *all* the country's various communities, according to their size, systematically began to absorb within their own "continuum" their share of the roughly ten to fifteen percent of underprivileged people still left behind by the postwar welfare revolution—the lonely old, the unskilled, the large or single-parent families, the handicapped, the migrant workers—probably no more than a couple of decades of sustained help and care would be required to establish a working balance. In this context, the policies followed by the Dutch in completely assimilating the Indonesian Dutch of mixed race and numbering 300,000, or two and a quarter percent of the Dutch population, in the hard years of postwar reconstruction could serve as a model. (The Moluccans have represented a special political problem.) Five percent of all new housing was assigned to the Indonesians throughout the country, an excellent example of how to avoid the concentration or ghettoization of problem groups. Social workers ran special boarding houses for training and preparing the migrants for new life. A prolonged and systematic program was laid down for assigning jobs and creating the skills needed for them. In less than fifteen years, the vast majority were absorbed.

Unhappily, the remarkable success of the program did not—such is the volatility of political will and human memory—persuade the authorities to apply it to the 300,000 migrant workers from other lands who arrived in the Fifties and Sixties to work for the Dutch version of the economic miracle. For historical reasons, they were not considered to have the claims of ex-colonial citizenship. They were only humans. Racial prejudice has also stood in the way of a similar policy of assimilation for the black Dutch citizens of Surinam. Yet the result has been a tenfold increase in dislocation and disorder which the continuance of policies carried through in far poorer but more generous times could have avoided.

If one considers this whole problem not at the large national level but in human terms, the scale of needed effort becomes more comprehensible. Suppose that on a lonely island of a thousand families, one shipwrecked family came ashore, stripped of everything by the disaster. It would be quickly helped and reestablished. This number is not much higher than the percentage of desperately poor people in most developed lands. It is by grouping them in what the British call "stress areas" that their place and status in the community is made into so bitter and self-perpetuating an evil. Unhappily, for historical reasons, the great conurbations include most of these stress areas and carry more than their national share. The Dutch answer for the Indonesians—a kind of "quota" insuring that a certain percentage of appropriate jobs, subsidized housing, and special assistance should be made available in a wide variety of communities—has been considered in other European lands. It would need to be operated in a flexible and informal fashion with maximum consultation and economic backing for the receiving community and no compulsion on the minorities to take up the new opportunities but equally no obstacles in the way if they wanted to move. It would involve neighborly community help in backing up essential services—education, retraining, child care, recreation. What is certain is that the longer the slums survive, the longer gross deprivation will produce citizens virtually unable to live elsewhere.

Market societies might also notice that whatever the complaints about services and community facilities in planned economies, segregation by housing and health and education in the ghetto sense is not among the criticisms. A few specialized communities—universities, for instance—may enjoy rather better housing. Rural conditions are generally worse. But sharp gradations of amenity based on class are not in evidence. To the frequently repeated wisecrack that this is "shared misery," the figures for health and literacy offer a reasonable rebuttal. The chief "misery" lies in the constraints that follow education—on free speech, on movement, on experiment and choice. But do the critics see some special value in unshared misery? Does it not matter that old people are dying of cold and one-parent families are going hungry in the midst of affluence because the majority basically feel "I'm all right, Jack"?

Once the priority of ending the worst urban conditions is accepted, the next question is how the renewed or newly built communities are to satisfy their wide range of social needs. A number of countries have adopted more or less explicit models of neighborhoods as the basic communal unit of a settlement, big or small. British planners in the 1920s began to talk of housing units based upon the population needed to sustain an elementary school—say, 6,000 to 10,000 people—designed in such a way as to insure that children would not have to cross any busy roads on their way to school and that they and their parents would have easy access to shopping centers, community offices, and also open space and recreation. This concept was adopted, in varying degree and scale, in the New Towns of the 1950s and the most recent and largest construction, Milton Keynes, uses a grid system to house 5,000 people in units of one square kilometer of land, with local schools, shops, halls, and offices established at points of intersection between the different units. They are all built at a fairly low density and entail considerable reliance on the motorcar.

A very similar approach to new town building has been the theory behind much of the Soviet Union's massive construction of new cities. Here, too, the "micro-region" houses a few thousand people, excludes traffic, and provides accessible schools, shops, services, and a communal park at the center. This basic unit can be used as a sort of building block and cities can be expanded simply by adding the necessary number of blocks and providing access to industrial and office work. In planning terms, of course, the employment comes first and this, too, has been subject to a general formula. The estimate in any community is that x number of productive (in other words, industrial) workers will need y number of further employees in the various services to support them. This equation then determines the number of houses and neighborhoods to be built.

14 THE SCALE OF COMMUNITY

THIS CONCEPT of small neighborhoods as the basic building block of human communities encounters strong criticisms, both of performance and of the concept as such. It seems a very general rule, in the building of new settlements, that the range of services—schools, shops, community centers, theaters—which are designed to turn an arrangement of houses into an active community very rarely get built in time to play their part in the early days of community building and, in some cases, lag behind indefinitely. In market economies, the reason often lies in the fact that commercial interests wait to see if a market is developing before they risk the necessary investment. This reluctance can be reinforced if, as with some of the New Towns in Britain and Sweden, some continued commuting to the main center and a lot of employment scattered over a wide region makes it somewhat unclear to the entrepreneurs which sites they ought to pick for their banks and offices and shops. A planned town center still full of premises to let has a subtly blighting effect. With luck, it does not last. But one or two new settlements, starting up with high hopes of becoming balanced communities, have drifted into almost a ghost-town atmosphere, not from having been lived in and deserted but from being insufficiently lived in from the start. The sudden withdrawal of federal funds to communities in the United States has left a number of such orphaned townships around the countryside, now waiting for the melancholy condition to be reversed.

It is significant that France is experimenting, in one or two of the New Towns, with a central service area built at exactly the same time as the local housing. For instance, Evry, one of the satellite towns designed to take the pressure off Paris, contains the largest multi-purpose town center ever constructed in France. It has three theaters, a skating rink and a swimming pool, halls for tennis, sports and dancing, the public library, assembly rooms and social centers for both grown-ups and young people. This "Agora" is surrounded by massive high-rise building, clearly testing the hypothesis that people will not miss private space if communal facilities are lavish and accessible.

However, since Evry is designed to serve nearly half a million people, subsidiary city quarters have their own clinics and social centers. And immediately across the Seine, at Melun-Sénart, the original intention of building Evry's twin was so violently rejected by the local communes that a totally opposite concept took its place. The old town of Melun has been enlarged by an unsensational sorting out of surrounding unplanned development, the whole forming a linked, low-density settlement, following the lines of hills and river, preserving woodlands and open space. The difference in the dates of the final plan—1966 for Evry, 1973 for Melun-Sénart—almost certainly reflects the increasing revulsion felt by French citizens for "life in concrete."

In the U.S.S.R., similar troubles have developed, not, of course, because of any dichotomy between planned and private enterprise but because of the overriding power and priority enjoyed by Gosplan and the central economic ministries. Many of the new industrial centers are, in a sense, still company towns where the responsibility for providing most services, both social and physical, lies uneasily between a strong, well-endowed industrial complex with all the state's resources behind it and an impoverished organ of local government, the soviet, which, according to reforms introduced in the late 1950s, was supposed to take on larger responsibilities but has lacked effective channels upward to the central sources of finance and decision-making. It is true that in 1960, the head of the highest Soviet agency concerned with settlements, the Soviet State Construction Committee (GOS-STROI) complained of the single-minded energy of Gosplan's dedication to industrial development and the consequent neglect of balanced planning for houses and services. In the Sixties, the provision of housing was given a wholly new impetus, both by allotting more funds and imposing fines for nonfulfilment of targets. Yet the provision of services seems to have fallen even further behind. This may be one of the reasons why, while the principle of a local community center in each micro-region is still honored, it is becoming usual, in fact, for a single central area to provide services for the whole town. And perhaps the gap between the planned and the commercial approach is not so wide as theory suggests. In 1972, *Pravda* quoted a builder's complaint that building services and amenities "are a lot of bother and the ruble profit is lacking."

This tendency to bypass the small neighborhood would not in the least surprise those who find the whole concept of a "micro-unit" to be only one rather small part of the problems of cities. A village is spontaneously a "neighborhood," but as you go up the urban scale, the small, self-contained community becomes less and less what people expect when they move to the cities. As a young British town planner put it: "A city is not a tree." You do not begin with the twigs and join onto the branches and finally, through the branches, reach the main trunk. This is an hierarchical arrangement of space that imposes restrictions and limits which the urban dweller does not seek or welcome. An open grid which permits access to the whole urban area is the best underpinning of the variety, the choice, the stimulus and surprise which are the big city's gifts to those that love them and which might make more people love them if only the dreary division of semi-abandoned core and surrounding sprawl did not drain the whole system of vitality.

A grid, of course, can suggest the most unattractive images— uniform blocks, roaring traffic, angularity of shapes and buildings, a depressing sameness in the use of materials and space. But this is only one possible form of a grid. It can move about, follow contours, climb hills, break into parks and squares, serve big blocks and small (including archetypal neighborhoods) and be freely combinable with walkways and pedestrian precincts. The point is that it is open-ended and gives access to all sections of the city without the cumulative bottlenecks of the "tree." In short, a grid pattern of access does not mean unshaped, undifferentiated slabs of urban tissue. The neighborhood is not a useless concept. Every house stands somewhere and its immediate surroundings affect the convenience and enjoyment of the residents. But it is still only a tiny part of a very large organism and must rely on larger groupings, mistakenly called "neighborhoods," which have, in reality, to be nearer the scale of boroughs or towns.

The genuine "urban villages"—Chelsea, Trastevere, Greenwich Village—are all in the 50,000 to 100,000 range of population. In any community that is much smaller, it will be found difficult to express and defend local interests or combine a necessary network of active people knowing each other and acting together for emergencies—the approach of the bulldozer, for instance. A larger scale of shops, schools, entertainment, recreation, and special services is also necessary to attract people from other parts of the city and at the same time satisfy the less mobile members of the local society—the elderly, the very young, the house-bound parent.

It is also the scale needed to allow for smaller cultural groupings—black, Irish, Czech, Polish—who in mixed populations like to join with immediate neighbors in a shared culture. Admittedly, these preferences can pose difficult problems if part of the difference to be protected is higher income, better services, and more successful schools. Then it helps to create the ghetto atmosphere elsewhere. But if North Boston is happily Irish, how many Anglo-Saxons or blacks should it be asked to include? If parts of Harlem are happily black, does the community have to be provided with some statutory whites? Many people simply like living next door to people like themselves. Provided the standard of services and opportunities, of good housing, parks, and amenities are about the same, the small cultural enclaves can add variety, not injustice. It is unusual for the Chinatown in any big American city to be thought of as a ghetto. It is a stimulus to variety and a place to visit. Cities must include such communities. They turn lethal only when poverty and color are the prime principles of exclusion.

There is a further reason for stressing the larger community. No center-city can be revitalized by mini-neighborhoods. The needed mix of classes demands a larger area to give it what one might call social breathing space. Nor can much be done with monumental office blocks by trying to insert dainty little terraces and miniparks between them. The whole scale has to be more arresting. One approach is to use financial inducements (and penalties) to office-owners to compel them to open up their lower floors to diverse uses—theaters, restaurants, concert halls, shopping malls. Another would be to follow the course sometimes forced on developers by reverses in fortune—to take over office blocks and turn them into apartments for different family sizes and incomes. Yet another is to preserve for renovation all remaining small-scale buildings, erase some of the more monstrous edifices (especially if they have remained empty to secure not rental income but capital gains, taxed at a lower rate) and build the schools, clinics, libraries, and social centers which are required for an urban scale of 50,000 to 100,000 people.

Since the erection of such portentous ziggurats as New York's World Trade Center Towers inevitably empties less prestigious buildings of a fair number of their tenants, the mistake can be turned to some advantage if the more modest buildings are returned to a much wider variety of human activities, including apartments, small-scale industry, and varied commerce. The saving of both Covent Garden and Les Halles from death by construction gives us working models of the kind of city district that keeps a center-city alive. But for a real reversal in living, in working, in lessening travel and increased amenity, the area to be developed needs to be the size of the whole Battery area in New York City or the whole of dockland now becoming available for inspired rebuilding in London along the banks of the Thames.

Yet another argument for the larger city quarter is that a reasonable variety of occupations keeps enough people from commuting and thus allows genuine local interests to take shape. This in turn gives the community enough political clout to make participation in local politics worthwhile. The mini-neighborhood can be served by a corner store, a primary school, and a small clinic. It can be an area for the kind of neighborly help that supplements such institutions. But communities of 50,000 to 100,000 people are necessary for wider needs, activities, and decision-making. Schooling and health, in particular, require a wider catchment area if they are to provide the underpinning of genuine communities.

There is no space in a brief overview of settlements' problems to enter deeply into such fundamental needs as education and health. Each requires its own report. But the concept of the just city is radically contradicted in affluent countries if its citizens are sick or illiterate from sheer lack of access to learning and healing. The basic success of the American public school, the French Lycée, the German gymnasium, or the Russian high school in producing, for the first time in human history, a population that is virtually completely literate shows that the communal provision of basic education is perfectly practicable and a well-established fact. Similarly, the success of medical insurance and national health services in Scandinavia and Holland or of public medicine in the urban communities of the Soviet Union removes any excuse for arguing that a wealthy nation cannot afford to prevent avoidable disease. If the service is inadequate, it is by choice, not necessity, and it is, as always, the poor minorities who are left out, schools and medical care going the way of housing in areas of special stress, standards slipping, literacy and competence declining, facilities falling into disrepair. The cycle is equally self-reinforcing. Poor schools and poor medical care produce sick and illiterate citizens and they become parents of children deprived in their turn. The only answer is the achievement of the needed continuum of houses, schools, and services and the kind of balance in income and talents, in facilities and staff which can begin to break the trap.

In every society, this outcome, however desirable, confronts the perpetual dilemma, equity versus free choice, variety versus equality. In any state system, for instance, should special provision be made for exceptional talents? One can see that there is not too much basic injustice in decreeing that some children can become ballet dancers without gross discrimination against the vast majority who are not offered the chance. But what about mathematics? What about physics? What about particular brilliance in languages? Are special schools or instruction an unacceptable privilege? Or must the brightest child be held back—and possibly destroyed by boredom—in order to keep in time with the slower-moving educational convoy? Is there to be no experiment, no variety even for less talented children? The Soviet Union appears to have opted for special treatment. Boarding schools bring the brightest young people from the rural areas. The brightest of all may end up in Akademoggrod, a whole city in Siberia devoted to the formation of exceptional talents.

Another answer, that would perhaps be more widely practiced if it were given public support, is the degree to which, in better integrated communities—and here the small neighborhood *is* important—citizens with time to spare and an educated background can help with the coaching both of advanced and of backward pupils. Probably much more could be done in this way if colleges and polytechnics were more systematically involved. It was one of the creative ideas latent in America's Headstart programs. Some communities on both sides of the Atlantic have offices where people can register what they want to learn and what they are able to teach. Thus the office links the needs and opportunities. Such cooperation reappears in all the myriad voluntary organizations that help with Youth Clubs and recreation centers. As a means of knitting communities together, such voluntary activities could hardly be bettered. The communities in turn may be suitably rewarded with less wayward scholars and fewer adolescent brawls.

Nor should we think of these "extracurricular" activities simply in terms of the young. Probably one of the most creative movements to supplement formal education in the twentieth century is the effort to extend the possibility of further education through the whole of the citizen's life. For women, especially, easy opportunities for retraining are an essential postlude to the years of close domesticity. No one has been quite so disoriented by the swift changes in industrial society as its women citizens. It is not a question of work. In most societies, women have always done the major share of it. But industrialism took a lot of "domestic" work, brewing, baking, spinning, weaving, out of the home and many women followed it—to lower paid jobs in factories. Tertiary and quaternary services also began to absorb—above all, in clerical and secretarial work—the products of the first general introduction of female literacy. As a result, in the twentieth century, just as for the first time a very large number of women also began to receive university training, domestic servants vanished and the Ph.Ds returned to the kitchen sink. With smaller families, close domesticity may only last a decade and in societies where nursery schools and day nurseries are provided, a total interruption in an educated woman's wider interests can be avoided (and incidentally a very creative use made of lonely elderly people who would happily be surrogates for grandparents if nurseries and old peoples' homes were close together). But normally "menial work," as it used to be called, does take the edge off a trained woman's skills and, so far, the sons of even the most glorious revolutions of liberation do not much care for washing up. So the result can be a dulled and frustrated human being, with no means of resharpening the old tools of learning—a tragic waste of society's scarcest resource, alert and reasoning minds which biology does not seem to distribute solely on a sexual basis.

But if local institutions for retraining were available, if the deadly barrier of empty suburban living were broken by the reclustering of communities, as in French planning, around new universities and research institutes, "re-entry rockets" into the post-menial life would be available. Husbands, offered the same opportunities, might, as in some Scandinavian countries, opt for part-time work and a larger domestic role in the decade of rearing young children. In a curious way, such a domestic "mix" might be nearer to the joint tasks of peaceful Neolithic times than the strict segregation of our recent and aggressive cycle of "civilizations."

But short of this new dawn, the provision of a wide range of institutions for changing skills and interests could have a permanently enlivening effect on local communities. After all, more and more people live to seventy. Forty years in the same work is a long time. Perhaps some of the new growth we need might be the new interest, not the new car, the second skill, not the second house. What is sure is that such institutions as Britain's Open University, providing university degrees by a combination of media teaching and personal coaching, has a vast, unsatisfied waiting list. Universities, business schools, polytechnics are extending the possibilities of refresher courses and widening it to include changes of profession and skill. In West Germany, a citizen is paid ninety percent of his or her previous salary if new training is sought. A distinguished British scholar once said: "To stop learning at fourteen is as unnatural as to die at fourteen." Backed by suitable grants and institutions, learning can become a lifelong process—*une éducation permanente*.

One unintended bonus of a wider community commitment to the idea of continuing education is to give new value and use to schools and colleges which all too often have long fallow months simply because up to the eighteenth century children were expected to help with the harvest. Many new towns, notably in France, are designing schools and community buildings so that they can become day-long and year-long centers of activity for all their citizens, young and old.

The involvement of the local people in educational development can take other forms. Voting by parents for local school boards and active parent-teachers' associations can be helpful. Yet, as America has discovered, it can also entrench wealthier suburbs in their determination to drop out of the nation's problems of deprivation—in education, in health, in everything—by the simple expedient of excluding the problem people.

This is perhaps the fundamental difficulty in market economies with wide cultural and racial differences. Are parents to be forbidden to save and send their children to private schools because they want them, say, to receive a particular kind of religious formation? Have racial or national groups the right to be integrated or not according to their own choice? As a number of American colleges have discovered, many black students prefer their own company. Yet some mixture of races and nations seems to be required in schools in order to make sure that segregation is not being introduced by the back door of residential arrangements.

The chief hope in America must be that the stride forward in educational opportunity for the black student achieved in the last two decades will begin to have its wider impact as the coincidence and concentration of all forms of deprivation—poverty, ignorance, ill health—in one or two minority groups begins to give way, and new skills, new leaders, and new confidence emerge. This type of solution, it must be repeated, is far more likely in a larger community than in neighborhoods conceived on too restricted a scale. There must be a feeling of elbow room and space and choice. The community of 100,000 offers a much better chance that variety will cease to be a threat and will become an enrichment.

Perhaps the nearest we can approach to a general principle is to say that, ideally, public schooling and public health should themselves be excellent enough to make the need for other schools or hospitals a matter of choice, not necessity. Such a principle may involve higher spending on these public services. We are back to the problem of the "tax bite" and its presumed unacceptability. Yet of all the needs a society has to recognize, the education of its young and the health of its people surely deserve the highest priority. And the alternative may be a still larger "tax bite" for police, law courts, prisons, not to speak of such monstrous sums as Britain's $1,000 million in one year to repair the effects of vandalism. It is better to try not to provide the vandals.

Until the nineteenth century, there was neither education nor care for most of the poor. Our present standards would have seemed Utopian to Victorian great-grandparents. Why then must we assume that we cannot do better still? Or that expenditure to do so, provided it is wisely spent, is not of more value than a new deodorant or that trip to the Bahamas? It is easy to say that money alone will not solve the problems. This is true. The community, especially the wealthier members, must give their personal backing and involvement as well. But try solving any of these problems without money. No amount of goodwill would offset the physical absence of schools and clinics. The truth is too easily forgotten in our often inward-looking consumption-minded societies that general social excellence can become as much an accepted aim of society as national security, provided citizens make it so. An in trying to achieve it in the new urban regions, the effort will be easier in larger communities, better able to absorb minorities, live with and even relish a range of cultural differences, and acquire some of the hallmarks of genuine urbanity—tolerance for the stranger, courtesy for the chance acquaintance, links of friendship in many areas and occupations, and an outlook on life generally able to accommodate the strangeness, the largeness, the excitement and stimulus of the wider family of man.

15 ACCESS, NOT MOBILITY

HOWEVER COGENT the arguments for rethinking national land use policy or the patterns of work, homes, and leisure in the big conurbations, any hope of real improvement depends on one fundamental problem: Can anything be done about traffic? If mobility, based upon man's most treasured and possibly most lethal domestic convenience—the private car—continues to be the answer to all mismatches of employment, residence, and recreation, we shall have the same old "slurbs," the same old pollutions, the same old swallowing up of local parks and distant beauties. A reconsideration of the use and misuse of the private automobile is central to a saner use of space—and resources. In many countries it is also, to risk a wholly inappropriate analogy, the very largest of sacred cows.

Space and resources are closely related, of course. The further the commuting distance, the larger the amount of energy that must be expended. But resource use is also determined by the type of vehicle, and before we look at the problem of alternative spatial arrangements, it is as well to recall that the relationship between passenger miles and a U.S. gallon of fuel (or the energy-equivalent, 130,000 British thermal units) can vary from the seven miles per gallon of the helicopter to the 1,000 miles of a bicycle. In between, an average car with one passenger does just over twenty miles to the gallon, a city bus (in the rush hour) ninety-five miles, a city subway (again in the rush hour) 120 miles, and a standard-gauge train 390 miles. Cars manage a better average if passengers double up. A small car with four passengers manages about the same as the rush hour bus. On the other hand, a microbus with seven passengers clocks perhaps 175 passenger miles to the gallon. All the arguments from cost and waste reinforce the need to use space more wisely and to see whether secure access cannot be achieved by other means than an almost mindless mobility.

Let us begin where present patterns of car use seem, even to the most devoted drivers, somewhat short of rationality—in the center city. There are two problems, the one exacerbating the other. To commute by public transport for, say, over half an hour, morning and night, with a further journey at each end, is not in itself perhaps intolerable. Newspapers can be read, books studied, the day's program of work reviewed. But these useful pursuits do demand a seat, elbow room, breathable air, reasonable punctuality, and some measure of cleanliness. If most of these factors are missing, then commuting by public transport can become, as it is for the citizens of Tokyo, their top index of "disamenity." Yet the chances of a decent service surviving a large transfer of commuters to private automobiles are slim. A vicious circle sets in. As riders diminish, the costs of the public system rise (with an extra push from inflation), its services deteriorate, its fares and tariffs go up, and more riders and users drop away. To this dilemma, the initial response of public authorities in most highly motorized societies has been to give the vicious circle some vigorous extra spins. More and more road-building, requiring more and more elaborate and land-consuming intersections—this has become standard practice on both sides of the Atlantic. Some of the interchanges have been vast and elaborate enough—one thinks of the end of New York's Bruckner Boulevard—to suggest the temples of some exotic cult. One can easily be led to speculate what the archeologist in 5000 A.D. will make of such an expanse of asphalt, ruined pillars, broken arches, and fallen concrete.

Yet the very scale of the constructions carries with it the reminder that the whole system could be moving to within reach of its limit. As we have already noted, roads and parking spaces make up over half of Dallas and Los Angeles and over a third of Washington D.C. and New York City. The loss of taxable space is in fact one element in New York's near-bankruptcy. At present, at least a quarter of the city's commuters travel by car. When one remembers that more than three million people move in and out each day—virtually the equivalent of moving the whole of central Paris—it is easy to see that if the domain of the private motorist were still further increased, there would simply be no more city. There is, spatially, no alternative to public transport.

But it is a crumbling system.

Nor are the consequences of center-city commuting any less dubious for the drivers. The departure from home may still be a matter of free choice. But once the vehicles join the solid commuting convoy, their owners are estimated to get only about six percent of useful work out of each gallon of gasoline. The rest is lost in idling engines and polluting emissions. Even before the rise in oil prices, one estimate put the annual loss in extra costs to private motorists caught in New York City's traffic congestion at $180 million.

Commuting to the center is not the only pattern. It also includes moving long distances to work around and about the whole suburban belt. Admittedly, this circulation increases the commuters' opportunities to choose between jobs. Equally, it closes them for the poor and handicapped without cars, spins out and out the metropolitan sprawl, devours land, and extends the areas affected by direct air pollution. Nor should we ever forget the horror of steady, accepted killing. Altogether, even when every convenience, utility, and enjoyment are, as they should be, conceded to the automobile—cover for wet days, space for the family, combined golf bag, luggage holder, and shopping basket—even with all this, the price paid for the Great Car Rush in the Fifties and Sixties in the world's developed urban regions is almost as cataclysmic as the cause.

The position becomes even more of a paradox when we remember that little of this mobility is an end in itself. Idling out into the countryside on a fine weekend is mobility pursued for its own sake, with the added pleasure of a mountain or a lake or a picnic thrown in. But virtually all mobility is really getting somewhere to do something. In other words, it is access that matters, not the means used. Once urban regions exist, a fundamental aim in their redesign is precisely to improve ease of access. Reviving and diversifying the center-city, taking pressure off it, lessening the load of people and work, clustering alternative centers of activity and attraction in the periphery offer more hope than any alternative yet devised of getting people, homes, work, and leisure nearer to each other.

This is the first principle—access instead of mobility. The second is to fit the most convenient strategy of movement into the new pattern. The shift of direction is bound to be uneasy at first, even though higher gasoline costs are an inducement to fresh thinking and there is some evidence from Europe's most highly motorized country, Swe-

DALLAS—The vanishing city

PARIS—''When you've seen one, you've seen them all''

CZECHOSLOVAKIA—A house is not a home

ST. LOUIS—Pruitt-Igoe

WESTFALENHUETTE, WEST GERMANY—"Dark Satanic mills"

BUDAPEST—Home and play

THE NETHERLANDS—Formal and informal energy

LONDON—Human scale

LONDON—Equal density, different scale

TAPIOLA, FINLAND—Human scale—modern

LEVITTOWN, LONG ISLAND—Aerial view

ABIDJAN—Water on the head, drains at the foot

BOMBAY—New slums for old

RIO DE JANEIRO—The great divide

PERU—Drinking water for half of mankind

GUATAVITA, COLOMBIA—A village built in 1969

COLOMBIA—The village builds for itself

CHINA—Medical teamworkers assisting farmers with the harvest in Yenan

den, that a surprisingly high percentage of people (nearly eighty percent) do not consider that the private motorcar makes much sense in the center-city. But in most countries, the habit of the car has taken tremendous hold and in public transport the rise in costs and decline in standards are in full swing. Moreover, a lot of the work on "clustering" employment and housing in new regional centers still lies in the future. How can citizens be lured away from their cars while public facilities are inadequate and, for inter-suburban travel, virtually do not exist?

Perhaps the first decision to take is to accept a general strategic direction—the restoration of comfortable, viable, public transport —and then to pursue it not by one particular policy, say, the extension of subways or the taxing of cars, but by a whole array of tactics, each supporting the other and cumulatively moving the citizen, without too much disruption, toward the new goal.

Some of these policies can be developed without major structural changes. Or rather they can be used while the changes are taking place. A simple one, now being experimented with in over seventy American cities of more than 50,000 people, is to stagger working hours in the areas of dense employment so that there is at once more space in the commuting trains or buses and a wider spread of use over the whole system. When we remember that seventy-six percent of all passengers within a ten-mile radius of Tokyo use public transport every day, that the percentage goes up to eighty percent in Paris, the immediate relief offered by thinning out the flood a little would be enormous. The area covered for Tokyo includes 21 million people and observers have remarked that subways can be packed even more tightly in summer because clothing is thinner. Even so, the official pushers still have to stand by to give the extra shove that gets the door closed.

Another simple change is to give tax advantages and fare rebates to city taxis and to encourage the carrying of more than one passenger. In the United States, taxis account for over two and a half thousand million passengers a year and if they could, say, treble the figure, more private cars could be left in the garage at home—especially if informal arrangements linked group-riding with the stations and bus stops of interurban public transport.

Another innovation, which does not demand too much structural change, is to introduce closed bus lanes for full time or simply for the peak hours of commuting. In the Lincoln Tunnel, which connects New York City and New Jersey, one lane is reserved for buses and in the hour of heaviest commuting, four hundred buses move 25,000 passengers—a figure that is eight times higher than the normal rush hour flow on one lane of a city freeway. Another technique for giving priority to buses is to set traffic lights so that they automatically turn green on the approach of a bus. One or two of the French New Towns are trying this out.

Over a hundred cities in Europe—including Vienna and Florence—have introduced pedestrian precincts and traffic-free areas in the city centers and this change, quite apart from the enjoyment it creates in itself, can discourage some traffic since the way around the pedestrian zones often leads to a lot of devious rerouting, turning back on oneself, and simply getting lost in less familiar streets. To a degree, therefore, it can be classified as one example of a wider strategy—that of "attrition," simply arranging traffic in city centers in such a way as to make it encounter a whole series of tiresome obstacles—lights that stay red for annoyingly long periods on approach roads, major arteries barred to all but buses and taxis, private traffic diverted into an endless merry-go-round of one-way streets with a high possibility of finding oneself back where one started, a large absence of parking spaces, and heavy fines for street-side parking. Attrition seems to be one of the purposes behind the traffic scheme introduced into London's longest shopping street, Oxford Street. Pavements have been enlarged to encourage shoppers and, during the main commercial hours of the day, no private car may do anything on the street but cross it on traffic lights which stay red for the side roads for a very long time. The street itself is reserved for buses and taxis. Private traffic naturally becomes more and more congested on each side of the blocked artery and it is on the lateral streets that "attrition," assisted by a bewildering network of one-way sections, really takes hold.

The danger of attrition is that it may madden rather than discourage the privately driving citizen. In Nottingham, the techniques of attrition include prolonged red lights, prohibited areas, diversions, priority for buses; but after months of experiment, the impression seems to be gaining ground that the motorist is being harassed with no great gain either for the bus-user or the pedestrian. This is the kind of scheme that risks failure because of an angry withdrawal of citizen compliance.

Perhaps the most direct disincentive is to compel private car drivers to carry the full costs of their journeys. In most motorized countries, the costing and financing of the sudden vast eruption of the private car have been inadequate and indeed irrational. This fact reflects many facets of travel, including the obvious and valuable flexibility of motorcars outside urban centers, the vast popularity of private movement, the scale of institutional interests—car manufacturing, road builders—which are supported by its growth. But inadequate cost-benefit analysis also reflects fundamental defects in our accounting systems. As a result, for about twenty years in market economies, the motorist has led a subsidized existence with a strong consequent bias against public transport and hence against the needs of the carless, often poorest groups.

One of the "subsidies" until 1973 was, of course, the extraordinarily low price of fuel which has allowed drivers in developed countries to run down millennial reserves of petroleum to within sight of exhaustion in less than a century and to do so for what is arguably the most wasteful use, simply burning it up. An Indian peasant burning cow dung is in the same short-sighted class, but with fewer alternatives.

Other biases are less obvious and have simply slipped unnoticed into the system. Any effective transport system must have a track, a signaling system, rolling stock, and terminals for goods and people. Railroads are compelled to finance and provide all these elements. Road users are much less clearly involved and there is very little careful calculus to see whether car license fees, fuel taxes and road tolls—their direct contribution—and their share of rates and taxes cover the full costs of all four basic elements.

The tracks—in other words, the roads—are built with central or local tax funds to which both private motorists and nonmotorists contribute. Since the financing is by public grant, roads are not expected to pay interest on a large public debt, the source of ruin for a number of railways.

The "signaling system"—traffic lights, traffic police, lighting at night, road signs—again all come out of rates and taxes, paid by car users and nonusers alike. Their inefficiency is such that—it must be repeated—90,000 people are killed every year on Europe's roads. In contrast, the railway record is all but impeccable, in spite of the ferocious publicity surrounding any single accident.

The rolling stock is provided by private firms and individuals with some fairly casual estimates of the cost-benefit of use—idling time in traffic, "dead" periods in garages, the balance between prestige and cost when top executives and visiting dignitaries still roll off to ceremonies and luncheons in long black limousines, regardless of the fact that 1,000 pounds taken off the weight of a 4,000 pound car saves twenty-seven percent of the cost of fuel. One thinks with affection of the Archbishop of Canterbury's "mini."

When we come to the terminal points, the road system pays very little. Street parking in the past has usually been free. Municipal authorities have often built multistoried garages with parking rates that do not fully cover maintenance, interest, and amortization because they wish to attract visitors and shoppers. Unhappily these buildings are, virtually without exception, the most hideous ever erected by man, resembling nothing so much as a pile of thickly cut concrete sandwiches with some dark, dubious substance spread between. Shops and offices also provide "free" parking space and add the costs to their sales. Or tax inducements may be given to developers to build underground garages, thus giving indirect aid to a building's heightened density and capacity—indirect aid, in other words, to tower blocks which in turn increase the pressure of commuting. To these more official subsidies, one should add the large spaces added to trunk roads for commercial parking and the degree to which, in some communities, trucks are simply left for the night in residential streets, and often started up, explosively, at five in the morning.

Now this calculus is not designed to recommend a blanket return to railways for virtually all purposes of movement. This would make as much sense as to have advocated a total return to the stage coach when the dirt, smell, pollution, and intrusion of the railways became apparent in the 1840s—how nostalgically Charles Dickens evokes the cozier days of coaching! The aim is first to contrast the public subsidies paid to railways—accompanied by shrieks about their "bankruptcy"—with the vast subsidies paid to roads which no one even notices. The second aim is to introduce this contrast into public accounting methods. It could then be one tool in an integrated transport strategy according to which *all* the modes of traffic and movement are designed to play a rational and mutually supportive role. If the first effect is to make motoring, either for passengers or goods, more genuinely representative of costs and hence more expensive, this is a first step toward rationality.

16 TOWARD A TRANSPORT STRATEGY

SINCE COSTS are at their peak in heavily built-up areas, it is here that private motoring costs must be most sharply increased and added to the resources required to improve public transport. A citizen can be said to have an inalienable right to a car but not to a large public subsidy. As the Mayor of Toronto put it: "Sure, everyone has the right to come downtown, but he doesn't necessarily have the right to bring a ton of metal with him." And, we must repeat, there is an issue of justice involved. The hidden subsidies go to those who can afford to pay the costs of private motors and at the same time help to undermine the public systems which are the only ones the poor can use.

If the priority in urban regions is clearly given to public tranport, the question remains: What kind of transport? And to this the general answer must be: all kinds, according to suitability, cost, and existing installations, but designed to support, not compete with, each other and to produce an integrated system. Of course, developed countries (and increasingly developing lands) do not start from scratch. They have vast investments already made in traffic systems. But as the nations, as it were, come up dripping from the sudden deluge of the private car, the first need is not to repeat the carelessness and wastefulness of the last quarter of a century but to devise integrated traffic systems that work for all citizens.

Most of the developed world's large cities are served by railways, some of which run, part of the time, underground. This is the form of tranport which, as we have seen, carries over three-quarters of the commuters in such centers as Paris and Tokyo. The system has been growing, with new subways in Rotterdam, Munich, Milan, Washington, Atlanta, and many other cities. Long-established systems, such as the New York, London, and Chicago subways, are being extended. It would hardly seem necessary to underline the primary point that, where these networks exist, the first need is to make them efficient, attractive, and (with greater difficulty) less expensive. An equally obvious point is that the different modes of public transport should support and supplement each other. The degree to which downtown surface transport in Toronto—buses and trams—is linked to the stations of the metropolitan rapid transit system is a better model than the tendency in London and New York to have buses duplicating the underground routes.

In the wider "commutershed," railway networks that have already been built should be used as the underpinning for the strategy of clustering work, houses, commerce, and recreation into more dense and balanced communities. The oldest of Britain's New Towns—started soon after the war to take the pressure off Central London—are all linked to the center by rail. But since each has achieved a reasonable degree of local balance between employment and residence, their commuting to the center is less than that of people still living in the scattered, unorganized "slurb" areas. According to estimates made in the mid-Sixties, less than ten percent of the New Town workers were commuting into London and the percentage seems to be shrinking. At the same time, ease of access has allowed the inhabitants an intermittant but reliable share in some of the advantages—the entertainment, the intellectual exchanges, the urban vitality—of the capital city.

Where commuters' railways do not exist, as in France's new "urban regions," there are plans for experimental high-speed links between the major centers. The new readiness in the United States to provide federal subsidies for public transport in dense urban regions at least suggests that the over-mighty automobile is losing some of its sovereignty. The risk is that without land control and a proper emphasis on clustering, the renewed railway systems will simply serve an undifferentiated suburban sprawl. In that case, it may prove extremely expensive, and difficult, to avoid two opposite dangers—underuse of parts of the system, overloading of others. Viable urban regions require rapid linkages but not empty or congested ones. Dispersed New Towns or concentrated employment centers are the necessary complement to any successful organization of systems of public transport. Incidentally, the first decade of experience with the French Ring Towns around Paris suggests that this balance is beginning to appear.

The more successfully transport policy lessens commuting by car, either to the old centers or to the new "clusters," the more public transport inside the centers must be improved since people no longer bring their own transport with them and not all of them are able to take advantage of the much greater range of free movement for pedestrians. In parts of the city, presumably, taxis will continue to operate. But group riding should, as we have noted, be encouraged by variable fares. There is also evidence from some developing cities that small buses, with rather flexible routes—the "jitney" taxis—perform better than traditional bus routes. But this may be largely a result of the present degree of traffic congestion. In many cities simply lessening the private load of traffic will allow traditional bus lines to be more effective, eliminating the long waits at cold street corners and restoring schedules to reasonable reliability and spacing. It is, above all, periodic traffic blocks that produce the curious phenomenon of buses on the same route, with the same destination, apparently traveling in convoy. (Once when an angry passenger asked the reason for six successive "Number Elevens," the conductor equably replied: "Well, Madam, like this we never lose one.") In parts of the United States and Canada, trolley buses are coming back into favor, partly because some cities never abandoned them, partly because of their relatively cheap costs of installation, which can be anything from three to ten times less expensive for each mile of track than any subway system. Their attraction might well increase if one promising line of research succeeds. Britain's Motor Industry Research Association believes that with newly designed equipment the unsightly overhead cables of the trolley systems could be reduced by three-quarters if coverage were concentrated where a number of routes overlapped. The trolleys could pick up enough power at these points to carry them over their whole route.

Another much more formidable innovation is being tested out, not surprisingly by some of the large elevator manufacturers. One of the most effective mass movers of people, admittedly for very short trips, is, of course, the elevator. When buildings of over 100 floors have to be served, elaborate programming with express elevators and local elevators and the proper interchange and balance between them has to match the flow of people with the services they require. One could almost call the planned balance between the flow of daily users—87,000 of them—and the elevators needed to carry them that has been achieved in New York's Twin Trade Towers a model of controlled mobility if one did not recall that no effort was made to relate the twice daily tidal wave to the streets outside.

But since elevators can cope so effectively with vertical movement, could not their horizontal use be expanded? A number of airports already have long moving strips to carry passengers to the more distant jumbo jets or to handle luggage. Such carriers could go at the slow, steady speeds now used at airports, which allow walkers to step on and off the moving belt without falling over or to remove their bags without dislocating an arm. It has even been suggested that if such "people movers" were installed inside buildings, say, at the second floor, they would be weatherproof, permit streets to be used for other more interesting purposes—bicycles, walking, gardens, cafes, sitting about—and also allow parking space to be released for housing, shops, and offices. They might even introduce what could be charmingly designed crossovers at the intersections of streets—bridges of sighs, old New England covered bridges, elegant modern "flyovers," according to the style of the city.

But the airport speed is perhaps only suitable for short journeys around pedestrian precincts and traffic-free shopping centers. If, as some researchers hope, the "people mover" can become a cheap and environmentally acceptable alternative to taxis and buses, then the system would need to be speeded up and in place of bus stops, there would be landing and leaving areas, with moving belts timed to go slowly at the point of access and exit, speed up, and then, for a time, run parallel with the main mover at exactly the same speed. Users would simply step from one to the other. There would, no doubt, be a few falls and a few collisions but it is better to collide with another human than with 3,000 pounds of metal in their cars. If, on first thoughts, the whole concept seems fantastic, we have seen men on the moon. And we should remember that the system is designed to replace buses, not the use of the human leg.

This new sense of matching use and density can do more than rationalize travel between the new "clusters" and the old center or make movement more flexible within various centers themselves. Most plans for new towns or new high-density areas in the wider urban region have a further purpose—to try to lessen the sprawl effect, shorten and concentrate suburban journeys, draw workers from unorganized suburban areas to the new clusters, and thus lessen the likelihood of their continuing to drive their cars to the center-city. This lateral attraction—for work, for shopping, for recreation—seems to be growing. The mid-1960s survey of London's New Towns suggest that nearly forty percent of citizens working in the professions came in from surrounding areas. For lower paid work, the percentages were less, but this seems to be largely due to a high coincidence of local work with local residence. A longer-term effect might even be to release land for recreation and open space between the emerging communities. In short, the new clusters are designed to be magnets in their own right, reducing the old overloading of the center and giving more shape to the whole sprawl.

But in every urban region which has grown up by successive waves of fall-out from the original center—in other words, in the majority of the world's conurbations—it has to be said that lateral movement round and about the center is much more difficult to regulate than along the old radial pattern of roads and railways. There usually are no railways. The entire region is served by roads. But the density of housing is so relatively low, the scattering of factories and shops so random that regular bus routes lack sufficient users and it is difficult to think of any workable alternative to the motorcar—or even two motorcars, if one or other spouse commutes by car and is not anxious to leave the other one marooned. In the Los Angeles urban region, for instance, over eighty percent of the families have cars and nearly fifty percent of these have two. Yet if the traffic planners were to feel obliged to "accept the inevitable" and let the car continue to be almost the sole mover, there is still no solution for the twenty percent who do not have cars at all. As we noticed earlier, it was sheer inability to move about and find work that sparked the Watts riots in Los Angeles in the Sixties. Ten years later, there are not many more cars—or jobs.

Of course, one of the chief arguments for clustering housing facilities and employment is precisely to create the "critical mass" that can make regular bus services a working expedient. There still remains the problem of luring people out of their cars. In Stevenage, one of Britain's New Towns, a "Superbus" service has been set up, connecting one of the residential neighborhoods with both the town center and the industrial area. It is reported to be clean, fast, reliable—and subsidized. At least a quarter of the people formerly using their cars seem now to be traveling by bus and the town is considering the extension of the system to the whole of its potential catchment area. Oil price increases will encourage the trend and as passengers increase subsidies can decline. The old vicious spiral turns back on itself and begins the beneficent upward spin. This is the hope. The turnaround would be more quickly achieved, here as everywhere else, if private cars were compelled to cover their full costs.

There still remains the problem of sprawl so shapeless and dwellings so dispersed that no regular routes can serve them. Here a relevant experiment may be the system of Dial-a-Bus that has been the basis of pioneering experiments in a number of cities in the United States and Canada. It is exactly what it is called. Users simply call up a central exchange connected by radio to small buses and they route themselves to pick up the would-be travelers. In the Dial-a-Bus experiment at Milton Keynes in Britain, orders can be booked in advance for specific times. As an alternative to both cars and regular bus routes in low-density areas, it is clearly a useful and possibly successful innovation.

But the urban region, however redesigned, is itself part of two wider systems: the circulation of people and goods in the country at large and the international and intercontinental movement which has provided the most revolutionary explosion of growth in the postwar world. (If we include space satellites disseminating words and pictures, inter-planetary movement is, as we shall see, a third context of interest to many more people than cosmonauts and astronauts.) National connections between city regions are now served by rail, road, and airways. The last twenty-five years has been marked by a vast switch of passengers and goods to the roads and the airlines and, since no country has a coordinated transport policy, the balance between the services has no discernible rationale and has produced and is producing costs and wastes that could, perhaps, have been avoided if accounting practices had made more sense.

This is a difficult issue to determine. There are limits to human foresight. Perhaps no one could have prophesied the instant, overwhelming appeal of free choice offered by automobiles or the opening up of frontiers of contact, business convenience, adventure, and new experience all locked up in man's conquest of the air. These developments, vastly accelerated by the research and mobility of war, belong to cataclysmic change which human beings rarely handle with complete wisdom. All too many railway systems, often ably assisted by their managers and workers, slipped into their downward spiral before people were fully aware either of the fact or the cost. In the United States, between 1950 and 1970, passenger travel on trains fell by forty-five percent, the proportion of freight carried by road rose from 15.8 to 21.2 percent. But even if people had been perturbed by the shift, it was easy, with oil at less than two dollars a barrel, to argue that worrying about the future of railways in 1950 resembled worrying about the future of horse-driven stagecoaches in 1840.

Yet, quite apart from the skew in accounting that has already been mentioned, there are further reasons for taking a new look at the role railways can play in providing successful service to human settlements. One must, of course, begin by accepting the fact that some change in the balance of use would occur. The new cars and trucks enjoy a flexibility which train services cannot begin to imitate. If we take a square mile of land as the yardstick, France has 4.4 miles of road compared with 0.10 miles of rail, West Germany nearly three miles of road and 0.21 miles of railway, the United States one mile of road and 0.06 miles of rail. It is clear that access by motor vehicle is infinitely more flexible and a large number of places can be reached by no other route. Moreover, the drivers delivering passengers or goods are not tied to railway schedules. Above all, they can make door-to-door deliveries and particularly efficiently with fragile or perishable goods. It is the bulkier goods that tend to stay with the railways, particularly on the longer hauls.

But the way in which, on balance, the railways have handled catastrophic falls in customers and revenue has not helped to make the best use of large existing capital structures or to encourage governments and users to take a fresh look at transport costs. For freight, they have tended not to introduce smaller, faster trains. Yet goods piling up while a 2,000-tonner is being put together (or later sorted out) can tie up more working capital than companies can afford. Very few systems have introduced really sophisticated computerized routing systems which could speed up the whole movement of both passengers and freight. A really grave error, particulary in Britain, has been to shut down railway sidings. (France has 11,000, Britain only 2,200). A sizable expansion of these facilities would allow trains to carry a larger proportion of goods for quick and convenient transshipment to small, local delivery services. This would help to get juggernaut trucks out of built-up areas and lessen their wasteful competition with railways for bulk goods over long hauls. The railways have too often failed to seize the opportunities of the new containerized roll-on-roll-off revolution in maritime, land, and air transport which would make them even more competitive on long distance routes—for instance, from sea to sea in Canada, cutting out the Panama Canal—and conceivably on some shorter ones. If they had more well distributed sidings and freight depots, these could receive the containers for breaking down into local loads—and would do so more smoothly if the railroads cooperated fully with local haulers. It is instructive, in this context, to remark with what prescience Canadian railways removed their large sidings and marshaling yards to areas outside the cities to become centers of freight collection and dispersal and used the sites freed of their intrusion, noise, and traffic-generating congestion for new urban developments such as the Chateau Lacomb complex in Edmonton.

Given this more consistent and flexible pattern, it would be reasonable for governments to encourage new industries to choose locations near the new sidings and marshaling yards. The railway network, instead of being half-dismantled, might be used as one of the elements, as in French planning, in the establishment of new, balanced urban regions. In spite of very heavy subsidies being paid to railways in France and West Germany (and not offset, in the popular mind, by the even larger hidden subsidies to roads) there are projects in the making in both countries to draw a revived railway system into a more constructive role in an integrated national transport policy.

The French are experimenting with hover-trains for high-speed connections between Paris and some of its satellite cities and the new stations are directly designed to give the easiest possible interchange between the various modes of transport. At the same time, the "balancing metropolitan regions" are to be linked by new, high-speed turbo-trains of advanced design.

West Germany is experimenting along the same lines. High-speed trains, using magnetic suspension above the track, would move passengers and goods all around the country at top speeds of 300 miles an hour, bypassing the cities with their stations situated on the outskirts, usually near the local airport. They would be equipped to carry automobiles and trucks and there are optimistic forecasts that at least a quarter of present intercity freight will be diverted to the railway system. Sweden is also considering such an integrated shift, removing from the roads all freight carried for more than 160 miles. Such policies might show the way to a structural change needed everywhere on motorways, the physical separation of lanes for heavy traffic and, in the neighborhood of cities, separate bus lanes as well.

By staying outside the dense urban centers, the German system is designed to preserve Germany's highly decentralized and concentrated urban pattern. The trains, as in France, would also lessen the need for short-haul air journeys which, in Europe's uncertain winter weather, would in itself save uncounted hours of wasted time, nerves, and energy in the unrelieved boredom of "identikit" airport lounges. If railways took up a larger part of internal travel, airports could then serve their major function—to provide for rapid international and intercontinental flights.

One can sense in all this the first, dim emergence of a genuinely integrated strategy for transport—with each mode designed to fit into its appropriate place in relation to density and speed. In ascending scale it would include people movers, bicycles, group taxis, jitneys, and buses to supplement walking in the streets and pedestrian precincts of city centers; rapid transit underground and overground, by rail or special bus lanes, to the new centers for work and residence within the urban region; Dial-a-Bus or group taxi-riding to draw in more scattered districts; high-speed passenger and freight trains between city regions to lessen road congestion, link up with the seaports, and take the strain off air services—and incidentally prevent any more airports from being built over acres of good farm land. Last of all, long distance jets would carry the main load of intercontinental travel and some of the frieght until, perhaps in some calmer time, the businessman, the traveler, the convalescent, and the home-mover rediscover the benefit and refreshment of travel by sea.

And just as this vision of a system emerges, there are those who warn us that it is already out of date. What is happening, they claim, is as radical as the emergence of either railway or automobile. Telecommunications, telexes, video-telephones, simulated direct experience by television, computer terminals in the home, the whole postwar

explosion in accumulating and transmitting knowledge and information make the whole idea of moving about almost obsoluete. Why
dash around the country when the facts, the feelings, the conversations
and controversies can all be conducted from the home itself or at the
most from group terminals for computers in the immediate vicinity?
Once again, the gods of irony in history are at work. Marshall McLuhan compares the present state of our technology of movement with
the state of the automobile industry in 1910. Who would then have
guessed that every aspect of urban and rural space would be reordered,
whole economies built up on automobile manufacture and servicing,
peoples' entire range of expectations and styles of life changed beyond
recognition? Now, he claims something similar is about to occur:
"The car . . . has quite refashioned all of the spaces that united and
separate men and it will continue to do so for a decade or more, by
which time the electronic successors to the car will be manifest" * It
is a fascinating, cataclysmic idea—all the separate little units glued to
their screens and their computers, experiencing everything, but everything at second hand and never needing to leave their own front doors
as they telephone their shopping lists, join their colleagues in televised
conferences, swap business decisions, or speed investments on telex
circuits and press the buttons which turn one wall into an odorous pine
forest, another into a sighing ocean, and a third into the stage set for
La Traviata. Indeed, a novel has been written describing this solitary
paradise, which has become necessary because the external world has,
rather gloomily, reached a point of no return in pollution. Then a child
escapes and wanders down to the sullen, oil-slicked ocean beneath its
leaden sulfur skies, and falls into an ecstasy at this first contact with
"the real."

Although the future remains dark to us, we need not fear either this
degree of degradation nor any need for such unacceptable isolation.
That telecommunications are about to play a much vaster part in peoples' lives is not in doubt. And if both more leisure and "permanent
education" become firmly embedded in the habits of developed societies, a great deal of movement may well be eliminated. But one of the
most careful studies of this trend—undertaken for Detroit's Regional
Transportation and Land Use Study by Doxiadis Associates—does not
suggest any really large-scale changes. The number of people working

* Marshall McLuhan, *Understanding Media*, p. 225.

together, say, in local computer centers—for research, for decision-making, in banking, insurance or commerce, for advanced education—might increase with the growing tendency to "quaternary" occupations. This could reduce commuting to the center but could equally stimulate the need for personal contact in other centers or regions. Already, the world has seen the emergence of communities of scholars and specialists who have more in common with each other than with their physical neighbors. Little suggests that video telephones will satisfy their need for contact.

Shopping journeys could decrease but recreation would be likely to pull people outwards and, if the taste for leisure does increase, with earlier retirement, the journeys may be longer. General mobility will not lessen. But possibly the most congested parts of it will do so.

This could be the hope and indeed, there is some reason to suppose that the patterns of decentralization proposed for city regions fit rather well into the possibilities of the "information society." For instance, a Los Angeles insurance firm recently compared the cost of having its 2,500 officials commute to a central office with the alternative establishment of eighteen offices in various dispersed centers in the region. These offices were chosen to suit the convenience of the employees and all were linked by telecommunications to the head office. Commuting fell from an average eleven miles to an average three. The annual cost of installing and amortizing the network was no more than $500 for each employee and this was less than their savings on travel—quite apart from the intangible saving of wasted time and personal frustration. The rents of the offices were also cheaper and the city itself gained by having 2,500 fewer cars on the roads. In terms of the economy as a whole, the gain was as great. A commuting automobile consumes twenty-five times more energy than the telecommunications system. Even a normally loaded mass transit system uses around ten times more energy. In fact, the concept of a "communications society" fits very easily into the strategy of urban regions with dispersed centers of attraction. It reduces but does not do away with the need for mobility. Indeed, in terms of recreation, of higher quality and interest, a population of increasingly well educated people may need more movement and more choice. But on this, the limits may prove to be not so much the limits of transport or energy but the still unreckoned and unpaid bill of environmental costs.

17 THE CONSERVING SOCIETY

THE REDUCTION in pointless mobility that could be made possible by better arranged and more compactly designed settlements has consequences that go much beyond greater convenience for everybody and greater justice for the carless poor. Better management of traffic is a paradigm for the better management of many other services and goods, all tending in the direction of less pollutive use and a wiser conservation of society's resources. Since emissions from motorcars account for a large percentage of air pollution in highly motorized societies, a large shift to public transport automatically helps to clear the skies. Since lowered use of petroleum would cut the need for giant tankers to carry petroleum across all the world's oceans, the risk of truly gigantic oil spills would decline. And although most motorcars are recycled, the number of unsightly junk yards and the final discards would decrease and thus lessen the pollution of the land.

At the same time, there could be a steady saving in the actual use of fuel and the personal cost of journeys—the mileage per gallon of gas would increase while expenses would as steadily decrease. This double process, of cutting pollution and conserving resources, is a complete break with the slosh-it-on approach of the cheap energy decades of the Fifties and Sixties. And it is applicable over a very wide spectrum of the community's activities.

Electricity generation is a polluter second only to motor cars. Since roughly a third of the energy consumed in developed societies is used to heat, cool, and service buildings, they are a major area for conservation policies which also lessen pollution. Recent estimates in the United States suggest that although many existing buildings have been put up with little thought for insulation or for better fitting doors and windows—standards have been standards of design, not of construction—it would be possible to save up to twenty-five percent of the energy now used if greater care (in other words, switching off lights and turning down thermostats) were combined with some quite small investments such as upgrading domestic boilers or weatherproofing roofs, doors, and windows.

The saving in large new buildings could be doubled again, to fifty percent of present use, if builders were obliged to consider not only the cost of installing light and power but also the cost of running them over the life cycle of the building. Better insulation, more efficient air-conditioning, recycling waste heat by using heat pumps, installing windows that open and shut to take advantage of moderate weather when external temperatures are perfectly comfortable—all these may cost more in the original construction than sealed glass towers which will go on requiring simultaneous heating and cooling all through their working lives, even on the balmiest days of spring. But cumulatively these energy gobblers cost much more than buildings designed for more rational uses of energy, and building regulations in a conserving society should be designed to insure that these costs show up in the original specifications.

For all buildings, new regulations could also rule that full advantage be taken of a building's natural surroundings, catch cross breezes, admit winter sunshine, and be sited and constructed so as to avoid midsummer glare. The builders should also be invited to consider the increasing number of solar devices—solar panels, thermal storage walls—which are coming on the market to supplement traditional energy sources and, since heating by electricity is twice as wasteful as by gas or oil boilers, the "all-electric house" might be quickly phased out. These are the kinds of innovation which underlie one British estimate that if house builders and owners invested in better means of conservation, a fifty percent cut in energy use could be secured.

It is not simply buildings but whole communities that can be designed in a more conserving pattern. In fact, one of the advantages of more compact clustering of houses, offices, services, and industry is the possibility of reducing both costs and pollution in providing them with energy. In district heating systems, widely used in Sweden, Denmark, and West Germany, individual boilers are replaced by a large district unit which distributes hot water or steam to homes, shops, and factories. At Malmo, in Sweden, where three-quarters of the houses are linked to such a system, there is an added bonus. Pipes under some of the roads return the water for reheating and keep ice and snow off the streets in winter.

Even larger savings can be derived from what are known as "total energy systems." Normally, the thermal efficiency of a power station is between twenty-five and thirty-five percent. The balance of wasted heat has to be disposed of in the air and in the waters. But if the power station is connected with a district heating system, the wasted heat can be used for space and water heating in the neighborhood and efficiency can rise to something like eighty percent. The Soviet Union and Eastern Europe make considerable use of this method. At Vasteras in Sweden, a community of 120,000 gets virtually all its heating and electricity from a total energy system, has experienced a drastic reduction in air pollution, and sells any surplus electricity to neighboring communities.

There are further advantages to be gained from "total energy systems." If a highly productive invention for the better utilization of coal—the fluidized bed combustor*—is used as the basic furnace for the system, it not only produces electricity from low-quality coal; it can incinerate a proportion of municipal refuse and still achieve an eighty percent rate of efficiency with minimal air pollution. And at this point, we enter a whole new field of expanding and inventive techniques which contrive at the same time to save and recycle raw materials, increase supplies of energy, and do so with much decreased risks of pollution.

It is easy to forget, amid the gloom of the sudden quintupling of oil prices, how creative the more realistic price of fuel is proving to be. It is difficult to keep count of all the new uses—all more conserving, all more productive—that are beginning to stir in inventors' minds, reach the drawing boards, go on to experimental plants and,

---

* The principle of fluidized combustion is that the fuel—in this case, finely crushed coal—is burned in a bed of inert particles such as coal ash. Air is blown upwards through the bed at such a speed that the mixture of burning coal and ash bubbles up like a boiling liquid; the bed behaves as if it were a fluid. This gives a highly efficient combustion process. The temperature of the bed, which can be up to one meter deep, is maintained between 750°C and 950°C, low enough to avoid the formation of slag or clinker. At this temperature, too, nitrogen oxide and sulfur dioxide emissions can be controlled.

many of them, move into full production. The energy bonanza encouraged wasteful, throw-away, unproductive uses. The new pressures are, as usual, proving to be the mother of invention and of inventions that are of necessity more cost-conscious, less lavish, and more concerned with wasting nothing. As a result, most of them are less pollutive as well. In spite of some discouraging setbacks—such as the American President's 1975 veto of environmental restrictions on strip coal mining in vulnerable areas—it can be said that the energy crisis and the world's environmental concerns are not, as so many feared, contradicting each other. On the contrary, more careful use produces less to waste and throw away. It is in itself essentially conserving.

We can follow for a moment the clue of municipal waste. There are various ways in which the mountains of garbage produced by the throw-away generation can be dealt with. In the past, they have all too often been pollutive and wasteful—burned off to fill the atmosphere with smoke and soot, dumped raw in rivers and oceans, used as landfill, often so carelessly that poisons have seeped into underground waters or ill-chosen sites have been used, such as the marshes which act as sponges for nature's occasional overproduction of water. The result has often been land compacted into building sites flooding heavily just as the houses are completed.

But all these careless ways are increasingly seen not only as dangerous in themselves, not only in need of the disciplines of Clean Air and Water Acts, regulations, fines, and even, in extreme cases (for instance, careless poison-dumping), of imprisonment. They are also seen as stupidly wasteful. As a result, the positive methods of prevention—which is better use of the wastes—are beginning to catch hold.

Broadly speaking, three-quarters of municipal garbage is made up of organic matter—paper, wood, cloth, remains of food. Metals account for just under ten percent, glass eight percent, nonferrous metals one percent. The small balance is unusable dirt and rock. For some time past, a number of countries have been using part of their garbage for more constructive uses than incinerating and dumping. The organic matter once separated can be allowed to decompose, in the presence of oxygen, into usable compost. In Leningrad, for instance, or the Netherlands, it goes to the country's farms. The Dutch produce about 200,000 tons of compost each year, a fifth of what the farms could use, and receive a commercial price for it. Organic waste can also be used as a fuel. In Düsseldorf, a municipal incinerator, servicing a city of some 800,000 people, has for some time past provided district steam heating and hot water from its waste-fired boilers, recovered scrap iron from the furnaces, and used the remaining ash for landfill and cinderblocks. Industries using the incinerator are charged so much a ton for the right to put in their wastes—"the polluter pays." At the end of the process, the city makes a modest profit and has got rid of the rubbish.

Such incinerators were the first steps in a technology which is now becoming steadily more efficient and complex. The first step in the new processes is usually shredding, to reduce the bulk of waste to a manageable size. Then the shreds go into a high-velocity tower (a process known as "air classification") where the lighter, mainly organic materials are blown off and the heavier metals drop down for further treatment. This is the stage at which the organic part can be used either for composting or directly as a fuel according to local priorities. And there are other options besides composting and incineration. Pyrolysis—thermal decomposition in the absence of air—reduces the wastes to char and releases valuable and salable gas, light oil, tar, pitch, and ammonium sulfate. Or anaerobic decomposition can be used by excluding oxygen and leaving microorganisms to produce methane—the main component of natural gas—and ammonia, carbon dioxide, and hydrogen. The remaining sludge can, like compost, be used for fertilizer.

The next stage is to put the inorganic material through a series of processes designed to separate the different kinds of metals from each other and from glass. There may be more shredding, more air classification, screens, magnetic separators, froth flotation systems, and so on. The aim is to produce the most salable mineral or recyclable glass at the most reasonable cost, and the whole technology is now in a state of continuous research and experiment. For instance, nearly $4 million has been spent on an experimental plant in St. Louis which shreds and "air classifies" organic wastes for feeding into a 125-megawatt boiler as a supplement to pulverized coal in the production of electricity. Magnetic separation sorts out the ferrous metals and they are resold. The local utility company is now modifying some elements in the process and plans to go ahead with it. The company is expected to build a $70 million plant, using 8,000 tons of refuse a day from the St. Louis area for the production of recovered metals and fuel supplements. The experiment, incidentally, has shown that trash-based fuel has a low sulfur content and admirably meets air pollution standards.

This is only one example among hundreds. Some schemes are more ambitious. The State of Connecticut, for instance, has set up its own Resources Recovery Authority to encourage experiment and construction throughout the state. Nearly $30 million has been spent on a Bridgeport plant for the recovery of glass, metals, and the production of fuel supplements and $70 million on two plants, one in the Housatonic Valley, the other in New Britain, for the conversion of wastes to boiler-fuels for industrial plants and for power companies.

These patterns of profitable reuse are not confined to municipal wastes. They can be applied to municipal sewage. Too much muck is still dumped in the water and never sees a treatment plant. Primary treatment only removes grit and scum and lets the wastes fall into a sedimentation tank. The resulting sludge has to be disposed of and it is still pollutive. But secondary treatment, like aerobic decomposition, makes use of oxygen and bacteria to produce an "activated sludge" which, if disposed of in water courses, no longer produces explosions of algae that consume the water's dissolved oxygen. The more important point is that the sludge can be used to refertilize mined or poor quality land. The price can cover the costs of processing and turn a burden into an asset.

There may be further important innovations ahead. One of the world's profoundest injustices lies in the degree to which ever more grain is fed to animals to provide high-protein foods for developed countries. Of North America's 1900 pounds of grain a year for each consumer, only 150 pounds is eaten as grain. The rest comes to him or her via cows and pigs and chickens, which are far from being the most efficient processors of grain—the wastage in meat production is of the order of eighty percent. Recently, whenever bad harvests drive a major food importer like Russia into the market, absolute shortages develop and the Indian can barely afford his nominal 400 pounds of grain. Of course, if the animals graze on grass or forage, the position can be entirely different. "All flesh" may be "as grass," but humans cannot eat grass. Animals grazing on land that cannot be used for crops are therefore highly efficient converters. It is feedlot animals or grain-fed poultry that compete most grossly with starving children—

and often pollute the water courses as well. Meanwhile, a lot of Russian and American meat and distilled spirits continue to be consumed at the expense of the poorest of the poor.

But suppose animals could be provided not only with grazing but with other sources of food? Suppose the process had the double advantage of reusing organic wastes? Grain for all humans could be increased with no loss of beefsteaks for the wealthy. Such possibilities exist. The Thames Water Authority in Britain has recently made an initial contribution to a pilot project for converting sewage into animal food. Animal feed producers are interested. So is the government, reflecting, no doubt, on the $1000 million Britain has to spend each year to import grain for fodder. The process consists of using electrolysis to separate out metals and chemicals and sterilization to kill possible microbes. The resulting stew, which is sixty percent pure protein and fat, is mixed with dropped straw and turned into feed pellets for use on poultry farms or as cattle feed.

The economics are no less interesting. The cost of producing a ton of the new feedstuff is estimated to be about thirty-two dollars, which is a quarter of the price of a comparably nutritive amount of feedgrain. Even if one assumes that sewage-feed would only sell for half the present price for fodder—at, say, sixty dollars a ton—the estimate for a municipal plant serving 250,000 people is that it might make a million dollars a year in sales to fodder merchants and farmers. Since the costs of treating sewage at present run at about the same level—and must in the main be paid for out of taxes—the new use for the city's organic wastes could leave the municipality with a gain of the order of $2 million a year. Obviously, such possibilities could revolutionize the readiness of city authorities to install proper treatment plants. This encouragement is vital wherever rivers—the Rhine, for example—are within sight of a degree of contamination that rules out their retreatment for drinking water. For threatened inland seas like the Mediterranean, where it is becoming increasingly difficult to bathe without having to skirt raw sewage, the prospect of municipalities actually earning income by cleaning up would be more potent than a thousand exhortations in the finest environmental rhetoric.

When we turn from municipal wastes to the discards of industry, they are often the same, since a fair proportion of the wastes passing through municipal treatment plants originate with industry. An essential policy in conservation is to see that firms are charged fees which cover actual costs—the American city of Cincinnati discovered that industrial wastes fell by a third when such charges were introduced. This is more than a financial issue. The more industrial systems can use air and water as cost-free dumps and cleansers, the less easy it is for them to escape from the throw-away mentality and, as a result, the more likely they are to miss possible and valuable opportunities of saving, both in materials and energy. Since, in the developed world, industry uses about forty percent of primary energy consumption, greater conservation could profoundly affect all extrapolations of future energy use.

It is here that a conjunction of interest can arise between better methods of metals recovery by municipalities and the readiness of industry to increase its use of scrap. Internal scrap left over in the factory itself accounts for much of the increases in the recycling of metals mentioned on an earlier page. But the help of scrap merchants is also enlisted. If municipalities were to become well organized sources of usable scrap, the proportions of reuse in industry could go up still further. Taxes on the use of virgin ores could encourage the switch. To recycle steel requires only twenty-five percent of the energy required for new ore. For copper it is between five and ten percent, for aluminum below five percent. Paper is not so attractive. Recycled paper requires sixty to seventy percent of the original input of energy. But who will despise a thirty to forty percent saving in a world of steadily rising fuel costs?

To make full use of these possibilities, industry and government have to overcome the most expensive aspect of waste-recovery—its collection in the first place. This is a point to which we must return. But quite apart from the saving of materials, industry can make a vast contribution simply by a more conserving use of energy itself. We should not overlook the effectiveness of direct campaigns for economy. A large British commercial enterprise reduced energy consumption by fifteen percent simply by consultation with the staff on switching off lights and levels of heating and lighting. An American firm achieved a similar fall simply by requesting a daily report on energy use from each of its departments. One of the world's large multinationals has put the unnecessary energy cost to Britain of poor insulation in offices and factories at some $1,200 million a year. Japan, on balance, uses thirty percent less energy per ton of steel than does the older American industry. Modern cement kilns in Europe use fifty percent less energy per barrel than their American competitors. Studies made by the Workshop on Alternative Energy Strategies organized by the Massachusetts Institute of Technology show that Sweden uses a quarter less energy (per dollar value added) than the United States in its food industries and a remarkable fifth of American use in the production of chemicals. Such contrasts crop up everywhere. West Germany shows many of the same Swedish-American ratios. In 1971, France, hardly a backward country, used about half as much energy as the United States or the United Kingdom per unit of GNP. Yet in national wealth it has now pulled well ahead of its British neighbor.

That the scope for a far more sparing use of energy is possible was shown decisively by the most thorough study yet made of energy in the country which uses thirty percent of the world's supplies. The results of the Ford Foundation exhaustive Energy Policy Project make it quite clear that if energy consumption in the United States were to continue to rise at the accelerated rates of the Fifties and Sixties, the amount of energy available by the end of the century would actually begin to surpass any foreseeable uses. With a more stable population, a large shift to less energy-intensive industrial processes, based upon automation and the flow of data rather than blast furnaces and steam hammers, with an increase in miniaturization and a vast growth in electronics for entertainment and learning, sheer raw energy uses would be likely to decline. Used efficiently, they would decline still further. With social changes no more devastating than a smaller use of cars in center-cities and a shift to public transport, the need for growth in energy might well become stable by the year 2000. Other studies conducted for Holland and Sweden reached very similar conclusions. And it should be noted that none of them imply the sort of heroic cuts in living standards that would be appropriate, say, in a wartime economy. On the contrary, the American "scenario" presupposes the continued use of all of today's appliances, twenty-four percent more travel, and a more than doubling of personal income. This is hardly a spartan proposition.

18 FAUSTIAN BARGAIN OR NATIONAL THRIFT?

IT IS WITHIN this context of large-scale possibilities for conserving energy and of cutting, often by half, its present use that we must look once again at the most fateful of environmental hazards, the development of the nuclear economy. The two arguments that are being used to hustle humanity toward the nuclear option are, first, that energy must rapidly increase to give mankind a "civilized" existence, and that there are in any case no alternatives. The examples already given show that, on the contrary, a more sparing use of energy and a greater effort of general conservation would give human society a more truly civilized existence—less filthy, less noxious, with cleaner waters and clearer skies. Another energy binge would lead us back to the old careless waste; this time its nuclear pollutions would be uniquely toxic and some of them last half a million years.

And there *are* alternatives. If extrapolations of future use are cut by a third to a half, as some conservation measures would make possible, traditional, nonrenewable resources of energy, the fossil fuels, would give technological man well over a century to develop safe alternatives. And some of them are beginning to appear. It may be that fusion power is one of them. Apparently it does not produce deadly byproducts for millennial storage. Its basic raw material, deuterium, is virtually endless. Its vast thermal pollutions could possibly be diverted to industrial use. Its sheer scale is risky, both in terms of centralized power and of the difficulty of protecting particular plants. We know too little about risks of fusion reactor malfunctioning to say whether an accident would be the equivalent of a thermonuclear explosion. The basic technique is, after all, the same—the release of energy through the fusion of nuclei, as at the heart of the sun. All in all, it is an awesome decision, to reproduce the sun's processes on earth *inside* the atmospheric shield. But, just possibly, continued experiment is in order.

What is certain is that mankind could be on the verge of a different kind of breakthrough which would make fusion, with its vast costs and uncertain effects, entirely obsolete. This is the very rapid development of solar cell technology by which electricity is produced directly from the sun's radiance and can first supplement and finally take the place of the world's present reliance upon fossil fuels. At present the cost and reliability of the process is not fully established. The turning point, expected within a decade, will be the production of solar electricity for less than $500 a kilowatt, which would be under half the present nuclear costs and could be even lower ten years hence. Solar power could be essentially decentralized—either in small power stations serving the new "clustered" communities or attached as energy units to individual buildings. They could be connected to a traditional grid which would be used as a sort of energy store or back-up system. This could be drawn on when houses or communities or industries need more than their solar plants can supply and could be turned down or used to convert electricity into other fuels that can be stored—such as hydrogen—when the solar plants produce more electricity than is needed. The excess electricity could be fed back into the grid so that both charges and credits are registered. So flexible a system would have the added value of delivering communities from the single knockout blow of a flicked-off switch at the central generator—by accident or design.

Nations which have already made a considerable commitment to atomic energy by nuclear fission will no doubt require time to phase out the unfortunate experiment. Meanwhile, we must hope that no accident occurs in the reactors or in the disposal of lethal wastes. No one denies the care and vigilance of the managements concerned. Yet it is disconcerting that the two largest nuclear power plants in operation—at Brown's Ferry, Alabama—had to be closed down precipitately in April 1975 to avoid the risk of a major "melt-down." The cause of the accident would be almost comically trivial were it not so horrifying. Here is a contemporary account of the accident:

"A workman was using an unshielded candle to detect airflow and accidentally set light to cables under the control room. More alarming than the fire itself was the fact that the emergency systems, designed to keep the reactor cool in the event of an accident, appear to have failed. When his instruments began to show something was wrong, the operator 'scrammed'—shut down—both reactors as quickly as possible. Later he noticed that the water level in reactor one was dropping, creating a danger of overheating in the core and possible fuel meltdown. He operated the emergency core cooling system (ECCS) but nothing happened, apparently because the control cables had been damaged by the fire. The plant operators brought the reactors under control by using other pumps, not intended as safety systems, to maintain the water level. But the accident has renewed anxieties about American-designed nuclear plants, which have suffered a long series of accidents and setbacks."*

For scientists or nuclear engineers or public officials to reassure the public by saying that every precaution is being taken is not the same as saying that every precaution will work. Indeed, the risks are obliquely admitted because no private corporation in the United States will carry on in the nuclear business without the special insurance of $560 million for each reactor provided in the Price Anderson Act. Moreover, some nuclear problems have not yet even been considered. No nuclear power station has yet come to the end of its working life. When it does, how can it be safely decontaminated or sealed off? Nobody knows.

In spite of the gravity of these problems, they are as nothing compared with the central and terrible reality of the so-called "Faustian bargain." It is not technical. It is not scientific. It is historical, human, and moral. There is no society on record in which, at some point, public order has not broken down, and we can be absolutely sure that in the future, undisturbed good order will not last out the 24,000 years of plutonium's half-life. Yet the nuclear option, through fission—using conventional reactors or the further step to the breeder-reactor—means that the world's indestructible nuclear wastes will steadily accumulate.

When every conceivable technical safeguard has been put in place,

* *The Observer,* April 5, 1975.

every alarm in position, every fabrication plant, reprocessing unit, and reactor surrounded by protective devices that make a medieval fortress look like an open city, we still come back to a Japanese Red Army man or an Ulster terrorist or whatever brand of Trotskyism is enflaming the latest vanguard of the world's proletariat—or plain lunacy, which is never in short supply. Plutonium, like heroin, will find its price and its market. We know already, since an MIT student has done it, that an atomic device can be cobbled together. If a few determined men carrying only conventional small arms can kidnap every one of OPEC's Ministers for Energy, what could stocking-faced terrorists with stolen plutonium not accomplish, especially in a world driven toward ever deeper poverty for the many and ever more bull-headed egoism and escapism for the few?

The conclusion is inescapable. Nuclear power, whatever the interests, both public and private, that may be vested in it, whatever the—unproven—technical safeguards, whatever the blind confidence in man's eternal ability to find the right "technofix," must be steadily phased out of current use and removed from the drawing boards and from the future of humanity. We are going to have enough to do to hold back "the blood-dimmed tide" of anarchy in the years ahead without gratuitously adding a "final solution." It would exceed even the excessive limits of human folly to choose such an epoch of potential disorder to multiply the risk of placing in terrorist hands the infallibly ultimate weapon. It will, no doubt, be objected that armies already possess such armaments. True—but it is hardly an argument for increasing still further an already existing menace. Moreover, the way in which weapons are controlled within a military system—by intense, continuous surveillance—is a reminder of what sacrifices of essential civilian freedoms, what centralization of authority and spread of police power would be required for "peaceful" nuclear installations, deemed to be fully safeguarded, in an age of violent social disorder. Between police states and terrorists, the political price is not one humanity should be asked to pay.

The decision to phase out nuclear power would naturally need to be accompanied by a very greatly increased governmental emphasis on the conservation of energy and on research into the alternatives—higher and safer rates of return from coal mines, possibly by more automated methods of extraction; the development of oil from tar sands and maybe shale; gassification and liquefaction of coal—the former providing a supplement to natural gas, the latter being used for electricity generation and possibly motor fuel; the solar option; the use of windmills and geothermal energy where appropriate; the encouragement of more hydro power, particularly on a small scale in developing countries.

Government policy should also use tax inducements, fines, and penalties to cut down all wasteful uses of energy in private and public establishments. A general increase in energy prices would be helpful. Taxes on virgin ores have already been mentioned. Incidentally, the American states of Arizona and Indiana already reduce the property tax assessment on houses fitted with solar devices. One useful suggestion put forward by the Ford Energy Study is that an energy tax be introduced at a future date—say 1985—and increased steadily over a ten-year period. This would give business firms time to shift to less energy-intensive technologies before the tax began. Goods would then be taxed according to their energy consumption. To prevent these measures hitting the poorest citizens hardest, income tax rebates and welfare benefits would offset the cost. Bonuses for energy-saving industrial usages and inventions, prizes for "the saver of the year"—all such means should be used to keep the country alert to the basic unacceptability of wasted energy or, indeed, of any form of waste. A similar battery of inducements and penalties is needed for the salvaging and recycling of materials and the prevention of pollution. An Agency of Conservation, preferably situated in the President's or Prime Minister's office, would be an appropriate instrument for a sustained commitment.

Nor should we forget the progress that is being made. The Japanese are beginning a ten-year clean-up program under which two percent of GNP is to be devoted each year to ending air and water pollution. Since 1973, the Americans have begun to spend about the same percentage on their own "spring cleaning." They also lead the world in institutionalizing the need for environmental action with their Council on Environmental Quality and its watchdog—with real teeth—the Environmental Protection Agency.

Some individual American states intend to go further. Oregon, for example, has banned the pull-tab can and required return deposits on all beer and soft drink containers. Clearly, much more could be done by the public authorities to encourage greater reuse of materials. Containers both of glass and metal should be manufactured to specifications—of uniform composition and manageable shape—which permit easy recycling and, in the case of glass containers, reuse. Taxes should be imposed and government orders refused in all cases of noncompliance.

Above all, the effort must be made to end the throw-away mentality in the place where it does most harm—in the minds of the peoples themselves. That culture and education play a part can be shown by the vast differences to be found in the world between clean and messy cultures—or in the transformation of China before and after its revolution. This is more than a question of decency and environmental respect, important as they are in changing over from the wasting to the conserving society. Some problems of waste are all but insoluble without public cooperation. At least eighty percent of the cost of municipal refuse, for instance, lies in collecting the rubbish in the first place. Technology can help a little. But in most communities, the willingness of citizens to sort their own trash and the willingness of garbage collectors to keep it separate is an essential part of the answer. This requires discipline and respect—on both sides. All too often sanitation men are allowed to feel not the most valuable but the least liked members of society. In Munich, for instance, every garbage collector is a "guest worker" and it is almost as though Europeans were allowing a new race of untouchables to grow up in their midst. The work is, in fact, indispensable and should be more highly paid than a great many of the spotless jobs in the "quaternary" sector.

Any increase in public respect and cooperation would have the incidental effect of improving the service. But in the last analysis, the quality of life will be determined by the people themselves. If every city had its citizens' committees for cleaner neighborhoods, with children retrieving the returnable bottles and getting their money back for the old people's Christmas party; if housewives—and house-husbands—sorted bottles, cans, and newspapers and saw that they were separately sacked; if youth groups cleared out back yards and did the heavy jobs for the elderly; if the kind of spirit that has led to the cleaning up of decrepit tenements and rundown terraces were extended to the streets around, the fears expressed by Sir Colin Buchanan might be reversed. The decline in squalor could mark the beginning of a decline in violence.

And in such a reflowering of effective citizenship, one might, without too extreme an optimism, see the first shoots of a wider hope. To love, cherish, and clean up the particular corner of the planet where one's own home is built need not be an exclusive dedication. The earth and the sky are the same for everybody. The task cannot be carried out alone, even in four streets and a little square. And since respect and care are states of mind that become intensified with practice, if we start wherever we are, perhaps the sense of needing to be less wasteful and more careful can be extended to wider aims. In place of the self-regarding, self-centered consumerism drummed into the citizens of developed technological societies, there might open up a little space for reflection and comparison, for a realization that, in spite of all the inflationary pressures and disappointed hopes, wealthy nations today are still the privileged elite of an increasingly hungry and despairing world. At least a third of humanity would be glad to consume the food that the rich throw away, at least half could live on what they discard. The first step is to stop the waste. Perhaps the next might be a greater willingness to share the wealth that has made such waste possible.

19 THE RURAL–URBAN BALANCE

THE DEVELOPED world's experience with controlling the use of land and allocating the nations' resources according to more just and acceptable standards has led to certain conclusions—that it is not wise or politically possible to take no notice of regional imbalances, that a free-for-all in the land market is not a reliable guide to community-building, that vast overblown conurbations exact heavy economic and social costs, that gross disparities in income, further exacerbated by inflation, are hardly the recipe for the good life. These experiences of the already developed countries may, like the *enfant terrible,* serve rather as a warning than an example. But developing nations may find it rather more acceptable to learn from the errors of those who have so often suggested themselves as models. In any case, their own margins are so narrow that it would be folly not to avoid as many as possible of the mistakes already made by other, wealthier communities.

The first conclusion, that serious regional imbalance in a country's development is politically disadvantageous and probably economically so as well, is most clearly illustrated by the example of France, whose whole strategy is based on a determined effort to reverse the trend to overcentralization. Virtually the only states in Europe which are not actively trying to revise some of the development patterns first established by the free play of the market are those which, like West Germany or Switzerland, had greater regionalism built into their historical experience, constitutional structure, and local geography. Virtually all America's present planning is, in one way or another, concerned with lessening the effects of an unintended distribution of population, industrial activity, and urban sprawl. It may take the form of advocating greater concentration—for center-cities—or smaller concentrations—in Florida or Colorado. In either case, it implies discontent with land use arrived at by an almost solely economic calculus.

In developed socialist economies, the degree to which the regionalization of economic activities and the consequent spatial distribution of population are actually planned is naturally carried considerably further. The "sucking pull" of growing cities which, by their ability to provide services, supplies, and a ready market, set up their own chain reaction of further growth is rejected in favor of a search for some kind of optimal size for the community and optimal distribution of communities throughout the national economy. Socialist planners point out that in earlier city building, the real costs of agglomeration have been distorted by the ability of industrial enterprises to pass the entire social costs of their activities, *via* the public authorities, on to the taxpayer. Would cities have grown with so strong a centralizing thrust if social costs had been more equitably shared? Planners can also point to the fact that a number of studies, in many different countries and types of economy, do suggest a certain consistent pattern of costs changing in cities in relation to their size. There are economies of scale in concentration—in other words, more houses, institutions, commercial undertakings, and factories can be served for each dollar (or ruble) spent on roads, lighting, water, and sewerage—as the city increases up to about the half a million mark. Then, somewhere within the next million, a number of factors making for economy are reversed. The expense of transport and its irregular rush hour concentrations are usually among them. The distances that need to be covered to satisfy water demand may extend a city's catchment area to a hundred square miles, often competing uneasily with that of a neighboring conurbation. The filling up of accessible sites for landfill can be yet another item of rising cost. So, in northerly cities, is snow clearance. There is so far no precise rule for infallibly estimating the relations between size and cost. No "optimum" is generally definable in some conveniently applicable general law. Climate, topography, types of industry, density of housing, cultural traditions all help to decide what scale of city its inhabitants do or do not find manageable or affordable—or desirable.

Over the years, for instance, American public opinion polls have shown, with remarkable uniformity, that a majority of people when questioned in large cities, declare their preference for living in smaller ones. In the latest U.S. census, there is even some evidence that, reversing the trend of the last fifty years, people are leaving not simply the center-city—*that* move began in the 1860s—but the whole metropolitan area and heading toward the equivalents of Springfield, Illinois or Springfield, Mass. But however inconclusive the argument, planners in Eastern Europe are tending to put the "optimum" size at between a million and two million people. And since many of the nations in Eastern Europe are nearer in their stage of modernization and industrialization to developing countries, their experience with planned decentralization and regional development may be of more direct relevance to developing lands than that of older industrial centers whose condition can now be removed from theirs by a century at least of urban growth and changing technology. The possibility is increased by the fact that much of the strategic land use planning seems these days to be less concerned with devising new patterns of work and community than with mitigating past mistakes. It is at least arguable that it might be better for developing countries not to make the mistakes in the first place.

A second, fairly general conclusion in developed economies is that a wide variety of reforms may be required to offset the antisocial effects of an unregulated market or of exclusive property rights in the community's finite supplies of land. On the side of agriculture, it is simply an historic fact that no developed state contrived to launch a full-scale program of modernization and industrialization on the basis of a traditional feudal structure. The movement of industrialization eastward from Britain almost seems to move with the modernizing break from the feudal past—in France in 1789, in Central Europe after 1848, in Russia after 1866 and the emancipation of the serfs. As though to confirm the connection the latecomers to the nineteenth-century process, the Japanese, made the break with that undeviating thoroughness the world has since come to expect of them. After the Meiji Revolution in 1868, the entire feudal superstructure was dismantled. All federal dues were abolished, tenants became owner-farmers, the Samurai class of traditional "rent collectors" were paid off in bonds which they could invest only in the nascent industrial sector.

Although a high land tax was used to divert the necessary resources from farming to industry, it was still lower than the old plethora of feudal payments. Thus it provided a direct incentive to greater agricultural output. It was a sort of textbook operation of a whole economy's synchronized move into a new phase of development.

True, after some fifty years of urbanization and modernization, a profound world depression and Japan's full involvement in the Second World War, the peasant farmer had not kept pace with the community's general expansion. Concentrations of ownership were reforming in the wake of debt, and "feudal" relationships of dependence began to reappear. But the Japanese were fortunate enough to be defeated by the United States, which wrote a new land reform into its policy of occupation—a step which was accompanied by a very great strengthening of Japanese cooperative structures. In the Fifties and Sixties, the farm sector moved forward to become one of the most productive in the world, a farmer earning a middle-class income from his average of eight acres of double-cropped land.

Japan is unique in developed countries because of the small scale of the farms themselves—only seventeen percent of that mountainous country is arable at all. But its social structure conforms to a more general pattern throughout developed market economies. The private farm, sometimes vigorously supported by a cooperative network—as in Scandinavia—sometimes less so—as in Britain—has become the norm in a sector so productive that ten percent or less of the labor force is required to work on the farms. Yet they still supply butter mountains for Europe and the world's entire grain reserve from Canada, the United States, and Australia.

Much less uniformity is evident in the patterns and uses of developed urban land. But the pressure is steadily toward the recognition of its social dimension. The more trouble governments have encountered in trying, by way of taxation or special levies, to secure the increased increment created for urban landowners by the multiplication of public needs on or near their lands, the stronger has been the trend to turn to forms of direct public controls—by advance purchase at the value of present use, by the creation of land banks, by outright municipal or national land ownership. A free-for-all in urban land is increasingly recognized for what it is—a disastrous invitation to speculative land gains, to skyrocketing urban prices, to the exclusion of more and more citizens from the possibility of land or home ownership, and to a sharp upward spin to the vicious self-feeding spirals of inflation.

And inflation is a key element in the third lesson from developed societies, the lesson which turns on the degree to which a society's progress toward a more fair and acceptable distribution of its rewards can be stopped short and even dangerously reversed unless its economic system can escape from the sometimes opposite and sometimes concurrent trap of price inflation and job deflation.

How and to what extent are these storm warnings—of regional imbalance, of delayed or neglected land reform, of imbalances in wealth further aggravated by inflation—relevant to conditions in the developing lands? We must begin by reminding ourselves again of the many reasons why the position of nations developing in the late twentieth century cannot be strictly compared with the progress of the more fortunate pioneers. The early industrializers all set out on their journey with much better lined purses. Two or three centuries of active trade and technical improvisation preceded the eighteenth-century breakthrough. Even the gin-soaked ruffians we see lying about in the contemporary caricatures of a Rowlandson or a Gillray certainly subsisted on more than $75 a year. A growing merchant and professional class already enjoyed what the Victorians would call "a modest competence." Today $75 or less is the annual income of nearly a thousand million human beings, or about a quarter of the human race. This is the base of desperate poverty from which over the next three decades populations in the developing world will continue to grow rapidly both in the countryside and in the cities.

This is another critical difference. We are not talking, as in the nineteenth century, of the rise in urban industrial jobs "pulling" people off the land while farm productivity falls. By the year 2000, the world's rural people—at present nearly 2.5 thousand million—will have grown by almost another thousand million, overwhelmingly in developing lands. Urban populations will have more than doubled, two-thirds of them in the poor countries. Thus the pressure on land and city will be equally intense. Moreover, long before reaching even the halfway mark toward full industrialization, most developing countries will have among them metropolises of a size simply undreamed of in the earlier phase of nineteenth-century development. When Britain was about at the level of most developing countries today, it had only one city of more than a million. The developing world today has 101 of these cities. Fourteen cities have over three million inhabitants, eleven others more than five million. We can dismiss entirely from our minds any nineteenth-century analogy of a vast convenient industrializing conveyor belt moving the needed labor force out of the rural into the urban economy, enhancing productivity and redistributing employment and income as it moves along. The nineteenth-century conveyor belt was, heavens knows, bumpy enough in spite of all the built-in advantages of a more manageable flow of people and a better match between numbers, skills, or types of technology. It also took many tragic decades of inhuman uprooting and degrading poverty before the process of distributing and redistributing the fruits of the new productivity began to work with even minimum fairness. But today no conceivable conveyor belt can both clear the countryside and employ the cities. The system is clogged at both ends.

And this essential dislocation begins to suggest that the processes of redistribution—the traditional pattern of producing first and distributing later—is equally blocked. The unstaunched movement from the land is a permanent depressant on the urban wage. The unstaunched growth of rural numbers is as permanent a depressant on rural output and earnings. It is against this background that we have to try to judge the relevance of the developed world's experience in regional balance, in land use planning and control, in direct interventions in the distribution of citizens' resources and gains.

The sheer, desperate dilemmas confronting most developing lands can, of course, be used as an argument for pursuing economic growth at the cost of bulldozing away any obstacles that may be held to stand in its way. Throughout the Fifties and the Sixties, the conventional economic wisdom was, as we have seen, to regard the most rapid forms of industrialization—and where possible, the heaviest forms of capital goods' industries—as the securest route to modernization. The U.S.A. and the U.S.S.R., mighty victors in battle, had followed that path. Now in the aftermath of war and empire, to produce locally what was formerly imported would reduce resented external dependence— had not the old colonial powers frowned on industrialization for just that reason? Also, as Stalin is reported to have remarked: "People cannot eat steel." A program based upon capital goods is, by definition, an enforcer of savings and a producer of capital for further expansion.

Given these preconceptions, urban-based industrial development enjoyed top priority—it was, for instance, "the core" of India's successive Five Year Plans. Every inducement of overvalued currencies, tax holidays and rebates, and manipulated tariff structures was introduced to encourage industrial investment. The "terms of trade" were turned against the villages by fixing food prices at a low level and in some countries by imposing quotas for sales to the government.

Agriculture in general enjoyed a low or no priority in planning and much of what it received took the shape, not of economic inputs but of rather vague and disjointed community schemes unlinked to either work or market. Any stimulus for development on sites or in regions not judged to be required by pure economic calculus was discouraged as "a wasteful diversion of scarce capital." The planners, in short, accepted the traditional strategy—first develop the resources, even if, for the time being, forced saving actually depresses personal and regional standards. The upturn and redistribution will come later. To this policy, clearly, the lessons suggested by developed countries' experience could have little relevance. Regional devolution would divert scarce capital and staff. Land reform, either rural or urban, could interfere with the maximum expansion of economic activity. To stop urban concentration would threaten growth. Redistribution would make no sense with nothing to redistribute. In short, the "warnings" could be seen as luxuries which, like antipollution or the preservation of endangered species, the already rich can afford for themselves. In the real world of hard survival, such extras have no part.

But the strategies of one decade can become the extravagances of the next. Two factors, above all, have radically changed expert thinking about development in the last five years, and in this new context the lessons of already developed societies are once again directly relevant. One factor is the emerging reality of a work force that grows in developing lands by as much as three percent a year—the nineteenth-century increase was never more than 0.7 percent. The other is the basic issue of man's daily bread. True, "men cannot eat steel." But suppose there is nothing to eat? Who will then produce the steel? The two issues of food and jobs come together to suggest very different priorities and they in turn dictate different approaches to regional planning, land use, urban growth, job creation, and the distribution of rewards. The key to all of them lies not, as it seemed to do in earlier development theories, with rapid industrialization. The key to regional development, to effective land use, to almost all aspects of income distribution, is to be found, as a matter of priority, on the farms.

This priority simply reflects the bleak fact that unless the farmers in the developing world who work on less than eight acres can be drawn into a more productive system of agriculture, there is, in sheer and literal truth, no hope of feeding the whole human family within the next two decades. Over 400 million children are undernourished now. Sudden disasters—a failed monsoon, devastating floods—already precipitate starvation. A slower but no less inexorable pace of decimation marches forward with the advancing deserts. In 1974, developing countries had to import nearly 27 million tons of grain. By the 1980s, if no drastic changes occur in local productivity, the deficit could rise to 80 million tons—by which time it would far surpass the ability of all the surplus producers in all the wealthy temperate lands together to make up the gap.

The small farmer with his eight acres or less may seem a ludicrously inadequate answer to deepening global scarcity. But there are over 100 million of him. Even with primitive tools and traditional practices, he can already produce more food per acre than larger commercialized undertakings. Figures published in the 1960s by the United States Department of Agriculture and Agency for International Development suggested that in countries as various as India, Taiwan and Brazil, the smaller farms were consistently outproducing the large ones in terms of output per acre. In Taiwan, admittedly, we are no longer talking of primitive techniques. The area is one of high agricultural sophistication, large inputs of fertilizer, and almost total membership in a strong cooperative structure. But the figure is remarkable. One-acre plots produced almost double the output of farms of more than five acres. Figures from FAO in 1970 showed Taiwan producing more grain per acre—3,510 pounds—than either Britain or the United States. But in areas lacking this exceptional development, the evidence is the same. At the end of the Sixties, the five-acre man in India produced forty percent more per acre than the "big farmer" (with more than fifty acres). In Brazil, the holdings of less than twenty-five acres produce around eighty percent more per acre (in money terms) than the farms of over 100 acres.

The general reason is simply that small peasants have to work much harder to keep alive and feed their families. But the Taiwan example shows something more. If to this driving energy of self-preservation is added secure tenure and the inputs of modernizing agriculture—water, better seed, fertilizer, cooperative services, storage, wholesaling, and, above all, credit, credit, and then again credit—the small farm can become, as in Taiwan now or in Japan since the beginning of this century, a powerhouse of food production. The FAO figures give other examples. Comparable efforts to get cooperative assistance and needed supplies down to the small farmer have been made in Egypt, South Korea, and Yugoslavia. The same pattern emerges. Egypt's output of grain per acre is higher than that of Britain or America, Korea's the equivalent of America's and not far behind Britain's.

At the top of the league, of course, stand Japan with 4,585 pounds of grain per acre and Denmark with 3,860 pounds. But these figures are also benchmarks of potential growth. Why should India produce no more than 945 pounds an acre, Iran 950 pounds, Brazil 1,225, Thailand 1,670, with every sort of level and variety in between? Climate and soil are, no doubt, part of the answer. But Japan's rib of rock, sticking out of the sea, mountainous, steep-valleyed, earthquake ridden, typhoon-prone, and only a fifth of it fertile is surely not what one would necessarily define as prime agricultural land.

Consider the plight of the average small farmer in most developing nations. He probably does not own even ten percent of the land in Latin America. Forty percent of the landworkers in India have no land at all. Less than thirty percent of the farmers in Brazil belong to cooperatives—the figure for Mexico is five percent, for Honduras two percent. Yet in Honduras nearly 400,000 acres are lying idle. Not surprisingly, landless farmers are beginning to agitate for an acceleration of land reform.

In most of the Indian subcontinent, the village is the limit for the cooperative—with perhaps no more than 150 members and not federated upwards in any way. This is too small a mass to afford modernization of methods or to provide any security for vital credit. In any case, the "big man" of the village is in fact in charge even of the nominal cooperative and in so far as it is used as a channel for government help, it is not difficult to guess in whose pockets the help ends up. Complete the picture with almost total isolation—dirt roads washed away in the monsoons, narrow mountain paths above dizzy Andean gulfs of emptiness, jungle tracks hacked and rehacked through the dense green curtains of clinging creeper, logs hollowed out for boats edging past rapids and alligators—and one has perhaps the faintest image of what life for the average five-acre man may be like, even if he is lucky enough to own his land, even if his health holds, even if his patient packhorse of a wife survives, even if his children live to help work the plot and secure his old age.

And having imagined it, one can ask whether it is a life that any human being will long persist in, once traditional fatalism begins to fade and rumors reach the distant places that cousin Jose has got his child into a primary school in Manila, that young Srinivas is earning $250 a year as an errand boy in Calcutta, that, after trouble with the landlord's agent, the Ramon family have simply given up and gone to Medellin where a cousin has started a small eating house and hopes to be able to help them build a lean-to shack in return for help with marketing, serving, and washing up. So it goes—from one end of the universe of misery to the other. The smallest report of possible advantage dislodges the desperate people like stones before an avalanche. And, indeed, they possess so little, gain so little, hope so little that they have not much more stake in the land they till than the stones that lie on it. Yet these are men and women, it must be repeated, who can produce double the output per acre of sophisticated modernized farms. Collectively, they are probably the world's most neglected, most wasted, most exploited resource.

The reason often given by governments for overlooking this resource—at least until the recent eye-opening world-wide food crisis—was the sheer managerial difficulty of organizing thousands upon thousands of small peasants in anything like an efficient nation-wide effort to expand food supplies. One of the attractions, in the late Sixties, of pinning public hopes on the so-called Green Revolution was that by securing the new improved hybrid seeds, encouraging a large increase in the commercial sales of fertilizer, and subsidizing the purchase of tractors, output could be increased rapidly and massively, with large surpluses for sale in the cities, a sharp decline in food imports, and a general extension to farming of the high technology approach still dominant in industrial thinking. The sensational performance of the new seeds in India and Pakistan, producing a forty percent increase in food-grain, self-sufficiency in wheat, and even surpluses from one harvest to the next, encouraged the strategy and since only farmers with sufficient capital could afford all the new inputs—including mechanization—it could be argued that the managerial problem was, in a sense, solved at the same time since the commercial farm with up-to-date management would become the fundamental productive unit.

Similar decisions have been taken in many parts of Latin America. In Mexico, for instance, as the 1960s began, virtually the entire investment in agriculture went into the three percent of the farms that were organized on a commercial basis. The communal peasant plots— the *ejidos*—distributed in the earlier land reform, were largely bypassed. (Even so, they secured a better comparative return on the meager inputs they did contrive to secure.) Meanwhile, mechanization on the big farms very nearly halved the working year of day laborers and cut their income by nearly a sixth—if the word "income" does not suggest wholly exaggerated connotations for an annual money wage of $56. As a result, unrest is increasing in the Mexican countryside.

And these figures, of course, tell us what has gone wrong with the big farm calculus. Far from ameliorating the fundamental failure of food and jobs, it exacerbates both. By subsidizing capital and high technology which are scarce and should be expensive and *not* subsidized, it produces food that cumulatively will cost more. The quintupling of oil prices makes the overexpensiveness of mechanized agriculture even more sure. By sacking, reducing, discouraging, and generally undervaluing labor, it wastes the single resource that is totally abundant. It destroys jobs at once and increases food costs in the longer term—about as cockeyed a calculus as could be made for lands where massive unemployment, limitless poverty, and general hunger are the hallmarks of society. And it accelerates the inundation of the cities where the chances of feeding and employing the people will dwindle even more rapidly as a result.

However complex the managerial problem of building up a new social and economic framework for farming, there are enough working examples around the world to suggest that, in some societies, the managerial argument is not an explanation but an alibi. Whether it is Taiwan or Japan, Yugoslavia or Israel, South Korea or Tanzania, Egypt or Cuba or—a world in itself—the Chinese Peoples' Republic, there are certain common threads of policy, all of which reinforce the storm signals from developing societies and, at the same time, suggest that there are paths of hope ahead. A first thread is land reform. To suppose that feudal farm systems can feed the people over the next thirty years is to show an almost unnerving ignorance of history. If all the gains from the land remain with "the big man"—whether as in India he is a farmer with fifty acres (and cousins conveniently grouped in nominal ownership round-about) or in Latin America a latifundista with 40,000 acres, the result is the same. The indispensable productivity of the five-acre man is lost. Their "critical mass" in consuming power is lost. Their sons—and sometimes themselves—go off to swell the uncontrollable "cities of misery" on the fringes of every megalopolis. As in China's millennial cycles of breakdown, banditry will grow in the countryside, terrorism in the city. "The center will not hold." Under such conditions, it never has. There is even less chance in a world of open communications and entrenched revolutionary activity.

Land reform can take many shapes. Farmers may own the land but produce cash crops under central management as in the Sudan's Gezirah cotton scheme or Kenya's tea plantations. The land itself may be collectively owned by the cooperating farmers. This is the pattern in China, Cuba, and Tanzania. It is significant that all of them link earnings with performance—in Cuba after a premature plunge into an experiment with moral incentives only. For the latter, something closer to a Benedictine monastery than a peasant community is probably required. All encourage a certain amount of private pig and chicken keeping and vegetable growing on the side (in the Soviet Union, this "side" produces something like a quarter of the country's vegetables). The most productive systems are the Taiwan/Denmark type of combined private owning and cooperative organizing that gives the highest yields per acre in the world and, at the same time, in developing countries offers the highest chances of absorbing extra farm labor. In the mid-Sixties, even before the labor-removing onslaught of the Green Revolution, Taiwan, South Korea, and Egypt all employed more than seventy agricultural workers per one hundred acres. For India the figure was thirty-six, for Brazil seventeen, for Mexico only twelve.

But land reform is only the first step. The world is strewn with nominal schemes where land was distributed, but no support or technical support of any effective kind was thereafter provided. The new owners were left to scratch the earth, sell off to the old owners, and drift away to the city. Land reform can be effective only as part of a wider strategy to organize, both in resources and in space, the work of the community.

In most plans in the Fifties and Sixties, the spatial aspects of planning, particularly for the farm sector, went largely by default. Lip service was paid to the farm-to-market road. It remained unbuilt. And in fact the matter was perhaps not too important because no one had done very much about the market either. In India, for instance, the sense of actual physical space in planning tended to be so fragmentary that when "regulated agricultural markets" were set up to help to grade farm produce and stabilize prices—there were about 1,000 of them by the mid-Sixties—no one apparently had the idea of combining them with small-scale industrial estates which were being set up at the same time. Only about a quarter of them were built to overlap with the markets. In other words, no one had sat down to think out the needs of the farm and the village not as units for which "something must be done" but as essential elements in a local, regional, and national network of productive services, each level depending upon the efficiency of the rest. Traditional geological surveys were completed. So were some soil surveys. Large dam sites were chosen, but not the farm practices and crops that could follow future irrigation. One or two countries—Malaysia, for instance—attempted a thorough inventory of its natural assets, forests, minerals, farm lands, natural lines of access and communication. Similar surveys are being attempted in Colombia and Brazil. But few have followed up their findings with the sort of spatial planning practiced, say, in Rumania and now, very late in the developing day, in France.

This type of planning would have involved the choice of active regional market centers, endowing them with cooperative banks, light industries serving simple agricultural consumer needs, warehousing and storage, secondary schools, a small hospital with a mobile clinic, and all-weather roads leading to the number of villages it would be supposed to serve. In Israel, where very careful spatial organization has been devoted to the placing and servicing of agricultural communities, regional centers serve six villages. In Denmark, the figure is eleven. But in countries where the spatial integration of the nation has played little or no part in economic strategy, the deadening isolation of the villages can be measured by such figures as 185 villages to each urban center in India, 269 in Iran, a remarkable 355 in Indonesia. The lack of roads reflects the same phenomenon. In the mid-Sixties in Taiwan there were 2.6 miles of farm to market roads for each square mile. In Pakistan, the proportion was 0.7.

These intermediate centers could in their turn serve and be served by a nation-wide distribution of big cities designed, like France's *métropoles d'équilibre,* to provide all the employment, education, research, tertiary, and quaternary services and advanced industry required to keep some of the strain off the monster megalopolises inherited from the past's lopsided colonial commerce. Here again, the communist models are relevant. In Eastern Europe, the intention is evident to build up stronger intermediate centers to serve the farms and decentralized employment. Russia's agricultural setbacks are likely to increase its emphasis on new "agrovilles." Nearly every developing country can, without too much difficulty, pick out the cities of a million—or advancing toward it—which show every capacity for development and diversification. Throughout Latin America, medium-sized cities have been showing a rapid increase. But few of them seem then to receive that systematic backing in, say, the placing of a new university, the establishment of new industries, the development of easier communications—a new airport, perhaps?—which, taking France once again as an example, we find being mobilized to build up the middle-cities against the overcentralization of Paris. When one considers that present extrapolations would bring Bombay and Calcutta between them to somewhere near 100 million inhabitants in the early twenty-first century, it is not utopianism but sheer common sense to suggest that 100 cities of a million, scattered all over India's vast territory, acting as economic energizers of their regions, servicing an active, productive small farm population and concentrating on all the labor-intensive activities of city building, servicing small-scale production and the "bazaar economy," would be better instruments for development than Kipling's "packed and pestilential" city with Death looking down.

The megalopolises exist—possibly the worst of all legacies from the still unreformed system of dependent colonial trade. They cannot be wished away. On the contrary, the urban order is destined to absorb a higher and higher proportion of the world's peoples. The point is to diversify that order, to slow down by positive measures the rural exodus, to build up intermediate centers, to see to it that in no country does over half the population congregate in the capital city. The need must be faced, if necessary, to use disincentives to reduce and redirect the rural flow away from the biggest concentrations; such a policy has been adopted in China, and however repugnant to the pure theory of liberalism, some direction of movement, as in wartime, may be a lesser evil than the alternative price, which can be death by cholera, jobless and shelterless on a city pavement.

A number of positive measures required for civilizing the megalopolis will be examined in more detail on a later page. But two should be mentioned in the present context of land use and income distribution. The margin of resources available to the poor world's largest cities is so narrow that they cannot afford, over and above all their other pressures, the luxury of private land ownership creaming off the meager surplus and adding to inflationary costs. There have been attempts by taxation, variable rating or capital gains taxes, to secure the financial resources necessary for community-building. Unhappily, the lack of skills, trained surveyors, tax officials, administrators, coupled with the highly professional exploitation of tax loopholes and frequently the desire to attract business at all costs has, so far, not offered much hope that tax measures alone can deal with the problem. In fact, the models of Stockholm and Amsterdam, with their high degree of public ownership, offer more interesting and reliable precedents. One reason why Singapore has been able to achieve a remarkable record in housing and employing its citizens lies in the fact that it owns a large part of its own land and can control and make use of developmental increments. Hongkong, too, for all its special problems, has a firm hold on the city's basic stock of land. Where this is lacking, land values can add catastrophic costs to tottering budgets and land speculation hold desperately needed urban land out of the market in the expectation of further rises in price. In Rio de Janeiro, two-thirds of the registered sites are not yet built on and land prices, in certain areas, have been known to jump by over 2,000 percent in a couple of years.

Thus the structure of ownership in the big cities simply adds, inexorably, to the radical skew in the whole distribution of national income. Add to it public services—of education, health, and sanitation—which reach the wealthy, not the poor. Add forms of highly capitalized investment which can provide 40 jobs in the modern sector while wiping out the livelihood of 5,000 artisans. Add the lack of public transport and add again the numbers who cannot even afford a bus. Add all these and the big city, like the feudal countryside, can be seen as an organized and structured system for insuring that ten percent of the people will continue to engross some seventy-five to ninety percent of the wealth. Land reform, regional development, labor-intensive activities in town and country are not simply keys to higher productivity. They are the only keys to more equitable income-sharing, to a greater measure of fundamental justice in the nation's life. And if any social order can contemplate an existing maldistribution of the 80/20 order—eighty percent of the wealth for twenty percent of the people—if it can in addition estimate that in the next two decades the eighty percent of the people will have doubled in numbers with no necessary increase in the relative share of income, if, having done all the necessary arithmetic, it can still believe in the possibility of its own survival in affluence and stability, then one can only repeat the reaction of the great Duke of Wellington who, when greeted by a stranger as "Mr. Smith, I believe," retorted: "Sir, if you can believe that, you can believe anything."

Part Four: The Poor World's Settlements

20 CITIES UNDER PRESSURE

IN MOST WAYS, the experience of developed societies in producing reasonable housing within socially just and environmentally acceptable communities has not too much direct relevance to the infinitely more daunting problems facing the settlements of the developing world. As we have seen, their historical experience has been profoundly different, the scale of resources at their disposal infinitely less, the scale of the problems correspondingly more vast. The figures bear repeating. Between 1950 and 1970 while world population grew from 2.5 thousand million to 3.6 thousand million, the numbers in the developing countries grew four times as much as in the developed. Their rural populations increased by 500 million, while, in developed countries, they continued to fall (from 422 million to 391 million). Urban populations increased by about 250 million in developed societies to 693 million, making them, overall, more than sixty percent urbanized. But in the developing world, urban numbers increased by 366 million, from 256 million to 622 million—in other words, to an urban population only a little lower than that of developed societies where urbanization, industrialization, and full scale modernization have been in progress for over a century and have produced a cumulative gross national product of 2,972 thousand million dollars in 1972. The wealth available to developing countries in that year was 650 thousand million. Extrapolate these trends to the year 2000 and we can end up with over five thousand million people in developing countries, over half of them rural and 1.4 thousand million in the developed world with only a quarter of a million still on the land. Even allowing for the new wealth of the OPEC countries, nearly three-quarters of the world's

SLUM AND SQUATTER SETTLEMENT POPULATIONS
Selected Cities (millions)

	DATE	CITY POPULATION	SQUATTER & SLUM POPULATION	PERCENTAGE OF CITY POPULATION IN SQ. S. & S.	ANNUAL GROWTH RATE —SQUATTER & SLUM POPULATION (PERCENTAGE)
South Asia					
Manila	1972	4.4	1.54	35	5.5
Jakarta	1972	4.6	1.19	26	4.6
Seoul	1970	5.54	1.2	24	—
Karachi	1971	3.43	0.8	23	10
Bombay	1971	6.0	2.48	45	17.4
Calcutta	1971	8.0	5.33	67	9.1
Latin America					
Lima	1970	2.88	1.15	40	13.7
Caracas	1974	2.37	1.0	42	5.7
Rio de Janeiro	1970	4.86	1.46	30	5.5
Bogota	1969	2.29	1.38	60	
Africa					
Kinshasa	1969	1.29	0.775	60	—
Ibadan	1971	0.76	0.569	75	

WORLD HOUSING SURVEY, 1974.

resources will still be commanded by the developed minority.

Nor do the general figures display the most startling and potentially unmanageable aspect of the change—the dominance in urban growth of the developing world's biggest cities. These are accelerations that tend to induce a sense of helplessness. And it is not lessened by the fact that today's megacities in developed countries—New York with over seventeen million in its metropolitan area or Tokyo with rather more—give little good cheer when it comes to questions of finance, management, environment, or the plight of the poor. If the affluent do so badly, how will the underprivileged manage better?

But three points should be made from the outset. As in the urban

issue of location, there may be clues to wiser policy in the outsized
mistakes the rich countries have made. Next, not all these vast cities
are yet built. In fact, nearly half of them are not. There *is* elbow room.
There *is* scope for learning and improving. And even the factor which
from one angle of vision can seem the most discouraging is, from
another, a possible spur to hope. The flood of new people who will
come to live on this planet between today and the year 2000 is an inescapable fact. The mothers are born. However responsible the choices
of future parents, the world's six to seven thousand millions are inexorably on their way. But if societies can find some way of seeing in
these millions not a drag on the living standards of those who have already "made it" (one of the most unattractive features of so much of
the population policies advocated by the already rich) but as a prime
source for the energy, intelligence, dedication, and work needed to
build the new settlements, it will first be discovered that prodigies can
be performed. And then it will be found that self-reliant and responsible citizens are being shaped who themselves are able to see the injustice of bringing into the world children they cannot support themselves
and whom society at large can barely either feed or employ.

In any case, there has been enough experience of family planning
over the last two decades to show that hopelessly passive and apathetic
people—the "marginalized" men and women thrust to the outer fringe
of decisions and benefits—do not in any area of life grow in responsibility as a result of handouts. They cannot be "scolded into continence
and thrift." Responsible decisions imply self-respect and self-reliance
as well as information and material help. That is why Victorian duch-
esses did not do very much for the destitute workers on the London
dockyards and why much twentieth-century effort in the area of population control might have had more effect if it had not been too often
accompanied by a stark indifference to every other social lack and difficulty—of food, work or shelter—that contradict and cripple the life
of man. It is above all in societies where the mass of the people have
been more directly drawn into the building of their own societies that
birthrates begin to level off. Whether the means of citizen involvement
are mixtures of private, cooperative, and public action as in Taiwan or
South Korea or the forms of decentralized socialism evolved in main-
land China, whatever the technique, there is no doubt about the outcome. Treat the masses as problems and they remain so. Treat them as

cooperating and productive citizens and this is what they have a chance to become.

Before we look in any detail at the policies needed to secure active citizenship in the great cities, one disaster of the developed world needs to be underlined and at all costs avoided. This is the general failure to keep basic control of the land market. The image of Tawney's prewar Chinese peasant, up to his chin in misery so that the least ripple can drown him, is valid today for millions upon millions of citizens in the developing world. In the poorest countries—the vast majority in Asia and Africa—average per capita income is rarely above $150 a year and is nearer $50 for the poorest twenty percent. Up to 80 percent of that income is spent on food. Savings are infinitesimal, the amount that can be spent on rent or travel no larger. If any element in the economy—a food shortage, a spurt of inflation—adds to regular costs, the ripple goes over the citizens' heads.

A first principle in developing countries must therefore be to insure basic control over urban land prices. They can follow the path of the planned economies and vest the land in the municipality, the region, or the state. They can follow France in zoning areas for urban development where land can change hands only at the price customary for pre-urban use or prevaling in a given year before development was due to begin. They can study the effectiveness of Euopean land banks or the negotiated prices secured for the whole urban site by the Development Corporations of Britain's New Towns. But they have to be clear about one thing. If, at a time of breakneck urbanization, the public authorities have no controls over the land market or of the gains to be made there, the whole process will be skewed in favor of the skillful or lucky minority who use their private monopoly of ownership to engross fortunes created solely by the growth of the community. And with each new pressure—of natural increase, of fresh migration, of expanding demand for factory space or offices—fresh fortunes will be made while the ratio of people able to secure reasonable shelter in the growing cities will correspondingly decline. Moreover, the increment of value secured by private owners will be irretrievably lost to the municipal authorities responsible for providing the city's basic infrastructure—water, drains, roads, schools, the whole apparatus of "urbanity." They will simply fail to profit from the gains which they themselves create.

One or two other strands of policy in developed society have some relevance to developing cities and are, to some degree, interconnected. One is the increased emphasis on people owning their own homes. Another is the almost universal revulsion against massive, high-rise, public housing which breaks up smaller communities and the growing preference for urban renewal which can preserve all the ways people have found of living and working together.

Yet another is a growing unease over the private motorcar's costly conquest of the city's inner space and the *reductio ad absurdum* by which, as roads and parking lots rise to accommodate the increasing flow of automobiles, the city they come to visit gradually vanishes. Both the new emphasis on renewal and the new wariness felt for un-controlled urban motoring have one further aim—difficult, not fully formulated, sometimes impossible to achieve—and that is to secure a measure of social diversity in neighborhoods, the diversity of different incomes and types of employment. All these experiences in developed societies have some relevance for the city-builders of the developing world and can offer political leaders and planners in the developing cities a convincing number of examples of what not to do.

What *can* be done clearly varies from continent to continent. In parts of Latin America—for instance, in Chile, Uruguay, and Argentina—eighty percent of the people live in cities, birthrates are low, and no rural avalanche hangs over the urban areas. In other parts—Brazil, Mexico—wealth has reached a per capita level of between $500 and $800 * and although population still grows by well over 2.5 percent a year and rural migrations continue, there are resources to deal with the flood.

In most of Africa, south of the Sahara, intense poverty both in the towns and in the countryside sets limits to the scale of effective change, but in spite of a tendency for some over-heavy metropolitan areas to take shape—Lagos, for instance, with eighty percent of the country's industry—options are not, on the whole, already locked up in steel and concrete. The severest problems arise in Asia—indeed, India and China between them account for about one third of the world's entire increase in population. In countries like India, Pakistan, and Indonesia, population continues to grow in town and country alike. There is no prospect of a lessened migration to the cities before

* 1972 figures.

the next century. Yet vast metropolises, in the main a legacy from colonial times, already exist. Bombay, Calcutta, Karachi, Jakarta—not
only are they hastening to and beyond the 10 million level; they are
surrounded by peasant communities on tiptoe to keep their chins above
water. It is here that a transfer from desperate rural poverty to almost
equal urban poverty is the most likely outcome of migration. And the
sheer scale of the movement, millions a year in India alone, has a
floodlike, apocalyptic quality that seems to make even the discussion
of possible solutions a mockery.

But it need not be so. The analogy of the flood must be used with
caution. We are not dealing with mindless lemminglike rushes. The
migrants are usually the hardiest, most intelligent, and literate of the
villagers (this is part of the trouble for the villages) and evidence from
India suggests that the decision to move is carefully weighed. Movement into Calcutta, for instance, bears a fairly steady relationship to
the comparative level of rural and urban rewards and migration appears to have slackened off. It follows that if some of the options can
be improved, the choices they elicit have every chance of reflecting a
rational balancing of costs and benefits. The tragedy today is that in all
too many countries, whether in the village or in the metropolis, the
poorest seem to have little to weigh except costs and comparative
disadvantages.

What then are the possibilities? Perhaps the clearest way of finding
out is to follow a case study of what can go right and go wrong in a
particular developing country and then see if the lessons have a wider
application. Brazil, in 1964, had not yet reached an average per capita
level of $450 because the extreme poverty in the northeast held down
the national average. But in the south, in Guarnabara or Minas Gerais,
the possibility of rapid growth was a fact; resources, indigenous enterprise, a cadre of managers and skilled workers, and large and growing foreign interest had provided the potential launching pad. In the
area of housing, the position was much as one would expect—a lot of
rundown dwellings from earlier building (the national estimate was
that eight million houses, or half the total stock, were below acceptable standards) together with a rising tide of squatters building their
own settlements. In 1964, the government decided on resolute action.
The National Housing Bank was set up. Funds were drawn from the
growing industrial sector by an eight percent payroll tax (with a three-
year delay before interest began to be paid) and the Bank set in motion

a formidable boost to the whole construction sector. As a lender on building society lines, it built a million houses in its first decade and, by the steadiness of this stimulus, it undoubtedly helped to expand an industry which built another two million houses in the private sector. Sixty percent of the BNH homes were reserved for poor families, and since its founders saw housing not as an end in itself but as one component in a larger complex of humane and healthy communities, it accompanied its home-building program with a large-scale effort (the so-called PLANASA) to provide eighty-five percent of Brazil's city people with water and sewage disposal by the mid-Eighties.

A further vital effect of this stimulus was to make housing and its related services one of the lead sectors in an economy which soon began to grow steadily by ten percent a year. By the early 1970s, the construction industry alone was providing 500,000 extra jobs a year with a considerable upgrading of a primarily unskilled labor force. About twelve percent of each year's intake could apply for further training in government centers. Personal savings grew to nearly $500 million as confidence in public lending institutions, such as the Bank, increased. At the same time, its ability to siphon off a steady share of the gains from rising industrialization had a certain redistributive effect at a time when something like eighty percent of the gains were accruing to not much more than ten percent of the people.

But by the early Seventies, some of the difficulties already encountered in developed societies began to appear like reefs under the flowing tide of building. It had not proved possible to keep control of land costs. As a result the price of even the cheapest dwelling tended to be out of reach of the poorest workers. True, in a booming city like Sao Paulo, higher wages and growing skills allowed the bulk of the workers to find new accommodation. Squatting was reported to have fallen to as little as five percent of the inhabitants. Yet in Rio de Janeiro, the former capital, the investment of some $3 thousand million in housing over the Sixties still left half a million people in the *favelas* and migration continued to swell their numbers.

In the poorest Brazilian provinces, particularly the northeast, the pressures on the cities continue to be higher still. In Recife, for instance, the figure for squatting reported in the Sixties was as high as fifty percent of the population. And the pernicious effects of uncontrolled land speculation can be gauged by the extraordinary imbalance in a neighboring city, Goiana. There, by the time the households numbered 100,000, seven times as many plots were being held against the chance of speculative price rises. Even in a much more developed and sophisticated city such as Sao Paulo, some estimates put the land held off the market as high as fifty percent.

The cost of land entered into two other features of the National Housing Banks policy, both of which reflect similar discontents already experienced in developed cities. The expense of urban sites seemed to dictate high-rise apartment buildings. At the same time, the search for cheaper land led the authorities to build a sizable share of the subsidized housing toward the outskirts of the urban areas. Within a very short time, the familiar difficulties appeared. Many tenants, particularly tenants with families, came to dislike the tower blocks and, whether they liked them or not, were quite incapable of dealing with increasing problems of maintenance. In addition, rents were high even in relation to better urban wages. To this grievance was often added a doubling and tripling of the money that had to be spent each week on fares since the new housing and the traditional areas of employment could now be separated by half a city. The growing tendency to invest the capital made available for transport in roads for the private motorist and the failure to link the subway system with outlying worker settlements have further complicated the problem of mobility for the very poor.

It is an ironic comment on the continuity of urban problems that as the Seventies developed, tenants in Brazilian public housing began to express their disillusion by a steady falling behind in the payment of their rents. During exactly the same period, tenants in one of London's showpieces of rehousing—the large block at Thamesmead outside London, built with river vistas, courtyard pools and fountains, and a boating marina, but nonetheless an expensive wilderness of concrete—began to stage the same kind of protest, arrears in rents amounting to a kind of tacit rent strike. In developing as in developed societies, the superblock sometimes designed more for architectural prizes than for human use, situated far from available work and of its nature costly and difficult to maintain, provides accommodation which in physical terms—water, drainage, domestic facilities, shelter against the elements—is far superior to older buildings or the village "slums" so many migrants escaped from. Nevertheless, these blocks do not add up to a fully human environment. It is significant that in Thamesmead, experiments are going forward to turn the management of the blocks

VICIOUS CIRCLE

©1975 HERBLOCK.

over to tenants' committees as a first step away from the resentful passivity the whole form of the building tends to impose on them.

In Brazil, more radical changes are proposed. In the early Seventies two programs were launched. The first—the so-called Intra-urbs—was introduced in Recife, Salvador, and Sao Paulo, to see whether empty or rundown sites within the city boundaries could be developed by the government as complete communities—with housing, service, employment, and recreation all within reach—in fact, the "city-within-the-city" approach. The second program extended and developed the activities of the National Housing Bank. It set up a subsidiary, the Community Development Company (CODESCO) which uses the Bank's funds to provide families in the *favelas* with materials and components to build their own homes, or extend existing ones, according to their own design and with their own labor.

CODESCO's contribution is to be paid back over a couple of decades and, with PLANASA upgrading water supplies and sewerage, the new policy in fact resembles a rather different approach to the housing of the poorest—the so-called "sites and services" schemes whereby the government provides the communal facilities which each family has difficulty in securing by its own efforts and leaves the citizens themselves to do what they have amply proved their ability to do, build their own shelter. From the public authorities come layout, roads, drainage, water supplies, and such public services as schools, clinics, and assembly halls. In addition, they alone can provide two fundamental elements in any successful scheme for self-help—transport to insure access to work, security of tenure for the site on which the citizen is building his home. Here we can see a direct link with a similar discovery in developed lands—that to break up a functioning community, however poor, in the name of urban order and formal rehousing, may actually increase disorder and lessen the real acceptability and value of the shelter. So critical is this element of continuity to the success of the whole self-help enterprise that in 1972 the President of Colombia legalized all the land seizures that had taken place and thus formally recognized the right of squatter communities to remain and build further on their existing sites. When one recalls that in one Colombian city, Buenaventura, squatters accounted for eighty percent of the inhabitants, one can gauge the importance of the decision.

21 FORMAL AND INFORMAL CITIES

BRAZIL'S EXPERIENCE gives us a sort of spectrum of housing strategy in market economies—private construction for the well-to-do, public housing with varying degrees of subsidy for clerical staffs and workers with greater skills, various forms of sites and services with self-building for the poorest citizen. Take out the private construction element and the remaining sectors are relevant for planned economies. The proportion and mix of these elements will depend upon the overall wealth of the community and as income rises, one can expect a shift from less formal to more formal accommodation.

The speed or scale of such a move will vary enormously. Culture and climate make a very great difference in peoples' estimates of what they should or what they do want to spend on shelter. If we take the two largest areas of pressure where increased urbanization has to coexist with continued rural migration—China and India—the larger house is not necessarily the symbol of "upward mobility" in terms either of money or power. Modest urban standards of one- or two-room flats with shared kitchens and washing facilities are the norm in China's official building programs and vast numbers of blocks conforming to these standards have been built to take the place of the oldest and most rundown slums in the older cities. At the same time, self-help and rehabilitation of existing buildings by local tenants and builders are overseen by street committees. So is the allotment of space according to family need. In the countryside, the millennial tradition of peasants building their own homes continues. There are no available estimates of the balance between formal housing and construction by various methods of self-help. But it probably bears little relation to differences in income (or authority) in a society built upon a strongly egalitarian base.

In India, the position is rather different. As we have noted, an Indian entrepreneur who is doing very well for himself and his family is much more likely to buy his wife some more jewels than move out of his house, even if it is a crowded quarter of mid-Bombay. It does not occur to him to signal "success" by buying a mansion and leaving his familiar neighborhood. In Calcutta, the *bustees* thread their way all through the city. Neat villas in big gardens are a British legacy in Lutyens' New Delhi. Traditional Indian cities are more fluid and mixed. In South America the "casa" has symbolic value and rising income is likely to take the family out of the "informal sector." In short, the Brazilian spectrum provides only a very general framework within which to examine the "continuum" of policies for shelter in developing societies. Nonetheless, it does raise some critical and some hotly disputed issues.

It is clear from the whole scale of the National Housing Bank's achievement in Brazil that a strong, well-financed, expanding housing program can be a formidable advantage in creating direct employment and stimulating subsidiary industries—all the way from steel to plastics to curtain rods and cooking pots. A Mexican estimate is that a program of 100,000 low-cost houses (costing, on average, $4,000 for fifty square meters of space) would provide 126,000 man-years of employment, sixty percent in direct construction, the rest in indirect stimulus to other trades. In Singapore, where one of the most intensive construction programs in the world was mounted by the Housing and Development Board (set up in 1960) the result of the first decade was to build over 100,000 apartments (mainly in eight- to ten-story blocks) and to increase the proportion of employment in construction from three to fifteen percent. Beginning with a ten percent unemployment rate, the city-state purposefully chose housing as a "lead sector" and by the end of the Sixties, 30,000 workers were directly employed in building, 30,000 more in the industries producing raw materials for building, and uncounted others in the provision of domestic fittings and furniture. In the last five years, the 1960 levels of construction have been doubled again and the building of entirely new satellite towns planned for the periphery of the city. One can also point to the key role of organized construction in another small island city, Hongkong. Since the late Fifties, it has contrived to rehouse nearly two million Chinese citizens in the tall blocks which are virtually dictated by the island's size.

These large organized activities are also, as we have seen in Brazil's case, a considerable stimulant to the community's savings. Mexico, for instance, has followed the Brazilian National Housing Bank's example in setting up a fund, based on a five percent employers' payroll tax with extra governmental support, for the financing of low-cost housing. This Institute for the National Housing Fund for workers (INFONAVIT) aims at an annual output of 100,000 dwellings and its directors can hope to achieve the spin-off noticeable in Brazil—a greater readiness among poor citizens to save and lend, and the possibility, as a result, of widening the number of financial institutions—mortgage banks, building societies, savings and loan associations—which, by providing reliable channels for savings, have the effect of creating savings where there were none before. Once this type of beneficent spiral comes into being, it begins to be possible to think of increasing the share of construction in gross national product from the 3.5 percent common in many developing countries to the six to nine percent achieved in a few. Then, with a commitment of resources on this scale, the housing backlog can be lessened, a fair proportion of new citizens decently housed, and the construction sector firmly established as a durable stimulus to more rapid industrialization. The house is, after all, just as attractive a "consumer good" as the automobile. We have seen developed economies in which one worker in eight depends upon the motor industry. Is it not economically as sound to put housing in the same central position? And socially may it not be much more desirable?

A further advantage in developing the formal construction sector is the greater ability it confers on governments to plan not simply for housing but, as with Singapore's New Towns or the Intra-urbs "cities-within-cities," for whole communities, with all their services, factories, commercial premises, schools, clinics, and housing planned together and creating balanced urban patterns easy of access, pleasant to the eye, and with a new care for the environment. An increasingly urban industrializing society desperately needs in all its activities the scale of managerial skills, trained workers, specialized organizations—for finance and construction—and governmental institutions such as New Town Corporations—that the building of such communities can help to bring forth. The greater the delay in giving housing and construction their proper weight in the total economy, the more unbalanced the whole process of its transformation and modernization is likely to be.

Yet though this may be the aim, it is simply not yet a possibility in large parts of the developing world. The simple reason is poverty, poverty so deep that there is no way in which half to three-quarters of many countries' families can pay anything like an economic rent for even the cheapest "formal" housing. If eighty percent of income has to be devoted to food, fifteen percent is the absolute maximum that can be paid for shelter. Where average annual incomes are below $100, $15 a year in rent is about the limit. There is no way in which a government housing program can produce a dwelling unit cheap enough for so meager a sum to cover interest, let alone amortization and maintenance. Nor are governments in the poorest countries in any financial state to make up the balance with rent subsidies. Even if they tried, the poor would simply take the subsidy and rent the dwelling to a wealthier tenant. It is the all-but-universal experience of the poorer developing countries that public building is taken over by the better-off. The poorest live on as they lived before—in the *favelas,* the *callampas,* the *barriadas,* the *bustees,* and the *bidonvilles.* It seems that only when industrialization and modernization have reached a certain level, the $500 to $800 average annual income of a Brazil or Mexico,* that formal public housing can play a really important part and even then direct help for self-improvement in the shanty towns has still proved necessary. As we have seen, the $3 thousand million spent on new houses in Rio still leaves half a million people in squatter settlements that continue to expand.

Does this mean a hopeless verdict, a sentence of unredeemable misery imposed on the migrant millions for the crime of being too numerous, too destitute, too determined to leave their villages, too eager to try for better things in the city? Surely not—and it is precisely their determination that holds the beginning of an answer.

Over the last decade, the sense of hopelessness, the habit, de-

* 1972 figures.

nounced by William Penn, of "blaming the unhappy rather than covering and relieving them," has begun to give ground to a more positive approach. Miserable and cluttered as the serried shacks may look from the outside, minimal as are the sanitary arrangements and communal facilities, it is increasingly recognized that within many of the shanty towns live active, hard-working, hopeful citizens who, while perfectly aware of their present squalor, are convinced that the city offers, possibly for themselves and certainly for their children, the only chance of a better life.

There is immense resourcefulness in finding employment in the city's so-called "informal sector." The squatters are often the men who provide low-cost transport on tricycles and jitneys in Jakarta. They are the office cleaners and messengers, the street sweepers, bootpolishers, and garbage sorters; there are 40,000 ragpickers in Calcutta. They set up streetside food stalls—even in a city as "formal" as Singapore you can go from booth to booth around the parking lots and markets, choosing a different course from each cook with his own specialty. They mend and repair. They run tiny laundries and carpentry shops. And if economists of the more rigorous sort see in all this proliferation of services little net benefit to the economy—which is, of course, a stupid miscalculation since the tiny services are needed and paid for—we can add the thousands upon thousands of minibusinesses. Tailors, cabinet makers, manufacturers of household goods (often refashioned from cast-off materials) grow up in the shanty towns, find unused corners of warehouses or rooms in rundown property in the city, and add a usually uncalculated flow of goods to the output of the city and goods which the poor can afford to buy.

It is estimated that at least 140,000 of these little businesses are hard at work in Calcutta and they use all the informal networks of family and clan and village relationships to advertise their wares, inquire for help, mobilize mini-savings and send back to the countryside the news of business conditions—the kind of news which all over the world helps to make up the mind of cousin Shankar or brother Jose or the Eseagu family to pull up their country roots and make for the city. If it were not for this absorptive mass of small-scale economic activity, with minute rewards, survival-level wages, and occasional windfalls of a business expanding or child getting into technical school or a relative breaking through to real wealth, the shanty towns would hardly be expanding. Their people would, quite simply, have starved.

What the settlements reveal is thus not simply misery but an incredible tenacity in the face of odds more daunting than any Western society, even at the peak of a recession, can any longer recall. A hundred years ago there was something of this double urban life between the prospering city and the slums. We can read in Henry Mayhew's accounts of nineteenth-century London of the incredible variety of hawkers and whelk-sellers and rag and bone men that made up the city's miserable and colorful underworld. Charles Dickens' novel *Our Mutual Friend* has as an underlying theme and symbol a fortune derived from collecting a vast mound of garbage, a mountain, a vision of dirty dust.

But Western cities knew almost nothing of swamping inmigration utterly outstripping the formal industrial sector's absorptive capacity. What was on the fringe of London's problems is at the heart of Calcutta or Lagos or Lima. The task is to recognize the fact of a large "informal" sector and see whether the productive efforts locked up in it can be used to better effect. Here, as the World Bank has pointed out, one of the chief needs is an extension of credit facilities to the tiny entrepreneurs whom governments neglect in favor of large modern enterprise and thus stifle one of the sources of indigenous entrepreneurial capacity. The United States has its programs and credit arrangements for small businessmen. The developing countries need comparable help for the mini-entrepreneur. It is not a question of "cataclysmic" help that will swamp him into incapacity. He needs small loans, judiciously and selectively disbursed. He needs small contracts which will enable him, on the early Japanese model, to become a subcontractor for a larger business. He needs light industrial parks which put him alongside larger plans and, as Sir Arthur Lewis was one of the first to point out in his prescient Report on Industrialization in Ghana (then the Gold Coast) published in the 1950s, he needs advice and assistance in banking, bookkeeping, marketing techniques, and inventories which enable the small man, often illiterate, to work his way into a bigger league.

Since he rarely uses any but indigenous materials, works endless hours with entirely labor-intensive methods, and often provides just those low-cost goods which are all that seventy percent of local purchasers can afford, governments will not find they lose much needed growth by a new emphasis on the smallest sector. On the contrary, it is again and again the large imported technology, reinforced by every concession of tariff-free imports (and tax-free exports of profits), that settles down, year after year, to produce a local loss. The plastic shoe factory requiring an investment of $100,000, employing forty workers, and knocking out 5,000 local shoemakers and their supplies is a classic example of an ill-directed and directly impoverishing industrial strategy.

It is within this context that we should look at the problem of housing. The migrants follow the rural traditions of centuries and build their own homes. They lack the graceful materials of the countryside—local stone, local soil rammed into adobe or burned into brick and tile, palm fronds for thatch, wood from neighboring forest for doors and lattices. There is an inevitable disorientation in layout and order. All around the world, villages tend to have an almost instinctive ability to blend their building into surrounding contours, align their spires with more distant perspectives, cluster their cottages without self-advertisement at the edge of streams or below a mountain slope.

This instinctive sense of proportion is lost in the crowds and pressure and squalor of the city fringe. The materials are the cast-offs of incipient industrialism. The alignments are more those of barracks than the line of a stream or of a neighboring grove. But the shelter is built and, given even the first touch of urban prosperity, the shacks begin to improve—from tin cans and tarpaper to brick, from burlap roofs to tile or corrugated iron. Extra rooms are added for a lodger or an arriving cousin. Trees are planted. There are vegetables and fowl and pigs. Latrines get built and even if water has still to be secured from the itinerant water cart (at a cost twenty-five times higher than the water rate paid by rich families, often for watering their lawns) ingenious schemes are invented for tapping, legally or illegally, the nearest available source of electricity. And all the whole, small shops and small businesses spring up and, provided no catastrophic interruption occurs—a flood sweeping a whole hill settlement to the valley or, more ominously, the bulldozers of public authority driving out the squatters and crushing their vulnerable shacks—it is clear that before too long, a genuine community begins to emerge with its own internal systems of consultation and self-government, its own—often very tough—internal system of keeping order, and an increasing ability to make collective demands for minimal help—for a primary school, a clinic, for drains, for water.

One should not romanticize the picture. The *favelas* remain among the worst environments, for health and decency, endured by man. Some of them are in addition deadened by failure and the sense of helplessness—the "hope deferred" that "maketh the heart sick." But the basic fact remains. Any chance of housing, educating, and improving the lot of at least half the world's migrant populations depends upon helping them to help themselves, to build their own homes, evolve their own communities, and do all this at a cost which they can carry, given reasonable support.

Nor should this support be thought of as "doles" or "handouts" or "throwing good money after bad" or any of the other derogatory phrases invented by the well-to-do to express their sense either of their own superiority or of the hopelessness of helping people who, in being poor, are, by that fact alone, feckless and unworthy. There are very solid economic gains to be made from larger interest and investment in the informal sector. A man who builds his own house, improves it, extends it, lets a room, is adding to the country's capital stock and at minimum cost since he certainly uses local materials—imported steel and concrete are not for him—persuades unpaid friends and neighbors to help him or may, at most, hire at small cost a technician for minimal wiring and plumbing. We should remember, too, that the largest concentrations of squatter settlements are in hot, tropical climates where, for most of the year, open space, enclosed by a wall, is just as usable as a built room and much less costly. Nor is there much difference in density between single-story or multiple dwellings since high blocks have to stand farther apart. If the builder sets up a tailor's shop or a little eating house in the front room, the market economy is helped to grow. In some of the Philippines' squatter settlements, one can see the visible signs of this growth in street after street. "Master Plumber" is hung over one door, "dentist" over another, "help wanted" over a third. The settlement is growing its own variety, its own exchange of services. The relative modesty and speed of the house's original construction ties up savings for only a very short time. Income in the shape of the family's own shelter, a sublet, and perhaps a workshop begins quickly. As a result, the cumulative effect of self-help housing, if it were formally computed, could give a formidable rate of income derived from each unit of investment.

What sort of assistance is most likely to be effective to the self-help sector? Before discussing this point, two difficulties need clarification. The first is the question whether any formal help from outside interests and governmental institutions may not disrupt the often fragile links of cooperation that have been built up and turn what was a promising and increasingly self-confident community into a disorganized group of competing interests. This happened, for instance, in Madras when a large government scheme of public housing knocked out the small builders who traditionally built most of the cheap housing. There can be, it is argued, paternalism in giving, coupled with a bureaucratic rigidity which, like Mary Kingsley's elephant trying to hatch the eggs in a deserted duck's nest, destroys what it sets out to assist—even when it does so with great goodwill, a quality that is not invariably present. May it not therefore be better to allow the "young communities"—the *pueblos jovenes,* as they have come to be called—the chance to mature not only without the savage (and useless) attempts to do away with them, which was a feature of government policy all over the developing world in the 1960s, but also without the kinds of intervention which might come to resemble the disastrous mistakes of "urban renewal" in the developed world, the kind of renewal which leaves not a trace of the original community and destroys all the growing points of life, variety, self-confidence, and creative work? May not "benign neglect" be better than "cataclysmic" help, the vast concrete footsteps of Dickens' giant, overlaying and burying the frailer but richer human ecosystems that had flourished before?

Virtually every urban lesson of the developed world underlines the vital necessity of associating poorer citizens with the choices that form their destiny, the need to consult, involve, and encourage them, to end the sort of unconscious patronage which, as in Thamesmead's plans, even laid down stereotypes of resident behavior: "At this point a well-placed bench will permit the residents to secure an excellent view of the river. Here, the residents' children will pause in their stroll to admire the sunset." The whole project was described as a "fantasy to which the residents will come to subscribe." Their response has been, as we have noted, a rent strike. There are limits to guessing what people will really prefer when they are never consulted. There is even greater risk if the guess is incorporated into half a billion dollars' worth of steel and concrete. One of the added advantages of the "informal settlement" is that it can so easily be pulled down and readjusted as tenants and occupiers change their aims, their incomes, and their dreams.

Yet "benign neglect" is not a real option. The fundamental reason is simple. There are a whole range of essential needs which small, impoverished communities on the margins of subsistence cannot begin to meet. If any single physical service needs priority in the world's shanty towns, it is safe drinking water—the only competitor is security of tenure. The weariness, the pain, the loss of energy and hope to which perpetual dysentery condemns a human being are virtually forgotten now in the well-drained developed world. Contaminated water is a killer and a waster that only decisive action by the public authorities can bring to an end. To propose a trade-off between autonomy and dystentery is to talk nonsense. The preventible diseases must go, and there is surely enough wit left among men to see that proper water pipes do not undermine local democracy.

Access to the wider city is another physical service which the local community cannot provide alone. Since too many shanty towns are on cheap or unoccupied land on the fringes of the metropolis, walking to work becomes impossible, even for the hardy souls who are ready for two hours of it morning and night. Usable roads, bus services, links with subways—all these can be partially provided by local work and subscription. But the larger system must be ready to help to incorporate the smaller units.

The same principle applies to fundamental social needs. A local community can accomplish a great deal by way of self-help in the areas of schooling and medicine. Schoolhouses can be built by the community, the premises for a small clinic made available, literate citizens recruited for adult literary classes. But beyond a certain level of proficiency, the local system must be linked to wider educational and health services.

In any case, the divisions are perhaps described in too stark and heroic a fashion. There are all kinds of ways in which, with increases in development, with a general modernization of the economy, with a wider productive base, a steady, uncataclysmic change can take place in the squatter settlements which, without destroying their autonomy and integrity, gives them more participation in the city's general advantages and makes them urban quarters out of which people do not necessarily want to move as their wealth or education increases. Once again, we discover a principle already established in developed cities. The real slums are the areas from which everyone wants to escape. Provided governments are prepared to devote a fair share of the gains from the overall growth in productivity to the needs of the mass of the people—and not, as is too often the case, to the top twenty percent— the progress of a squatter settlement from a few shacks to an organized layout to water and drainage to schools and clinics to a wider variety of incomes and skills, to a true "urban village" is not inconceivably difficult. Almost insensibly, forms of self-help change. The man who begins by building his own house and his neighbor's sets up a small building business. If the economy at large is beginning to produce standardized fittings—brick, tile, piping, appliances—he and a dozen others will extend their work. Other community dwellers, now busily engaged in trading, will go to a builder for a new house or an extension. Diversification increases without the whole community falling apart.

What is critical is that governments should accept the need for basic security of tenure, check with all possible firmness the disruptions of land speculation, give the provision of services—which we will discuss in the next chapter—a more equitable distribution throughout the city, and, above all, treat the nascent communities as responsible cobuilders in the life of the state. And these directions of policy tend, not surprisingly, to conform quite closely to the patterns we first saw emerge in developed cities—the desire for secure tenure, the preference for renewal and reconstruction, not cataclysmic change, the desire to preserve the continuity of living communities, the mixture of incomes and occupations that make for variety and life. As the Seventies advance, we can perhaps observe a general trend toward these objectives. Certainly the change of mood and progress since the early Sixties is remarkable. What is still too often lacking is the energy and commitment needed to turn a trend, however hopeful, into settled policy and established fact.

22 SERVICES AND SELF-HELP

THE VALUE of a house in human terms—its safety, its underpinning of family continuity, its usefulness in the physical business of day-to-day living—is largely determined by the community of which it is a part, by the physical qualities of that community, roads, water, drains, power; by its psychic gifts—education and culture and beauty—with bodily health as the link between material and spiritual gifts. For the vast majority of the human race, shelter as such can hardly be distinguished from these wider services. If they are in good order, the simplest shack is a home. Without them, an elegant villa can be an unsanitary trap.

Sixty percent of the world's peoples still live in the countryside. At the century's end, half of them will still be villagers. Housing is not too much of a problem since the vast majority are in hot climates and misplaced modernity has not yet taught them how not to angle their doorways to the breeze, how not to shutter out the midday glare, how not to keep low-heat-absorbing well ventilated thatch and palm for the roof. The cottages, too, are malleable, easy to build, easy to extend, easy to knock down and often—one thinks of the towns of Northern Nigeria—of breathtaking beauty in simplicity of form and brilliance of decoration. The trouble in the villages is not with shelter. It is with the services which are not simply inadequate: some of them are all too often lethal.

Whether or not a government has decided on an active agricultural policy, villages which contain half the citizenry cannot be entirely left to "benign neglect." Their needs are simpler, smaller versions of the larger urban ones. They require access and mobility. They need water, drains, and energy. And, along with better health, they need the goods of the mind, not only the goods they have provided for themselves for the last five thousands years—in worship and song and dance—but also the newer goods, how to read the label on a seed packet or check the moneylenders' rate of interest.

With very little outside assistance—say, from survey teams and some general materials—villagers themselves can build an all-weather road to the nearest regional center. In Mexico, for instance, nearly half a million peasants have worked on a rural road project, converting paths and cattle trails into gravel roads. Provided their activities are firmly locked into a regional cooperative structure, they can finance their own commercial trucks—or bullock carts. Villagers can increasingly buy their own bicycles. A regular bus service will be well used but may need some subsidy, depending on the number of village centers to be served. Small multiple-use jitney or minibus services run by the villages with part-time drivers, can be a useful supplement—as they are in parts of still rural England. But they will emerge only with rising local incomes.

The most urgent village service is clean water. Nature has not stopped its billennial task of circulating, purifying, and renewing the earth's water supplies. But the risk that the purification process is not working with sufficient strength in the neighborhood of the village midden or past a long string of up-river farmyards is proven by the prevalence throughout history of endemic intestinal sickness. Cholera, typhoid, parasitic infestations are the normal accompaniment of the idyllic village to which some of the extreme modern primitivists recommend our return. In most parts of the developing world, standing water—flooded rice paddies, fish ponds, irrigation channels—carry the snail which completes its life cycle through the human bladder, leaving behind a relatively incurable state of infection and debilitation known as bilharzia or schistosomiasis. As many as 200 million people are its victims. Turbulent water, on the other hand, is the breeding ground in Africa of the small black fly which, laying its larvae under human skin exposed to water, produces a parasite which eats out the optic nerve and has produced villages with almost universal degrees of "river blindness." The estimate of the people affected is 20 million. Swampy lands are the watery homes of malaria, some of whose species are becoming resistant to DDT while DDT itself, as a long-lasting chlorinated-hydrocarbon, enters the food chain of various animal species with unpredictable and often dangerous results—hence the ban in a number of developed countries and the agonizing dilemma for developing governments, to balance malaria against more sophisticated dangers which cumulatively may be as grave.

Policies for water are thus at the very core of any effective strategy for essential village services. They will become steadily more important since the doubling of the world's population will call with steadily increasing urgency for the extension of irrigated land and the introduction of double and triple cropping. More farmers will be engaged in irrigated farming and hence exposed to the risk of schistosomiasis. Growing populations along each river system—whether in villages or towns—will load the watercourses with more and more human and animal excrement and increase the difficulty of securing uncontaminated water for drinking. Subsidiary risks are the overpumping of underground water with the ground subsiding (as it is in Bangkok) and wells running dry. And any lessening of local supplies will add incalculable hours to the time spent—usually by the village women—to collect water from more distant springs, streams, or wells.

And this is possibly a convenient point to underline the fact that in many parts of the developing world, the women do the major part of agricultural work. The men are responsible for those parts which are assisted by extra power—bullock, horse, or tractor. These tend to be cash crops. Women grow the food and do the weeding. The U.N. Economic Commission for Africa suggests that their share is usually sixty to eighty percent of the total village effort, with water carrying and the preparation of domestic food added. Cumulatively calculated, water carriage can add a fortnight a year to other work. It is hardly necessary to add that the women also bear and nurse the children. Unhappily, carrying heavy water pots on the head is a prime cause of pelvic distortion and hence of death in childbirth. The danger to babies of commercial baby foods using unsterilized water instead of their mother's milk is not in doubt. But those who—rightly—advocate breast-feeding should also pay equal attention to the fact that in most developing peasant societies, women are the last to be fed and a malnourished mother is not always able to survive the task of feeding another human as well. It is these brutal realities that can induce a certain impatience with some advocates of the simple and supposedly Arcadian life. One tract recently published by two young men from the

United States capped their argument for rustic utopias with the throw-away line that such societies have no population problem because heavy work insures that women tend to abort their children.

This is an extreme case. But those who honestly care for the wel-fare of country people will spend their time more profitably in adapt-ing all that modern science and technology can offer to the small-scale sanitary needs of peasant communities. Clean water, available energy mean quite simply that fewer babies and mothers will die. And, as more and more population experts are beginning to realize, nothing so quickly draws men and women to think responsibly about the size of their families than the realization that most of those born are not going to die. Country fatalism has one of its toughest roots in the hopeless resignation of overburdened mothers with dying children. Village ser-vices are not luxuries to be added once "real" development is under way. They are development itself, development of the innate powers, energies, and hopes of the human beings on whom all sustained prog-ress depends. And if people still insist on a cost/benefit tag, the Vene-zuelan Government has estimated that the provision of clean rural water can recoup its costs five to seven times over by the number of working days—and working bodies—it continues to save.

In fact, there is no contradiction between services and develop-ment. Water and energy are the key to both and some techniques can give a partial answer to both problems. The task is to get drinking water with the minimum permissible impurities and also to prevent the seepage into watercourses of excrement and infected wastes. If we begin with preventive action—and this is without exception the most rational principle to adopt in all matters of health and environ-ment—the first question is how to manage the wastes and effluents. We have already seen how big cities—in the Netherlands, in the U.S.S.R.—have long been using organic city wastes to produce com-post for the farms. This policy, enormously scaled down, can be just as effective at the level of the village. Another alternative, again based on developed country experience, is the production of gas from organic material. Any organic waste—refuse from food, human and animal excrement—produces methane gas, in the absence of oxygen. What is left when the gas is drawn off is usable fertilizer. The methane can be set to work to run a small generator for electricity or it can run garden tractors or provide fuel for cooking or run pumps for tube wells or do a bit of everything. The machine that does this separation of methane from organic wastes is the digestor.* The wastes from five to ten pigs can supply it with enough fuel to provide a farm family with both cooking gas and fertilizer. It costs only about $60. For $600, using the manure from five head of cattle, a village can secure a 1,000-gallon "gobar" gas plant and clearly, as the scale of the community rises, such plants, correspondingly enlarged, can absorb an even higher level of waste and excrement. Thus they provide needed energy, increase the manure supply, keep the waters clean, and virtually introduce a closed self-supplying exchange of energy and water resources.

Part of the system is, of course, as old as Neolithic man. Excrement to the fields is an immemorial principle. The frugal Chinese followed a peculiarly productive cycle in which the village pond's algae, enriched by night soil, could feed ducks and fish and the pond sludge be used to fertilize fields and garden plots. There was a catch in the system—the high rate of human infestation with worms and intestinal infections. But these can all be eliminated by using the sun's rays to kill off the pathogens. Painting the digestor black or using solar panels in hot climates absorbs enough radiation to raise the digestor's temperature sufficiently to kill off the parasites and improve the gas yield. Or the sludge can be dried out on land before being dug into the soil.

When we turn to water, simple solar water heaters are already in widespread use in Australia, Japan, Niger, Israel, and Florida and already being mass produced in Australia and Japan. A solar-powered pump in Chinguetti in Mauritania can provide the 3,000 inhabitants with a daily twenty liters of water which previously had to be obtained by hand power at the well. The pump operates for five to seven hours a day, using solar panels mounted on the schoolhouse roof. These collect sufficient power to drive the pump's mechanism. The process also cools the schoolhouse by as much as five degrees centigrade. The building of the school, the roof, and the storage tank (into which the water is pumped) was carried out by local labor using local materials.

---

* A digestor—a tank into which animal and human excrement and organic wastes can be flushed once a day. Anaerobic bacteria (that is, bacteria that work in the absence of oxygen) break down these organic wastes into methane—with some ammonia, carbon dioxide, and hydrogen—and a sludge that can be used as fertilizer. The gas generated is collected and stored for use when needed.

The new building blends in with the traditional village. The pump's mechanism is based on very simple principles and should have a long life free of maintenance troubles.

There are many other examples. For instance, a solar still in the Bakharden State Farm in the Karakum desert in the Soviet Union has for the past six years pumped saline water out of the ground and distilled it. This device produces three metric tons of drinking water every twenty-four hours. At the other end of the scale, there is a "portable well" which weighs only three kilograms and which can hold two liters of water and convert saline water into drinking water.

Small-scale energy technologies are also increasingly available. Village electricity units can be fired by methane or by fuel-crops (which are faster growing than wood). Alcohol, obtained through the fermentation of organic material, can be used as a fuel for machinery. The application of the windmill can also be invaluable in cases where intermittent supplies of energy do not matter. (For example, the pumping of water or the grinding of grain can be done by a windmill, the water being stored in a small reservoir for use when needed and the grain ground when the wind is blowing.) Solar cells may come into wider use later, while their present use in telecommunication can be expanded. In the immediate future they are unlikely to be of as much use as utilizing the sun's direct heat to power such rural installations as water distillation units, pumps, and produce driers. All these devices, incidentally, make possible a vital side effect—a check to steady deforestation as villages desperately search for fuel.

The advantage of putting this major emphasis on the reuse of household garbage and excrement is that with old wastes turned into new resources, the risk of infested water should be considerably lessened. The process can be strengthened if it is possible to provide simple filtration processes to reinforce safeguards at village fountains or wells. A caveat should be made that the water technologies used must not require highly skilled maintenance. Over the last ten to fifteen years, a fair number of newly installed village water systems have broken down and the villagers have slipped back to traditional sources, supplies, and dysentery. The equivalent of the simple "digestor" for water cleansing has not yet been invented. Yet probably nothing could make an equal contribution to both energy at work and bodily well being in poor communities.

Water is, indeed, the central problem of health in the villages. The chief debilitating diseases—dysentery, typhoid—are waterborne. They are the main cause of infant mortality, the chief cause, with malnutrition, of low adult resistance to disease and early death. These are not diseases which can be cured by the sort of medical services the developed world is accustomed to—doctors, big hospitals, multiplying hospital beds (usually in the cities). They belong rather to the development process itself and their prevention can illustrate once again a principle—that the most successful development is based on involving the whole community and will not really work until the people themselves become agents of their own destiny. We can take an example of this close intertwining of self-help, development, and better health from China. Of all the waterborne diseases, schistosomiasis is the most obdurate in its resistance to inexpensive countermeasures. But massive public campaigns can help. Chinese villagers are organized into teams to drain and scour lakes and irrigation systems. The snail's breeding grounds—at the point where soil and water meet—are sealed off with clay and the ditches relined. Farmers are encouraged to wear protective clothing; a simple rubber boot would be an excellent prophylaxis. In spite of the number of infected people, in spite of the rapid spread of irrigation, Chinese are convinced that after villagers have spent long hours draining and relining irrigation ditches themselves, while being forcefully told the reason for their activity, they are much more likely to understand the nature of the trouble and persevere in the right precautions. Learning by doing, the involvement of people in helping themselves, simple but fundamental instruction in self-care, the whole system decentralized enough to reach the majority of the people and arouse their concern in preventing disease—these are among the underlying principles in China's rural health service which few people fail to pick out as a model of what can be done for nationwide preventive medicine.

The general Chinese experiment in public health deserves a closer look. The evolution of the service had two stages. After 1949, all medical services were expanded. Yet in 1968 it was discovered that this expansion still served only fifteen percent of the population. As in every other developing country, the medical services tended to be concentrated in the cities, or, as one WHO official grimly described the developing world's bias: "Seventy-five percent of the diseases are in the countryside and seventy-five percent of the doctors are in the towns." Mao Tse-Tung's reported response was no less trenchant. The Ministry of Health, he said, had better be renamed the Ministry of Health for City Gentlemen. He proposed a halving of the six to eight years spent in preliminary medical studies, a widening of recruitment, concentration of research on preventing common diseases, and the dispatch to the countryside of a large number of the doctors. To these changes have been added a vast expansion of paramedical assistants who, while continuing their work part time as farmers (health aides and barefoot doctors) or as trained in simple record keeping—the patient's temperature or blood pressure, in vaccination, injection, acupuncture, and treatment for simple ailments. They also advise on sanitation and on family planning.

More complicated diseases go up the scale—to the clinic in the rural commune or city district and from there to a regional hospital. The chief strength of the service, the Chinese claim and no visitor disputes, is preventive work at the grass roots (and street cobbles) of China's vast population—the curing and cleaning up and care which people exercise for themselves. Prevention is the vital step, involving everyone. A clean environment, kept in that condition by clean and cooperative people, is worth a thousand hospital beds. The beds are needed, too, but they are the marks of partial failure. It was, it seems, a millennial tradition in China to pay your doctor when you were well and cease to do so if you felt ill. A popular and modern application of this older wisdom seems to offer the best clue to rural health.

The principle of local involvement may well be determinant not only of local health services but of local education as well. Most developing countries face one preliminary but overwhelming problem in thie field. By the tradition of at least a century, education has been seen by young people as the means of escape from the confinements of village life. It still is. A study in the Ivory Coast* at the beginning of the Seventies showed that for every one illiterate migrant to the city, there would be nearly eight with a primary-school certificate. And, as we shall see, the tragic counter-reality to this dream of emancipation in the cities is a rate of unemployment for young literates which is two

* Louis Roussel, "Measuring Rural-Urban Drift in Developing Countries," *International Labor Review*, Vol. 101, No. 3, March 1971.

to four times higher than the average level of worklessness. Must we then conclude that the kindest policy to be pursued in the villages is to shut down the primary schools—often built with great enthusiasm by the parents themselves—cut off the bus services, reroute itinerant salesmen, and ban transistors in the hope that ignorance and passivity will keep young people in their villages? The policy is totally self-defeating. No developing country can hope to survive the risk of famine in the years ahead unless it can count on a cadre of active, eager, well-trained young farmers. Part of the dilemma faced in such wealthy oil states as Venezuela today is that the legacy from past dictators—a Gomez or a Jimenez—is a peasantry kept illiterate to prevent unrest, a dangerous lack of skills, literacy, earning capacity, and enthusiasm in the villages and few intermediate centers of services, employment, education—and entertainment—to stem the surging flow to Caracas. The decision to build up a counterpole of growth at Ciudad Guyana, valuable in itself, was taken before the need to revivify the countryside was fully grasped. Today, in spite of all the gains of buregeoning oil revenues, it is, above all, skills and farming tradition and pride and self-respect that have to be created. All over Latin America, the legacy—and the presence—of military dictators with little care for anything but personal and family enrichment, lies like a coffin lid ready to fall on a debilitated feudal countryside. The hope of such newer types of military officers as those who introduced Peru's land reforms and now appear to be reconsidering the skew of wealth away from the mass of the people in Brazil is that they will begin to give the basic needs of food, health, education, energy, and mass employment priority over imported high technology, motor assembly plants, and the needs of rich elites in exploding cities. In any case, if the countryside continues to be a place of low earnings, low expectations, and low concern, the people will inevitably decamp. The hope of retaining them is about on a par with the expectations of King Canute's courtiers.

It is true that China has pursued the policy of sending millions of young people to the provinces. Some estimates speak of ten million in the last decade. Certainly, as we have seen, a check to urban growth has played an important part in China's priority for agriculture and, even with a rapidly declining birthrate, the evidence of relatively stable city size suggests that some siphoning-off has occurred. But few governments enjoy Peking's authority and, until the recent food crisis few of them felt the same urgency either.

If, however, developing governments over the next decade do begin to take seriously the fact that farm output has to achieve an annual five percent increase and pay more than lip service to the critical importance of improved farming, there are a number of experiments to be studied around the world that give some ideas about the possible content of a successful educational system for the villages. Perhaps one should say that the very first element in any strategy is precisely this recognition of priority for farming. We need not repeat the descriptions given on an earlier page of the profoundly depressing effect of government policy dogmatically geared almost solely to industrial expansion and city growth. If the villages felt they were second-class citizens, they were quite right. They were. That in itself was argument enough for the decision to give up and go to town. Teaching institutions reflected and reinforced the government's pro-urban strategy. At the peak, in new universities and teachers' training colleges, it was possible to find literally no one trying for an agricultural degree or showing the least interest in farming matters. Rural subjects belonged to traditional, often colonial life. Even when agricultural colleges were established, it was often found that over fifty percent of the graduates left to make their careers in other fields. Law, medicine, the liberal arts were the choices in a string of "Oxbridges" round the world— none of them unworthy or unimportant disciplines yet singularly unbalanced for nations with at least seventy-five percent of their people on the land and eighty percent of their report earnings from the farm sector. School curricula and teaching materials reflected the same imbalance, following earlier European models or the new urban, industrial priorities. Even growing a school garden has remained exceedingly rare. The number of countries insisting, like Tanzania, that students should work for a time in the country is minute.

Yet one or two experiments do give us pointers, if not to success, at least to its preconditions. The Tanzanian Mtuni Afya ("Man Is Health") campaign should be cited. It has three basic elements—the training of literate group leaders who learn how to conduct group teaching and discussion, the preparation of simple, understandable textbooks about basic means of preventing disease, and a twice-weekly radio course which repeats and reinforces the textbooks. This makes possible the participation of illiterate farmers. In the preparations for the campaign, which ran for twelve weeks in 1973, first 100 schoolteachers were trained. Then, in a series of two-day seminars, they trained between 60 and 70,000 "group leaders." Each of them was supposed to mobilize groups of fifteen people to read the books and follow the radio. But the interest aroused proved to be so great that when the groups formed there were more "drop-ins" than "drop-outs." The thirty-five percent who are estimated to have given up the course were far exceeded by new members crowding in. At the end of the first series, the results included the self-help digging of 750,000 latrines and insistent demand for more courses. Preparations began at once, with the same care and detail, for a series on nutrition. Over two million citizens, nearly a sixth of the population, took part and the estimated cost was about fourteen cents a head. It was the use of radio that made it particularly easy to keep expenses down.

Tanzania, with its strong emphasis on decentralized action, self-reliance, and mutual help—for instance, in the UJAMAA or cooperative villages—illustrates a further point. Introducing adult education, changing the curriculum, and giving local primary or secondary schools the kind of teachers and subjects which prepare them for a modernized rural life will lead nowhere unless the larger structure of farming is changing at the same time. If land reform is taking place, cooperatives being set up, regional centers expanded, rural industries introduced, and a sense of new life suffuses the community, it is possible to make the school part of the change. How much has to be changed is hard to say. Evidence from the private educational efforts of Colombia's *Acción Cultural Popular*—a movement devoted to general rural improvement and adult education—suggests that the readiest recipients of information have been farmers who own their own land, however small the holdings and districts in which official development agencies are at work—introducing cooperatives, bringing in piped water, building latrines, and in general showing practical official goodwill for local efforts.

The same kind of evidence comes from another continent. It was discovered in the rich rice-growing area of Tanjore in the South of India that by drawing the farmers into a cooperative research venture with the local extension officials—using their land for experiments, involving them in testing the results, and drawing them into consultations about the future direction of the program—the receptivity of the whole farming community for new knowledge increased very rapidly. And Tanjore also illustrates a wider point. By concentrating the educational effort—extension visits, radio, pamphlets, newsheets—on agricultural productivity, on increasing the crops, preserving them from wastage and getting them to market, the program had much greater impact than earlier experiments in which extension officials were supposed to do a bit of everything but never with any very clear direction of the efforts or measurement of the results. The conclusion that must follow is that the educational system—from primary school through adult education by way of regional centers of learning and extension services—can play a creative part if, in the region at large, institutions and income are improving and the whole countryside feels the breath of change and hope. Without this wider context of development, literacy will remain the biggest incentive to decamp. A five percent growth in agriculture may be the condition of survival of rmost developing countries. But they will not secure it by half measures or by inertia or in a fit of absence of mind.

One last word on services for the villages—the needed changes in health and education are themselves the best guarantors of the physical environment. The most urgent problems of pollution are contaminated lakes and rivers. The more wastes and excrement are used as fuel, the less the risk of pollution; the less risk, too, that the inexorable cutting down of the forests in search of firewood will continue unchecked. At the same time, the more intensively and carefully the land is developed by aware and educated farmers, the less the risk of soil erosion. Dams to control flooding, the replanting of reservoir banks and catchment areas, windbreaks lining the fields, fuel woods and crops near the villages, building and contouring in hilly country, a massive use of digestors and composter, complete avoidance of wasteful "slosh-on" use of artificial fertilizers, the choice of small agricultural machines, and the maximum use of labor—all these add up to a type of farming that sets man to work with, not against, the weave of nature and can produce for generations to come not eroding deserts but a settled, comely, and productive land.

23 SERVICES FOR THE CITIES

A NEW EMPHASIS on rural priorities does not mean that a steady transfer of the population to the cities will not continue to take place. It is part of the inevitable evolution toward the technological society. It is therefore just as important that improved health in urban life should be as strongly emphasized and a similar effort made to create a better relationship between educational expenditures and the kind of employment cities need and can supply.

To some degree, many of the same techniques—simple devices for converting human wastes into usable methane, or compost, paramedical assistants, small clinics, training on the job, school curricula designed to give not only basic literacy and numeracy but also a grasp of actual, contemporary neighborhood needs—are as usable in the new cities as in the old villages. Indeed, in many of the metropolises it is normal for forty to sixty percent of the people to have been born in the villages or the smaller towns. Very often they come and install their shacks and pitiful possessions next door to cousins and neighbors from the old life. In Africa, especially, the sense of clan, of the extended family, offers the bewildered new boy a sense of support not simply in Abidjan and Lagos but in the *bidonvilles* of distant France. Many developing cities are still almost constellations of villages and many of the small techniques still apply.

It is significant that China's rural pattern of simply trained paramedical helpers, concentrating on preventive medicine, at the level first of the overall commune, then of the brigade, and then of the smallest unit—the production team—is repeated in the cities. Responsibility in the large "municipalities"—we might call them metropolises—is similarly given to a series of urban units of smaller size. A "district" has anything from 200,000 to 900,000 people. A "neighborhood" is about the size of a Western city quarter or borough, in other words 50,000 to 70,000 inhabitants. "Street committees" cover between 1,000 and 8,000. The final "Group" includes a dozen to thirty families. At street committee level a health station is run by the committee and they are served by the housewives (Red Medical Workers). The neighborhood will have a hospital with fully trained doctors and nurses, part of whose responsibility is training the health assistants and taking them in for refresher courses. As in the countryside, these health assistants can vaccinate, take simple tests, treat minor ailments, and give guidance on family planning. With the public health section of the hospital, they help to keep the street committees and groups on their toes in such matters as getting rid of flies and keeping down garbage. The health workers also supervise the effects of contraceptives and no doubt play a vital part in the strong social consensus which favors late marriages and frowns on pregnancy out of wedlock.

The neighborhood hospital is responsible as well for local health units in industry where health assistants—the worker doctors—man the factory health station, concentrate on preventing accidents and illness, looking after minor troubles, and going through the same regular process of training and retraining. In the intervals, they continue with their ordinary work.

In these ways, a fifth of the human race, still at the income level of the poorer countries, receives elementary and far from ineffective health care. In general, however, the poorer countries' tradition of following more developed Western models has tended toward a different pattern—the concentration of a few highly qualified doctors and a few sophisticated services in the biggest cities and very little anywhere else. Some estimates put the number of people receiving no care at all as high as fifty percent. It is not unusual to find a ratio of, say, 1000 patients to one doctor in the capital city and one to a quarter of a million in the countryside. And the training of doctors to Western standards has a further consequence. Many of them leave for Western countries once their training is complete (or are trained and stay abroad)—a double drain since the country loses both the cost of their education and then the services that might have flowed from it. The number of developing nations which, like Tanzania, make service in the countryside a precondition of medical training is very small.

The same imbalance shows up in building and equipment. A single bed in a fully equipped modern hospital can cost ten times the average annual income in the country. Yet smaller clinics dispersed through the city, often built by the local people and concentrating on preventive medicine, could provide services which bear some relation to the country's income. This does not mean no "high medicine" and no teaching hospitals. It does mean constructing the whole pyramid of health, not simply the top of it.

The need is no different in education. The top of the pyramid is formal university education in the European tradition. One or two countries have followed to their advantage a later model—the American Land Grant College with its high emphasis on practical knowledge and research. But the lower parts of the pyramid are often simply not there. The expenditure per student-year in advanced education may be a hundred times greater than at the primary level. Yet these top-ranking institutions, again on developed models, are usually the sole avenue to better paid jobs, above all, in the growing civil services. And since the high bureaucrats make most of the decisions about national spending, universities tend to receive more than a reasonable share of the country's budget.

They also produce more highly trained people than the country can absorb so, as with the doctors, graduates finding no congenial work then depart to the developed continents. A 1971 attempt to estimate the "brain drain" concluded that one-third of the scientists in the United States and one-sixth in Canada had come from developing countries.

Meanwhile, the secondary schools which produce the sergeants and foremen of society—and cost ten times less per place per year—usually receive fewer resources and less well-equipped teachers. Nor is the curriculum designed for life in the real city. This is not to deny the value of literacy for its own sake, nor does it suggest turning secondary schools into vocational training centers. Such centers are not especially successful, do not relate skills to jobs, and often provide expensively what would be better learned on the factory floor. But there is desperate need for literate and adaptable minds, ready for the risks and possibilities of the new urban environment, as able to work in a modern factory as to help Uncle Amadeo with his blossoming bicycle business. Such a level of education requires from the community more money, more prestige, and more acceptance as the closing stage of formal education, not a simple stepping stone to the university. For in-

stance, if civil services recruited a steady proportion of nongraduates
on the basis of performance at work, the clamor for university education at all costs, with all its overblown expectations or risks of a brain
drain, might be lessened and there could be fewer repetitions of the
tragic Sri Lanka explosion in 1971 when unemployed graduates rioted
in the streets.

And in country and town at the base of everything is the primary
school where the first grasp on modern living—literacy—must be
achieved and then, by such efforts as Tanzania's education by radio,
by adult education teams, by literacy drives of the "learn one, teach
one" type, must be kept alive in young peoples' minds by the chance
to practice and use it. Today perhaps the biggest loss in the developing
countries' education systems is the number of scholars who pass
through quite an expensive network of schooling and emerge at the
other end virgin of everything save the desire to stop doing the tasks
for which they are equipped.

Naturally, these shifts in educational emphasis will not work
unless comparable changes are being made in society at large. If the
patterns of employment are dominated by large-scale, often foreign,
high-technology industries and by correspondingly large local, state,
and private bureaucracies, a policy of expensive university education
for the privileged, secondary schooling for a relatively small skilled
body of workers, and virtual illiteracy for everybody else would not fit
too badly into the overall pattern of available work. The only problem
would be that with growth rates of 2.5 to three percent in population,
the sheer swamping number of the marginal citizens would, before too
long, make the cities and the countryside as unsafe as a growing tide
of kidnappers and guerrillas could make them. Just as agricultural
training and self-help imply agrarian reforms, so does a more balanced
and productive educational system imply better balanced and more just
patterns of employment. The models of Japan and Taiwan, the light
industrial park, the "bazaar economy," labor-intensive workshops,
small firms working with larger contractors, spreading the availability
of skilled and semiskilled jobs—these are the types of employment
that can provide the framework within which literacy, apprenticeship,
night classes, and refresher courses are all seen to be a genuine investment in a better life.

And, we must repeat, the issue is not simply one of employment.
It is the avenue to a wider, more various, and more stimulating climate

of ideas, to greater self-confidence and a sense of grip on life. However trivial and even debasing some of the publications in this brave new world of literacy may be, to be literate and numerate and to have some sense of how society works is a precondition of full citizenship, of escaping from that tragic definition: "The poor are those whose plans never work out." Like malnutrition in infancy, illiteracy is lasting deprivation. In modern society, it becomes a more and more intolerable barrier to confident and cooperative civic life. Yet, as we have seen, it is chiefly to various forms of such cooperation that society must look for solutions to the enormous and proliferating problems of vast metropolises in the poorest lands.

However, there remains a network of essential services which citizen cooperation, however dedicated, cannot begin to provide and some of these determine what success mutual help and cooperation can hope to achieve. Not all the health assistants in the world can get rid of dysentery and cholera if water supplies are contaminated. Nor can apprenticeships and literacy classes and self-help forms of adult education launch the young worker if there is no bus service to take him to a job. The underlying rationale of orderly city planning and of a concentrated effort to carry out programs for "sites and services" is that easy access and basic sanitation cannot be provided by citizens acting on their own. But they can enormously enhance their individual and collective efforts.

The developing world starts from a frightening backlog of aging and inadequate services. Calcutta's basic water and sewerage systems were installed nearly a century ago for a city of 600,000. Now there are over eight million. The original system is running down. Many city quarters have no more than open drains. Again and again water has to be turned off when pumps or outlets are overloaded. The Hooghly River receives the filth and provides the drinking water, although treatment plants are on the same downward drift of deterioration.

The evils of pollution may reach a peak here but the problems are general. As the Seventies began, the World Health Organization reported that at least fifty percent of the city dwellers in developing lands had *no* regular water supply and that in more and more cities the point was being reached at which the growing amount of municipal wastes and industrial effluents discarded into the watercourses made it essential to begin to install treatment plants. Chlorination and a little filtration were no longer a sufficient defense. At the most modest level of service, the WHO calculus of cost for water and sewerage systems in developing countries for the decade of the Seventies is of the order of $20 thousand million, over half of it for sewers. In a sense, the sum is moderate—a mere $2 thousand million a year, or one one hundred and twenty-fifth of the world's annual arms bill. But what seems normal for "defense" against other humans is seen as spendthrift if the war is against life-destroying parasites and pathogens.

Overall figures do not solve the critical issues of the siting of services and the equity of their distribution. In densely built older settlements, there is a case for continuing with private and public latrines, cesspools and night soil collection by "honey carts" until the overall economy has reached a point where the financial burden of installing completely new sewage installations can be carried more easily. After all, central Tokyo has managed to this day to make do with what is basically a very primitive system.

A futher argument for delaying major outlays on sewage systems at this stage is that more and more effective methods of sewage treatment are being invented. It is only common sense now to link the collection of wastes (and possibly excrement) with composting plants for sale to the surrounding farmers. Smaller compacter systems may soon be available for district treatment. More sophisticated biochemical technology may permit animal feed to be developed by way of single-cell protein. Some of China's new urban districts are reported to have integrated sewage disposal systems which service grain and vegetable growing in the green belts now established around the older cities. This may not be the decade for a massive installation of traditional methods. A particular drawback in the system of wet oxidation proposed for Tokyo and Seoul, because it is very much less expensive than water carriage, is that the resulting residue is useless for fertilizer.

While new techniques of sewage disposal are being developed, a basic water service can be introduced at once. Priority should go to water treatment and piped water—or, as an alternative, government water shops with delivery by sanitary water wagons. If householders wish to link their own houses with the water pipes, the installations should be metered and the cost contributed to general upkeep. The worst solution is to establish Western levels of water supply—say, 200 liters a day per person—and then deliver the water only to the better-off parts of the city. Indeed, adherence to developed world sanitary standards advocated by foreign consultants and accepted often as a matter of prestige by local government officials (who are likely to live in the serviced areas) has come to be a serious obstacle to the achievement of more modest but still healthy standards for the mass of the people—for instance, communal stand pipes. What is intolerable is water playing on golfing greens for the tourist when children die of dysentery not half a mile away. In fact, one can argue that in most developing cities, it would be better to provide simpler standards for the whole city than have enclaves of expensive, modernized services for the few.

In fact, in many developing countries the whole issue of water standards borrowed from Western standards needs careful re-examination. It is easy to forget the enormous amounts of water demanded by various industrial processes and then returned to treatment plants or the rivers—40,000 gallons for a ton of steel, 200,000 gallons of water for a ton of newsprint. The dilemmas facing Taiwan illustrate the problem. Industrial use of water is going up by more than ten percent a year, personal use by two to three percent. At the same time, irrigation is being steadily extended and one ton of milled rice requires 3,500 tons of water. This explosion of water use, part of it supplied from over a thousand wells around Taipei, is steadily lowering the water table. Yet the basis of Taiwan's highly successful export drive is its ability to feed its own people and hence regulate its own basic rates of pay. Clearly, present water use threatens to develop into an overall water deficit. New answers are required. For instance, every industry should introduce its own water recycling techniques; one thinks of the Kaiser steel works in the United States cutting demand from 40,000 gallons to less than 1,000 gallons a ton. And tough metering must be used to hold down domestic demand. Desalinization may lie in the future when, if ever, water refinery costs no longer reflect rocketing energy prices. In fact, standards of water-use developed in the damp temperate climates of Western Europe or the Eastern United States cannot be taken as a sound technical base for countries with different endowments and ecosystems and their internationalization as universal norms can often do more harm than good.

Nowhere is this more obvious than in the related fields of transport and energy. The temptation to plunge on to nuclear power is particularly strong in some parts of the developing world because most of the southern half of the globe is not well provided with fossil fuels. Hydroelectric sites, though still abundant, are being, little by little, built (or silted) up and the whole scale of thinking borrowed from the developed North, capitalist or communist, is based on big installations, big grids, big use—and big waste. We will not rehearse again the totally unacceptable risks of the nuclear economy, although a reminder of its steadily rising costs is perhaps in order. What needs to be emphasized is that the world is on the edge of a whole new set of breakthroughs in the production, use, and conservation of energy. The need for new strategies was blanketed during the twenty-year oil bonanza. Now the hunt is on, and it is not too ambitious to guess that within a quarter of a century, energy produced from the world's income—of solar radiance, possibly of waves and tides, of winds, or, if it proves safe, of deuterium-based fusion—will have taken the place of present day fossil-fuel users, will have made fission power and the breeder-reactor mercifully obsolete before they are much used, and will produce systems which will certainly have less danger and may have far more flexibility than today's vast power stations and country-bestriding grids. To avoid big plunges into old technologies may be the wisest option at this moment for developing lands. Meanwhile there are enough margins in short-term conservation and in the basic availability of conventional fuels for prudence not to turn into failure.

The largest single energy-saving strategy is quite simply to forego the privately motorized city. There is every evidence that the developed world, having jumped in, is now trying to pull out again. So why step into the same river twice? The motorcar, after all, does more than swallow scarce and expensive energy. It is an instrument of profound social divisiveness. Abidjan, with under 13 percent of the population and 70 percent of the cars, Bangkok with only 8 percent and nearly 73 percent, Nairobi with 4.7 percent and 59 percent, Sao Paulo with 6.1 percent and 25.8 percent—everywhere the contrasts are the same. A small elite, in its own interests, slants the whole city system toward giganto-maniac road building while people use a bus if they can afford it—or otherwise endlessly walk. It is surely no coincidence that the developing nation with the highest combination of growth and of independence from foreign investment or assistance—China—has opted for public transport and the bicycle. Its total annual production of vehicles, mainly trucks, is not much above 100,000 for a population of 800 million. Perhaps 5,000 cars a year will be produced—for taxis and tourists. Otherwise, bus, rail, and bicycle will carry the millions and, since Chinese urban planners appear to be intent on clustering activities in communities of 50,000–80,000 inhabitants, much of the movement will be on foot. (With this decision, too, the problem of air pollution virtually vanishes).

The clustering of urban activities also makes it easier to bolster power stations' conventional fuels with municipal trash collections and, as in Sweden or Eastern Europe, to utilize thermal waste for district heating or industrial process heat. Developing countries should be alert to the plethora of new methods of conservation made possible by the reuse of materials and saving of energy that older—and sadder—municipal systems are beginning to explore after their extravagant love affair with petroleum. Half the poor world's cities may be about to be built in an era of infinitely more humane, adaptable, and inexpensive technologies. For once, history may be moving to their side.

The various opportunities to group urban activities in districts with their own jobs and services, to exclude all but the occasional car, to develop bus lanes or interurban rapid transit railways, to install basic services—power, water, sewage collection, with a keen eye for conservation and new techniques—become all the more practicable when one remembers that half the new communities will be on new land, not crabbed and confined within the existing metropolis. Provided land speculation is strictly stamped out, tenure made secure, and people assisted with the materials for building, the "young cities" can become exciting places of work and promise when the pioneers invent their own communities, build and extend their own homes, plant the trees, build the primary schools, send their children to the government-supported technical schools and training centers, and move easily on foot within their own streets and provide "critical mass" for the bus services to other centers. This is the dream, at least, for the new cities planned for New Bombay or New Bogota. It is not an impossible one. A weariness with overheavy bureaucracy, with standards that are too inflexible and norms that restrict human creativeness is not confined to the developing world or to the poor world's cities. It is a much wider mood. Its negative side is hopelessness in the face of officialdom, boredom, apathy, and on toward violence—the senseless violence of British football fans, the frustrated violence of young, educated Sri Lankans without a hope of employment. But its positive side can be a new environment of self-commitment, work, and hope. Of all tasks of administration in human settlements—which we must now discuss—to elicit this mood and respect those energies is certainly the most important task.

Part Five: Problems of Management

24 METROPOLITAN PATTERNS

WHAT ARE the administrative implications of the growth of monster cities all around the world? They have, all but universally, been unplanned. They have sprawled outward, swamping earlier jurisdictions. The "giant concrete footsteps" have trampled out the villages and surrounded the small towns. As they stamp about, they create the governmental problem of creating some municipal order, some principles of cooperation, some sense of direction, justice, and environmental control out of what is all too often one big muddle of overlapping, competing and even hostile authorities. The disorganization goes upward when conurbations, vast slabs of streets and masonry, intimately interconnected by networks of wider employment and movement, stride over old provincial and state boundaries. It goes downward in the flattening of active communes and parishes. Today, about a third of Japan's total population lives in the great cities entirely enclosing 300 miles of coastline around and beyond Tokyo—the Tokaido conurbation. New York City is the focal point for an area of work and travel which includes twenty million people in its commuting area and covers not only parts of New York State but also of New Jersey and Connecticut.

On the other side of the continent, the San Francisco Bay Area—including San Francisco, San Jose, and Oakland—contains 850 different local authorities for nearly five million citizens. In comparison, London's eight million, ruled by thirty-three Boroughs and a single "federal" Greater London Council—or even the Zone of Paris with its 243 communes—seems relatively modest in administrative proliferation.

Besides, as we have seen, a city area is not a settlement in the traditional sense of settled people living and working together. The commuter flood moves the equivalent of the inner city of Paris in and out of New York every day. Another less constant but almost as remorseless a flow is made up of tourists, visitors, and shoppers. For a city like Rome, the annual invasions can be the equivalent of four whole cities the size of inner Paris moving through in the summer months. These gigantic movements not only complicate administration at the center of the metropolitan region; they raise explosive political issues about the effective boundaries of the metropolis, about how much of the "commutershed" ought to be under city control, and whether, in the interests of the whole nation's earnings of foreign exchange, municipalities of great beauty or historical interest should be refused any rights of local self-defense.

All such concentrations of settlement and movement tend to create the same problems. How are they to be politically guided, administratively managed, and successfully financed? Since, in 1975, the two largest and wealthiest of such metropolises, New York and Tokyo, both did a cliff-hanging performance of near-bankruptcy, something must be seriously wrong with the handling of mega-urban affairs. Or, to cite another type of difficulty, if under the most unified, centralized, and comprehensive civic planning in the world—in the Soviet Union—the two major cities, Moscow and Leningrad, have contrived to double in size after all policies likely to lead to further growth had been strictly banned, there must be evidence of some innate, forceful, and all but uncontrollable influences at work behind the explosion of megaregions. This only makes the tasks of governing them more intractable.

To give some idea of the complexity of governing these vast, shifting masses of human beings between their homes, their work, their leisure, and their culture, it is perhaps best to look at the pattern of responsibility established in one of the world's large and reasonably successful metropolitan regions. Toronto, a conurbation of 2.7 million, stretched along the Northern shores of Lake Ontario, is part of the province of Ontario, itself a constituent part of the Canadian Federation. We will leave out the federal level of government, important though it is in the provision of subsidies, the setting of standards, evening out the distribution of wealth between the provinces, and providing, at the highest level, for defense, overall economic strategy, and the "general welfare." It is at the provincial level that the really inextricable interweaving of regional and local responsibility (and financing) begins. The provincial government of Ontario provides the Toronto Metropolitan Council—and all other municipalities in the province—with the capital needed for public housing, the financing (but not the administration) of welfare, the costs of law courts and jails and the hospital system. It also covers the costs of outlying commuter services by rail and road and gives sizable grants to education, to road building, and to the capital costs of public transport—building a subway, renewing the rolling stock.

At the next level of administration, Toronto's Metropolitan Council (set up in the 1950s) is responsible for overall strategic planning of the metropolitan area, the police force, major roads and parks, and the ambulance service. All these elements are partly financed from municipal taxes which are levied on the next level down of government—the boroughs. The Council also makes grants to a number of separate functional Boards or Commissions—the Metropolitan Toronto School Board, the Toronto Transit Commission, and the Metropolitan Library Board.

When we reach the boroughs—originally thirteen, but now unwillingly reduced to six—we find that they control local plans which in fact largely determine the content of the area's so-called strategic planning; they run local parks, the fire services (happily with considerable interborough cooperation), the administration of welfare, and the public utilities (gas supplies and the telephone are private monopolies).

It takes little imagination to see that this glorious Neapolitan ice cream of layers of government and responsibility is always on the verge of melting, and many areas do of necessity run into each other. Yet there is not a metropolitan area in the world that does not display similar complexity, and most of them are, like Toronto, tending to spread at the edges. The tasks of coordination, the achievement of needed measures of cooperation, the disputes over expenditure are simply built into the nature of the services and their inevitable degree of overlap. This, then, is the range of policies and problems for which effective government must be devised.

The world is trying out a number of answers but with widely varying degrees of effectiveness. In some areas, the attempt is being made,

either by a provincial or by the central government, to persuade existing communities to cooperate with each other over those issues which
they clearly share. In Japan, for instance, Osaka City, with a population
of nearly four million by day and nearly three by night, has
another four and a half million in its immediate neighborhood (excluding the city of Kobe.) To give some kind of order to this whole
densely settled area, a standing Conference of all the constituent cities
has been established and common policies are sought for land use
planning, for transport and communications, and for control of pollution. There is also some discussion of developing a large port and
shipbuilding complex with Kobe, whose population of 1.35 million inhabitants is virtually continuous with the Osaka area. But a strongly
entrenched sense of long-established divisions on the lines of separate
prefectures has so far inhibited any closer or more formal types of cooperation. Yokohama, another city in the total Tokaido conurbation,
has a population of two and a half million and no formal administrative links whatever with the other cities. And next door again is the
world's largest city. Tokyo, with over eleven and a half million people
in the confines of the city itself, has its own internal metropolitan pattern of government but again, no formal links with its neighbors.
Since, according to all recent opinion polls and also according to the
Japanese Government's own official attempt to measure "disutilities,"
pollution and commuting are considered the worst of Japan's urban
evils and one requires a sorting out of work and movement and the
other joint action to save the dying coastal waters, it would seem that
only more formal instruments of coordination would have any hope
of really improving the whole vast Tokaido complex. It would also
seem that the long discussed, promised, and postponed plans for de-
centralizing a number of industrial activities to other parts of Japan is
one the Japanese central government might be well advised to take up
again.

But the jealousy of old jurisdictions and the unwillingness of other
municipalities to carry new strains have inhibited change in Japan's
packed coastal regions. And exactly the same phenomenon occurs, on
a lesser scale, across the Pacific around San Francisco Bay. Here, too,
the distribution of work and residence, ease of movement, and pollution are basically insoluble if they are tackled separately, municipality
by municipality. The perception of this truth has led to the creation of

an Association of Bay Area Governments and to an agreement—now beset by severe financial troubles—to sponsor and finance together a new, ultramodern rapid transit system. But it cannot be said that, on the basis of San Francisco's experience, loose cooperative arrangements do much to tighten up and rationalize administration. We have already mentioned the number of separate authorities involved—eight hundred and fifty. They include a type of administration which calls for a word of explanation since it throws light on what is by all odds the greatest obstacle to balanced metropolitan planning and financing—the extreme unwillingness of wealthier communities to accept one of its implications, a more just and compassionate distribution of the areas' resources. In market economies, the planned city and the just city go uneasily together. The "Special District" is a small but telling example of the wished-for divorce.

A mood of exclusiveness is strong in these "Special Districts" whereby, in parts of the United States, including the Bay area, several counties group themselves together to form an area large enough to support efficient services—gas, electricity, sewage treatment, local transport—and these services are then let out on contract to efficient suppliers. The result is an improvement in the convenience and cleanliness of the district, no troublesome questions of becoming joined to larger and possibly poorer areas, and the preservation of local control, which is usually the control of reasonably affluent suburban families. One interesting and unintended side-effect is that some of the suppliers achieve a standard of performance in municipal services which could well be used as a yardstick to judge a lot of sloppy work turned in by uncompetitive municipal officials and unions. But, inevitably, it is easier to be efficient among the green lawns, handsome homes, and well-designed, well-stocked supermarkets of a Marin County than in the ghettos of Oakland.

To return to the larger scale of municipal administration, the weakness of a loose grouping of separate jurisdictions designed to achieve common purposes is that usually coordination is not enough and that, in any case, financial obligations are disputed or not spelled out, the administrative machinery for joint action is lacking, and by the time the supposed policy reaches the people it is supposed to help—the citizens themselves—it has been vaporized away in layer after layer of busy and time-consuming inconclusiveness. The argument for more formal and explicit cooperation is that it is the only means of turning cooperation into a reality and giving it the machinery and the finance to make it work.

The invention of one possible answer—what one might call federal metropolitan government—can be claimed by the London County Council established in 1889. Just as it was clear by the 1830s that you could not run Manchester with no larger unit of government than the parish—however imaginative the special commissions called in to run larger operations from the police to the gas works (or both)—so, by the 1880s, it was clear that London, containing incidentally *two* cities, Westminster and the City of London, and advancing, with its "commutershed," to six million souls, needed something larger than the 130 boroughs, wards, and parishes which had struggled, not unsuccessfully, to carry through the earlier revolutions of street paving, gas lighting, commuter railroads, magnificent sewage and water systems—and the less magnificent Poor Law. An all-London "county" government was established. Under it, in a sort of federal arrangement, were shortly afterwards grouped twenty-eight Metropolitan Boroughs and the City of London. The powers of each in the task of administering, financing, and cleaning up the city were specifically defined by statute. It proved to be a genuinely successful experiment in combining broad strategy with local autonomy and lasted unchanged through two world wars and nearly eighty years. And when in the 1960s it was expanded to become the Greater London Council with thirty-two Metropolitan Boroughs and once again the City of London, the structure remained essentially the same, the increase in scale simply representing a further growth of the "commutershed" and the need to include outlying suburbs in the area to be covered by the strategic powers of the Greater London Council.

Versions of this original model have begun to be repeated all around the world since the second world war. Tokyo may have no formal links with its two million and a half neighbor, Yokohama, but the city itself is now, by government fiat, the Tokyo Metropolitan Government. Its twenty-three wards roughly correspond to London's Metropolitan Boroughs. But the outer fringes of the "commutershed"—over fifteen million in it—have not been reorganized into local government units and continue to depend upon old-style, direct prefectural government. However, the elected Mayor of Tokyo doubles in the role of Prefect, so coordination is in some measure secured.

The fact that the Tokyo Metropolitan Government was brought into being by a decision of the national government is a reminder of an important point determining whether or not the large conurbations can secure rather more rational means of self-administration. If, in unitary states, the central government is hostile or indifferent to a sorting out of urban powers, nothing much will happen. Even in Britain, the home of urban "federalism," the principles were not applied to the dense urban regions of the north until the 1970s. The whole of France's strategy is, as we have seen, invented and imposed from the center—even if one or two genii may be showing signs of popping out of the DATAR bottle. In the United States, governments at the state level are often hostile to the idea of extending metropolitan government to a city's "commutershed" simply because suburban interests are strongly represented at the state level and the almost universal separation of the state capital from the "big bad city"—Albany from New York, Sacramento from Los Angeles, Springfield from Chicago—reflects an inbred American suspiciousness of the dangers, corruptions (and insidious delights) of bright lights and big cities. In the years before World War I, when the scale of urban and suburban change and expansion had not yet impinged forcefully on the national consciousness, it was relatively easy for growing cities simply to extend their jurisdiction and take in the neighboring county. This process has now virtually stopped or only takes place with considerable difficulty. A prolonged struggle with the Florida state government preceded the permission received by Jacksonville to form a metropolitan region with its surrounding Duval County in the 1960s. The state also consistently opposed the consolidation of Miami with Dade County and even lessened its financial support to both. It is virtually inconceivable that New York State would permit a change in New York City's jurisdiction to include a larger swath of its wealthy commuter-belt in order to offset the vast burdens of its urban poor.

In Canada, on the contrary, the provinces have tended to give a helping hand. The State of Ontario actively encouraged Toronto to federate with its thirteen surrounding communities and gave it extra financial support to cover the less popular implications of wider government—for instance, housing for poorer families. Manitoba was equally helpful in supporting Winnipeg's metropolitan federation, which has consolidated nineteen surrounding communities into thirteen city units, with an elected council and a fairly high degree of centralized control.

Where, as in Western Germany or Eastern Europe, city growth has been restrained either by an effective division of federal powers between central government and provinces (the *Länder*) or held down by the overall national plan, large metropolitan regions, concentrating several million citizens in contiguous and overlapping areas of work, movement, and living have not, in fact, evolved. The city of a million citizens can manage its affairs effectively with strong central administrative and elective bodies and local wards for more intimate representation. The powers of such cities—Munich, for instance, or Cologne or Hanover—help them to attract a high standard of technical staff and the compactness (and general wealth) of the community lessen the risk of inbuilt stresses between inner city and wealthy suburb.

There are a few serpents in the German Eden. Hamburg, itself both a city and a *Land,* finds that it is losing population not so much to suburbs as to neighboring Schleswig-Holstein or Lower Saxony and confronts some of the problems customary in larger cities—of seeing its tax base and even its employment shrink while the relatively poorer citizens remain. But, on the whole, the "million city" in a developed society does avoid the sharpest conflicts between center and periphery and has an easier task in coordinating the strategy of the whole city with the tactics of local wards and communes.

In planned societies, the unity of party control, running like a thread from the Supreme Soviet or central government down to the city block is, in theory, the generator of continuity and stability in policy, administration, and finance. In practice, things are naturally not so straightforward. It is clear from a steady underlying change in administrative emphasis in the Soviet Union that any federation on so vast a scale has problems in balancing central strategy with local performance and reactions. The pendulum has swung from stronger central decision-making to more local initiative and back again with some regularity since 1917. Nor has the difficulty we have already examined—the balance of power between the large industrial planning units, their policies of location, and the rather weak soviets or city governments which have to turn industrial locations into places worth living in—been thoroughly resolved. In highly industrialized cities, the balance of power seems still to remain with Gosplan and the central economic ministries. In provincial capitals, the soviets (the civil administrations) have larger influence. In Moscow, the whole apparatus of central government seems not to override but to enhance the role of the city administration. It controls land use planning and road construction. It has the resources to build its own schools and housing. It appears much less dependent upon the decisions of local industries and has the obvious advantage of quick access to the central planners. It is, of course, a very large city, an urban complex of over nine million—but it has not adopted any "federal" type of administration. In fact, part of its relatively large geographical extent is due to the decision taken in 1960 to include all its green belt and surrounding communities within the city itself. There are some complaints that this enlargement has greatly added to commuting distances—the Muscovite spends four times more of his work year traveling than his fellow commuter in Stockholm—and has not noticeably increased the city's open space and areas of recreation. The complaints are, however, reminders of the degree to which, under the apparent uniformity of party influence, a lively and often recalcitrant citizen body have their own ways of making their municipal government resonsive to their needs. The vast Soviet housing program of the last fifteen years, for instance, was in some degree a response to increasingly urgent pressure from below.

In the developing world, in part as a result of colonial control, in part of the shortage of trained administrators, in part of the swamping flow of migrants, there is often considerable weakness or even quite simply a nonexistence of representative government at the city level. The voting—if there is voting—is for central government candidates and the nearest thing to local representation is the responsible deputy in his constituency, listening to the grievances and difficulties of his voters, part mediator, part ombudsman, and often their only link with an administrative municipal apparatus directly run from the center— the position, we should remember, of the citizens of Washington and Paris until very recently. Even where, as in the Indian subcontinent, the apparatus of local government, with elected mayors and councilors exists, the cities, including the largest of them, are often not provided with independent financial resources, experienced officials, or genuine authority. As a result, a phenomenon we have already noticed—local government dominated by the activities of central functional boards or agencies—tends to flourish and in doing so to weaken local initiative. Such arrangements are not, of course, confined to developing countries. Some of the most important economic decisions in Australia, both for the states and the cities, are taken by the central Loans Council. There is hardly a municipality in the world whose water supplies do not depend upon other jurisdictions. And, as we have already noted, a recent flamboyant and dubious example of government by functional body, the Urban Development Corporation, was set up in New York State in 1968 to cut through all the local red tape, to get houses built, the "cities within cities" launched, the New Towns planned, and the construction industry geared to the highest level of productivity only to run first into a cold front of economic recession and then, in 1975, into insolvency.

The advantages a city in the poorer countries can gain by relying upon central government agencies seem so obvious—access to resources, skills, manpower, even foreign capital—that the difficulties are easy to overlook. Local needs get twisted about to fit in with a possible but not wholly relevant central program. Problems which require comprehensive and cohesive answers are unraveled to fit into the specifications of half a dozen different agencies. The definition of specific local needs can be buried under a flood of generalized central reports and statistics. During a two-year span in the mid-Sixties, the central ministries concerned with urban affairs in New Delhi, in addition to their own annual reports, published major reports on the financing and management of water and sewerage works, on national water supply and sanitation schemes, on the integration of urban housing schemes and land acquisitions proceedings, on housing and urban and rural planning for the Fourth Plan (this report included the findings of five subgroups), on rural-urban relationship and on urban land policy. All such reports and conclusions filter their way down through specialized agencies, housing trusts, and local boards. Equally, any request from a municipality, say, for a sewage system, would have to follow the same route upward. The exact point of decision remains unclear. The outcome is unintegrated development advancing at the speed of the most overloaded in-tray and very possibly no sewage disposal for another decade.

One possible institutional answer is the one developed in Calcutta—to attempt to counter the fragmentation of functions at the center by reuniting them in a single development authority in the metropolis. It can redetermine priorities, knit together the unraveled skeins of policy, and apply to the unique and local conditions the range of loans, grants, matching funds—and foreign assistance—that only the center can make available on a sufficient scale.

Such an authority is not and cannot be a representative government in any formal sense. But given the scale of poverty, homelessness, lack of all basic necessities, and grim day-to-day struggle to keep even a toehold on the shores of life, it is arguable that for some time to come, the citizens of the world's poorest metropolises will serve their interests best by developing their own small communities, their own self-help and building, their own job-getting and information, their own mini-industries and social aids. A city-wide development authority can help them where the scale of operations is too big for them—a safe water system, piping for drains, a gobar gas plant working off local latrines. But the immediate form of "representation" they require is confidence in their own efforts and day-to-day improvements in their own local environment. Out of confidence and better health, the demand for wide representation will no doubt grow. But, like the peasants of prewar China, they are in water up to their chin. They need to reach dry land before they can begin to think about political control of their monster cities.

25 INSTRUMENTS OF COMMUNITY

THERE IS NO WAY AROUND the dilemmas created by different levels of government. Some things can only be done at the national or, increasingly, the supranational level. Some demand a regional scale. Some are purely local. But by the time the full effect of all these policies has come together in the daily life of the people, it is the citizen who feels the effects, suffers the consequences, and should be the final judge of the total effect. It is all too easy to reverse the process and leave the citizen to carry the brunt of grandiose plans of industrial expansion, bureaucratic empire building, governmental dreams of glory, or—worst of all—national aggression which leaves his cities burnt-out wrecks and his children mutilated corpses. But how do the basic interests of the citizen, the living, hoping, suffering human beings in their settlements, achieve the primacy which should in the last analysis be the object of the whole governmental exercise?

Much of the answer will always lie in the education and cultural values of the whole society. If chest-beating, self-congratulating, "tough-guy" images are instilled in each generation, the result will be intolerant, repressive, and unresponsive leadership and a steady, ingrained contempt for those who do not "make it." It can even, as for so many years in Colombia, produce such horrors of personal machismo as *"La Violencia,"* which plunged the country into more than a decade of virtually senseless mutual killing. The vendetta, the duel, the gang warfare of "Mafiosi," are all products of vain, arrogant, self-glorious cultural images and make people useless servants of the city of man. The chief argument for elective government at national and local level is that it enables citizens to observe and check power whose tendency is to corrupt and enables the tempted officials to be removed, if necessary, from office. Single-party states can achieve something of the same kind of check by introducing primary elections, as in Tanzania, where within the single party, a number of candidates have to submit to local scrutiny and choice.

We cannot legislate for a humane education and culture. One of the tragedies of empire is the degree to which its apogee is marked by triumphant bullies and its aftermath by men too embittered to turn easily to the ways of peace. But a society can at least try to give itself the institutions, procedures, and checks and balances that offer some hope of offsetting what Hamlet called ''the insolence of office'' and ''the oppressor's wrong, the proud man's contumely,'' and to allow ordinary citizens, the men and women for whose well-being the whole structure of society is supposed to exist, to play a creative and cooperative part in their own social order. Nowhere is this need more intense than in developing countries where, if people are not allowed and encouraged to help themselves and each other—and indeed respected for doing so—the tasks of the next twenty-five years will, quite simply, surpass the capacity of any organized political system.

Let us now try to take these high abstractions down to the mundane level of concrete civic experience and pick out some of the ways in which citizen interests and public performance can be balanced in more effective planning, in the search for justice and in a better environment. Many of the details of these policies have already been discussed. Here we are concerned with the instruments of policy, management, and finance.

In the early stages of industrialization, whether the main executing agents are private or public, the whole process is, as we have seen, so uncertain, so urgent, so full of pitfalls and setbacks that nations scramble themselves into the urban industrial order against a background of priorities dictated in the first place by economic growth. But when a certain level of production has been achieved, the saner nations begin to reflect on the mixture of power and wreckage they see around them and begin to try to repair past ravages and improve the future.

Nineteenth-century sanitation, twentieth-century slum clearance belong to this phase of undoing past evils. Today, the more creative idea of not repeating the old mistakes lies behind much of the new thinking about land use planning, urban dispersion, and more livable cities in developed lands and behind a remarkable reappraisal of the agricultural-industrial balance in developing countries. These reassessments require a general strategy for land use and settlement planning. Overall, this must rest with the central government and here the citizens' political safeguard is the alertness of their elected or delegated representatives. At the level of county and borough, local government representatives have the prime responsibility for vigilance. Unhappily, it is in municipal politics that impartiality and a disinterested approach can, from time to time, be more easily offset by the lures of personal financial advantage. The street paving of nineteenth-century America seems to have involved almost as many felons as Prohibition itself. The recent scandals in northeast Britain over contract-peddling and the fixing of behind-the-scenes kickbacks surround the new Community Land Bill with a certain malaise, since all development contracts—some of them very lucrative—will now depend upon the decisions of not very highly rewarded local officials. The opportunities for graft are obvious.

A different form of the same dilemma appears to have arisen in some Russian cities where weak local soviets, desperate for resources to get the buses back on the street, have been compelled to bargain with a strong local industry for funds and in return offer immunity to, say, a flagrant failure to observe the local sewage ordinance.

But in the last two decades, a number of countries have devised machinery for more thorough explanations, inquiries, and discussions by local citizen groups. Public arbiters—the so-called ombudsmen—have been appointed to inquire into possible overuse or abuse of public authority. The procedures for public inquiries have been regularized and as the concept of positive planning has taken hold, more direct and formal citizen reaction has been institutionalized.

These are certainly needed safeguards. The designation of buildings of historic importance, the protection in perpetuity of certain areas of natural beauty, the preservation of open space in cities, the routing of highways, the siting of airports, even, in some areas, the building of a single house or the texture of its building materials are open to citizen inquiry. The plans are laid out for inspection at local offices, formal procedures for public tribunals are laid down by law, and, as the opportunities for the intervention of the concerned citizen have grown, so have the number of groups organized to take advantage of them. The only tragedy is that in many historic cities in Europe such processes of consultation have come too late and neo-brutal buildings of literally monumental ugliness have thrust up their pretentious towers of steel and glass above the human scale of city life and destroyed the balance and grace of a hundred urban landscapes before general public distaste for the high-rise fixation began to make itself felt. At least, in Britain, the Minister for the Environment has shown his sympathy for this revulsion in a recent decision to save some seemly, unpretentious, but not particularly distinguished buildings in the London borough of Kensington virtually on the grounds that any new architectural construction would be bound to be uglier and worse.

The citizen tribunal or inquiry is probably the most valuable new addition to the localization and humanization of planning strategy. It has been widened in the United States by some legal acceptance of groups' right to plead even if they cannot show personal damage. It needs, however, an added dimension—financial assistance for the defendants. Construction firms can charge their costs to business expenses. But the Davids who face these Goliaths have to find the price of every slingshot from their own purse. In one area in North London, determined developers have made ten separate applications for the same much treasured open site in less than a decade. Each effort has had to be refought by the local community. A graduated tax on the number of applications might strengthen the hand of the weaker side. In Sweden, all appeals against the expropriation of land are financed for the defendants by the state. Not surprisingly, their number has greatly increased.

Citizen action can, of course, be effective even when formal institutions are lacking—always provided that local groups have the will and the clout for opposing unpopular intrusions, public or private. An unusually effective example comes from Australia—the so-called "Green Ban" movement based upon close cooperation between citizen groups and the trade unions. The Green Ban movement began in Sydney in 1971 and has put a stop to forty-two developments, worth about three thousand million dollars, in Sydney alone. The first Green Ban, imposed by the Building Laborers Federation, was in response to a plea from a residents' association seeking help in preventing the development of a piece of open land which served as their local area for walking and for children playing and was also the last remaining piece of bushland on the river in Sydney. The group of women citizens who were seeking to save this land, called "Kelly's Bush," had tried petitions, going to parliamentarians, and making their point at the municipal office. As a last resort, they appealed to the Building Laborers Federation for help. A meeting was called, and 600 people from the area around Kelly's Bush formally requested that the union place a ban on all work on the development of the bushland. The union agreed.

The movement has proved flexible. When, for instance, a ban was imposed on a high-rise development scheme in another area of Sydney, an alternative plan of low-rise building was drawn up, on the local residents' initiative, which the union said they were happy to sanction and undertake. The example of the New South Wales Building Laborers' Federation was followed in all other Australian states, and by 1975 fourteen other unions have imposed Green Bans—the Queensland Labor Council has restricted development of Fraser Island for sand mining (the island being a great natural beauty spot); Victoria Workers' Council has put a ban on the Newport power station as it was going seriously to raise the level of airborne pollution over Melbourne; unions in Freemantle and Hobart are taking action against the demolition and redevelopment of historic areas and buildings in their cities.

This whole process illustrates once again a wider point—the extreme value in communities of small dedicated groups of people who, with or without the backing of their formal representatives (and sometimes indeed against them) are prepared to go to work, form a coalition of interested people, and make enough trouble for authority that problems and evils and oppressions are not hidden away either by the bland inertia of bureaucratic indifference or by the active scheming of vested interests—interests of money, interests of power. Kelly's Bush would have vanished under steel and concrete if an active group of citizens had not started the protest. And this habit of cooperation for specific purposes can give strength to what is often a rather lifeless level of government—the small ward or commune where what can be literally "parish pump" affairs do not stir up enough interest to get the citizens to the voting booths. (One notices the same phenomenon in free trade unions where perhaps five percent of the members bother to attend branch meetings and leave their affairs in the hands of officials or zealots.) Apathy toward small issues can reappear in any form of society. It is reported that a Polish neighborhood committee could not be persuaded to take much interest in local affairs until they were given responsibility for the local kindergarten. From this involvement, other forms of concern and action followed. Again and again in developed societies, it is through the small catalyzing group, fighting for a particular issue—to keep traffic out of New York's Washington Square, to save Oxford University's Meadows from a motorway, to keep Kelly's Bush—that political action at the lowest levels of government suddenly comes alive and the indifferent ward or apathetic commune begins to hum like a hive of bees.

But we must remember a possible other side to citizen action for local interests—for instance, determined efforts to keep out the less privileged and to keep havens (or Special Districts) of good incomes and good services under local control. The inability of many large cities to extend their jurisdiction to cover in any way the surburban citizens for whom they provide work and income is the commonest of all metropolitan problems. Zoning, restrictive covenants, arranged housing densities are as many dikes against a much-feared flood of less fortunate people. It is possible, however, that one cause for the recalcitrance is the bewildering suddenness with which some changes in metropolitan jurisdiction and financing are produced. It is perhaps instructive that in the East Massachusetts Planning Project, changes in land use, in jurisdictions, and in levels of responsibility are to be considered over a much longer span—into the 1990s—and citizens from every kind of group are being drawn into such basic studies as population trends, affluence and mobility, residential renewal, employment in the metropolitan region, and the distribution of families by level of income. It is the old story. A true community can begin to evolve only if the citizens themselves are involved in building it up. A "Master Plan" unconnected with the people, with its unpleasant undercurrent of "mastery," can tear a city apart more easily than it can build a better one. For that, citizen involvement is the only creative route.

It is thus when we turn to the concept of "the just city" that the most serious obstacles to policymaking, administration, and finance arise. The primary point must be repeated. If the central government is not interested in justice, income redistribution, and the right of the citizen to a human share in the national bounty, there is not too much to be done about the problem—in the short run. The hope is that increased education, the world-wide influence of the transistor radio, and the final difficulty of coping with deepening disaffection will change the priorities. Then a rational discussion of what to be becomes possible.

The general attitude of a society also determines the reactions of its public servants at the central and local level. The Victorian Poor Law is proof enough of the arrogance and inhumanity with which assistance to the needy can be administered if poverty is a crime and deemed to be evidence of the indigent citizen's unfitness to survive. Attention, care, respect are human qualities for which a system cannot legislate but which it can inspire. A typical twentieth-century temptation is to see the unfortunates as "cases," not human beings. Without any unkindness being intended, welfare officials' brisk impersonality can be almost as painful for the distraught widow or the abandoned child. There is also the perpetual risk to which all bureaucracies, public and private, are exposed, the risk of sanctifying the regulation to which the person must be made to fit, the fear of latitude and generosity which the rulebook does not provide for. One of the chief arguments for a basic national income to replace the direct receipt of a wide variety of welfare benefits is simply to avoid intrusive, not always well-intentioned, but always somewhat dehumanizing inquests into personal behavior—"But, Mrs. Smith, should you really have purchased two brassieres since June?" A considerable reduction in municipal staffs could also be the result.

This point underlines a prime financial principle. It is to allot to the national level responsibility for putting a basic floor under poverty by whatever means society judges to be most appropriate—social insurance, the negative income tax, supplementary benefits, guaranteed annual income. A modern industrial community cannot even speak of justice unless all its citizens are above the poverty line. This is not an obligation that can be fulfilled at the state or city level because, with free movement and increasing urbanization, the poorer people simply move from areas of inadequate income and pile up in areas—New York City, for instance—where the benefits are nearer the minimum required for human decency. The principle that the local community cannot carry basic welfare costs, particularly in times of economic recession, was well illustrated in the 1930s when, among other cities,

Grand Rapids, Michigan, was unable to meet its obligations and went into default. With impeccable logic, the state of Michigan eased the city's financial stress by taking over all welfare payments.

Admittedly, a national commitment involves some proportional difficulties. Life in the big city is more expensive than in Podunk or the Dordogne. In wage settlements in many large cities an element of "weighting" is introduced to offset the higher living costs of the conurbation. A similar case can, no doubt, be made for the extra welfare benefits in New York City. But the important point is that the proportions should be nationally worked out and agreed to on a realistic nation-wide basis and that the public payments necessary to keep poor, unemployed, aged, or handicapped citizens in decent self-respect be accepted as the primary responsibility of central government.

It is equally important that provinces, cities, and counties should have independent sources of revenue so that overdependence upon the center does not stunt local variety, choice, responsibility, and citizen interest. In most developed market economies, central government revenue is derived primarily from income and corporation tax, customs and excise, various forms of licensing, and the profits—if any—of public enterprises. The share of all this that finds its way in direct grants to lower levels of government is likely to be between forty and sixty percent of their total outlays. The balance which has to be made good locally is usually derived from various taxes on land and fixed property, on income from municipal services, on borrowing, particularly for capital works, and on a whole variety of lesser sources—sales taxes, poll taxes, sometimes from an income tax at the state level. Income tax is imposed even at the municipal level in Sweden and Finland and parts of the United States, including New York City. This very greatly strengthens the ability of municipalities to make and carry out their own plans and executive decisions. This, in turn, arouses considerably more citizen interest in local elections which, in many parts of the developed world, tend to be marked by an apathy which makes even a thirty percent turnout a "successful" response.

Yet, in general it must be admitted that the ease with which local governments can secure sufficient resources depends upon economic conditions they do not control. They have often little or no say in industrial location. If there is no central policy for controlling the price of land, cities are inevitably the most tightly pinched by the escalating cost of land they may need for public purposes. General inflation is, as we have seen, a disaster for them, both in rising interest rates and in the burgeoning wage bill for local services. But while they can contribute to inflation, they cannot end it on their own.

The forms in which central resources are made available can also have distorting effects. If, as in some planned economies, large funds are directed straight into industrial activities with no comparable release of resources for urban services, the local government and its citizens may have a fine steel complex but also put up with darkened streets and rationed water. Another bias can be introduced if the central government decides to give grants-in-aid only on a matching basis. Then wealthy communities can secure the aid while poorer ones will not be able to scrape together the matching funds.

And in the last analysis, local authorities have no say on the degree to which they can rely on central government to bail them out of the kind of difficulties inflation helps to create. The whole confidence-shaking, cliff-hanging public wrangle between New York City, New York State, and the federal government in America in 1975 would seem an object lession—at all levels—of how not to run a nation's finances.

One should emphasize the point. It must apply at all levels. One of the weaknesses in local authority administration, all too often exposed by the onslaught of inflation after 1972, has been a remarkable absence of financial discipline and an equally remarkable absence of any clear relationship between the amount of staff employed and the work actually performed. This is, of course, in part one more illustration of what, in more innocent times, was known as Parkinson's Law—the tendency of more and more layers of administration to be added while the quantum of work and responsibility actually shrinks. In Britain, as a whole, for instance, the number of public officials in local government increased by 62.6 percent between 1960 and 1974, in central government by 6.7 percent while manufacturing employment fell by just over twelve percent. New York City lost a quarter of a million manufacturing jobs in the early Seventies while there was a thirty-one percent increase in government jobs. Part of the British increase is accounted for by a large administrative reorganization at the regional level. But very little is known about the criteria for performance that have been used to check and judge this expansion and whether it has not itself become a serious cause of inflationary pressure—a modern version of the medieval conundrum: How many decision-makers can be balanced on the head of one coalface worker?

In New York City, municipal workers of all kinds increased by 300 percent in the last decade while the city's population actually declined. Did services genuinely improve? Were there audits of performance? Was there any check on some of the devices whereby, to give only one instance, retiring sanitation workers had their pensions geared to their final year's salary and contrived to fill that year with maximum overtime? (And, one could equally ask, in a city where virtually every large corporation tactfully arranges stock options for upper management, could a garbage collector be persuaded that he was doing anything outside the ordinary run of affairs?)

It seems likely that the question of degrees and effectiveness of staffing was simply not examined. Nor, in all too many cases, was the actual municipal budget. Can anyone, to give one or two concrete examples, explain why, in the London Borough of Camden the annual subsidy for a tenant in a house owned by the municipality has increased from $106 to $1700 in just ten years—while the national average is still only $464? Can one penetrate into the mysteries of a procedure whereby $4 million is to be spent converting some Georgian houses into council flats, a process which works out at about $146,000 for each flat and hence the need for a weekly subsidy of $300 to the tenant? The accusation that such councils "are spending other people's money as though it were other people's money" is difficult to refute. Inflationary pressures account for some of the alarming mathematics. But a larger part is a really dismaying degree of financial laxity and, presumably, a bland belief that there are no limits to which local rates cannot be raised or a central government bail-out secured.

That laxity plays the largest part is suggested by a comparison between London's metropolitan government—the Greater London Council—which in 1975 had to increase its budget by twenty-one percent to cover 1974's losses, and a much poorer local authority—that of Liverpool—which ended the year with a surplus and contrived to reduce tax rates by one percent whereas twenty to fifty percent rises are the general order of the British day. This achievement was not secured by cutting back on basic needs. It was the fruit of two very careful, difficult, and time-consuming procedures. One was a month-by-month balancing of the books to keep the Municipal Council exactly informed of the consequences of previous decisions and the impact of new ones—no more of "Let's slap another halfpenny on the rates, old boy." The other was even more demanding. It involved the effort by the Treasurer's office to get some idea of the number of people served by each program, the benefits and effectiveness of the service, and its actual impact on the city's efficiency and amenities. In the course of this audit, some astonishing details were uncovered—a municipal bathhouse used once a week by a single Chinese gentleman, for instance, or a municipal laundry of which a local politician said: "It would be cheaper to stand outside and give every customer two pound notes to go and spend at the launderette." Trivial examples, no doubt, but add together a sufficient number of such trivialities and the outcome is a large municipal deficit and a lot of furious taxpayers.

The answer at every level of government is as obvious as it is difficult—a severe and sustained audit of executive systems which, in both staffing and spending, have grown careless of the results of their actions—or inactions. That the difficulty is not confined to market economies is shown by the passionate pleas being made in planned economies to the citizens to increase their production and reduce soaring labor costs. And this appeal for cooperation is relevant in every society. Whether it is bathhouses or laundries, rented accommodation or garbage collection, playing fields or picnic spots, no account of public spending can offset careless, violent, dirty, and indifferent citizens. As we have seen, one of the chief arguments, under any kind of political system, for extending home ownership in settlements is the quantum jump in care that follows. In unfortunate Camden, annual management and maintenance costs, the highest in the country, reach $348 for each house. The national average is $94.

This need for sustained citizen support is nowhere more obvious than in the third of our three contexts—the maintenance of a clean and pleasing environment. There are, of course, needs for legislation and policy at higher levels of administration—national legislation to compel public and private enterprises to issue public assessments of the environmental impact of their activities, an area in which the United States, with its Council on Environmental Quality, its Environmental

Protection Agency, and its formal procedure for the publication of environmental impact statements, leads the world. Legislation on standards of emission—with adequate penalties—also belongs to the national level or dirty industries will move about looking for the laxest state. But in day-to-day living in the community, the quality of an environment is almost invariably the quality of the citizen's care. Municipalities can help by adopting performance standards for their sanitation services and rigorously insisting on an equal measure of service for each urban district. But as the Chinese—or the Dutch—have so clearly demonstrated in recent decades, nothing is cleaner than clean citizens and the best way to avoid an environmental mess is not to make it in the first place. With the increasing value of recycling, one can hope for greater local efforts to get the trash off the streets and out of the parks. But no city can afford to have an employee with a broom and a bucket following every group of beer-can-tossing, trash-throwing picnickers. In all the textbooks, cooperation is one of the hallmarks of good administration. But is the citizen in the throwaway society sufficiently taught that it is a two-way street?

And if, even in the wealthiest societies, the involvement of the citizens in the creative life of their settlements is a precondition of "the safe and happy life," how much more so is it in the poorer lands where neither manpower nor resources are available for elaborate governmental agencies and services at every level. Indeed, this involvement, achieved spontaneously in so many squatter settlements, can amount to the equivalent of effective administration. It must be reported. Provided there is the minimum provision of secure tenure, clean water, and construction materials which only government can give, there is life and fervor and work enough among the "urban pioneers" to sketch in the primary services, health, literacy, legal advice, employment openings, training in simple skills, to provide the first holds in urban life and begin the upgrading of "young settlements"—*pueblos jovenes*—into city districts. To achieve the right balance between these improving energies and the administrative help to supplement them is a delicate task. One recalls Mary Kingsley's analogy of the compassionate elephant. An instance of this overcare can be cited from Guatemala. In the 1960s, the government was worried that the squatter settlements in the capital city were becoming focuses for crime and political unrest. Government-sponsored committees were set up to help "solve" the officially defined "problems" and instead of the neighbors organizing their own neighborhoods, the city government tried to do it for them. Municipal workers started to install the new drain system—and did it inefficiently and at greater cost than the one already started by the neighbors themselves, many of whom were construction workers. The local community had included a varied number of skilled building workers. They also had their own information and social network, enabling them to obtain materials, tools, transport, and technical aid at minimal cost. The government's intervention disrupted the neighborhood and destroyed the highly effective informal self-help organization.

The trick in creative administration really is the textbook constellation of good administrative qualities—foresight to guide the migrants to usable sites, flrxibility to respond without overbearing authority to their still simple wants, economy to allow them to do all they can themselves—here, there is little choice—simplicity to concentrate on the basic needs and, above all, cooperation—the acceptance of every human being as a responsible citizen and the creation of the kind of dialogue that makes citizenship possible. If the symbol of the 1950s was the bulldozer flattening the tarpaper shacks, the 1970s offers better images of joint work and achieved respect. No doubt it is a journey of a thousand miles. Perhaps we can say that the first step has been taken and it is on the right road.

Part Six: The Universal City

26 A NEW ECONOMIC ORDER?

ALTHOUGH THE PRIMARY DECISIONS for human settlements rest squarely with national governments and their local authorities, there are areas where the consequences of urban and industrial living cross frontiers and require some widening of jurisdiction. The Joint Commission of the United States and Canada, overseeing the Great Lakes, whose shores they share, is an example of such a needed intergovernmental system of control. The Rhine, the Mediterranean, the Indus Valley are other instances where intergovernmental management is all the more important since progress toward effective action is obstructed and slow. But in the vast majority of cases, policies required to improve the condition of citizens living in their settlements, the national and local authority carry prime responsibility.

Nevertheless, all the world's settlements are not simply embedded in the local context. They are irretrievably part of the planetary system that has been in the making in the centuries between Vasco da Gama's first landfall in India, Guglielmo Marconi's first patent for a radio transmitter, and the first mushroom cloud above Los Alamos. The pressures of this world-wide system can be somewhat altered. Its benefits and disabilities can be differently shared. But, short of nuclear catastrophe, its interdependence has become an inescapable and irreversible fact.

It is also an unintended fact. Difficult as it is to insure some functioning order in the world's villages and cities and vast metropolises, at least the idea of better strategy and clearer policy is firmly lodged in the public imagination. But at the world level, there is no such consensus. Our present planetary interdependence simply reflects a series of chancey, casual historical happenings. No one planned a world society when, five hundred years ago, West Europeans sent out their little ships around the world or settled their first sparse colonies or opened up a mine here and a plantation there. Nor has there been much orderly or systematic attention since. In fact, two central facts in the historical inheritance we are experiencing in the last quarter of the twentieth century had so little intended design in them that we have all been taken totally by surprise.

These two facts should be repeated. No one foresaw that the control of epidemics introduced by modern medicine and spread around the world to save predominantly white soldiers in World War II would unleash an explosive growth in population. And no one foresaw the result of attaching little bits of distant continents to the Atlantic world's system of trade and investment and building around these "export sectors" the needed services for commerce, including growing seaports. But these ports and other dependent settlements have grown all into vast cities far in advance of any development in the local economy and have become the prime target of the exploding millions moving from rural poverty and stagnation to the hopes and disillusions of the urban scene. These tremendous upheavals have the casualness of forces of nature—of inundations, of ice ages, of mountain ranges thrown up by the collision of continental plates. Yet, however unintended, a kind of planetary framework has come into being and it does not need the highest forms of intellectual perception to see that it does not work well for at least half the human race and that it threatens to work even worse in the decades ahead. And it is, above all, in the developing world's megalopolises that the deterioration seem to be reaching its peak.

But if no one exactly planned such a world, we do at least have some clear ideas of how it came about and of what it represents. If we go back to our three contexts of examination—the intended society, the just society, the environmentally sustainable society—and take first the issue of an almost universal lack of definite planning or purpose, what we find in our planet is not an "economic order," old or new. It is not an order at all but a series of political, economic, and social arrangements and accidents inherited from the period of Western colonialism or Western revolution and held together, since World War II, by a shifting set of ideas, alliances, experiments, confrontations, and mistakes.

The Fifties saw the postwar reconstruction of Western Europe and Japan through the farsighted generosity of the United States, the relinquishing—easily or reluctantly—of Europe's political empires, the redevelopment of planetary institutions in the United Nations, and the setting up of two international financial bodies, the World Bank and the International Monetary Fund, which, as fundraising and disbursing bodies, were given weighted voting in favor of the major lenders. They thus reflected very specifically the world's immediate postcolonial balance of economic forces—seventy-five percent of the wealth in the developed "Northern" lands, seventy-five percent of the population in the largely undeveloped "South."

Across the innovations of joint international institutions there also fell the shadow of Cold War confrontation during which the Soviet Union confirmed a dominant position in Eastern Europe and China completed its communist revolution. Soon after, the Korean War in 1950 fixed for a time a gulf of hostility between the new China and the United States.

For Europe, Japan, and the Soviet bloc, the following decades were ones of unprecedented growth. These were productive, confident, and, for some, even halcyon days which, however, America did not fully share. In spite of almost as rapid a spurt of economic growth, its deepening involvement in Vietnam darkened the prospect. But in general during these years, the already industrialized powers succumbed to a certain euphoria. Western Europe forgot its ancient enmities and began to forge a new community, building it audaciously on a Franco-German compact; in other words, on the cooperation of two bitter secular opponents whose tribal wars had, in this century alone, cost half as many lives as were even born in Europe before industrialism began. Was there not a spark of hope here that, at last, after all the millennia since the Cities of the Plain, fiercely independent sovereign units could be relearning the arts of peace, of a common life under law: Could one faintly see in the U.N. Charter a similar hint of enlarging frontiers of order on a planetary scale?

In economic life, too, the winds of change seemed propitious. Not for a century had there been such a burst of world-wide economic expansion. Fueled by oil at under two dollars a barrel, underpinned by grain held steady by America's price support and land bank system, economies took to growing steadily by five to six percent a year—the nineteenth-century average was not above three percent—international trade expanded by an annual ten percent, and the faith was abroad that, provided the developing nations followed the same pattern—high capital investment (say, fifteen to twenty percent of GNP), rapid industrialization, quick expansion of educated manpower, massive investment from abroad—they would follow the same stages of growth and arrive with reasonable speed at the final felicity of the high consumption society.

Meanwhile, the process would be hastened and, for the West, communism deterred, if the industrialized market economies gave both concessionary aid and private investment to the Third World, especially to those countries which had been Europe's colonies only a decade or so before. It looked like an economic "order." It felt like an "economic order." In the Western world, publishing houses, universities, newspaper offices proclaimed it as an economic order based on the confidence the Keynesian full employment at home and judicious aid abroad had indeed banished the uncertainties of nineteenth-century growth and ended forever the risk of another 1929.

We should not exaggerate the halcyon mood. Moods anyway always look more halcyon in retrospect. The Vietnam shadow grew darker. The sudden, alarming Sino-Soviet rift presaged unknown future risks even though it did deprive Cold Warriors of the bogey of a great big bad Sino-Soviet bloc and was followed by a steady movement toward greater East/West trade and the beginnings of *détente*. But there were other preoccupations. One or two "eccentrics" began pointing out that planetary growth at a steady five percent a year was using up resources at a hectic rate and making a remarkable environmental mess. More "serious" observers began to look at the U.N.'s global censuses of the Fifties and Sixties and do the quick calculus that suggested a world doubled in size by the year 2000. But it was not until the 1970s that the house of cards of presumed "order" began to slide.

With hindsight, we can see how flimsy the structure had become. It had been maintained by America running a very large dollar deficit, swollen in the late Sixties by the inflationary pressures of war costs uncovered by fresh taxation. Not the careful prescriptions of the International Monetary Fund, not the trade negotiations undertaken under the General Agreement on Tariffs and Trade (GATT), not the organized lending of the new international and regional banks had been the factors underpinning financial stability for two decades. It had simply been confidence in the dollar. Now confidence in its value was eroded. The collapse of the whole system of fixed parities in 1971 was the first card pulled out at ground level from the shaky house of the world economy. A universal boom, forcing up all raw material prices, pulled out a second. Then came the Russians buying up virtually the entire American grain reserve and tripling world food prices; another card fell. Then OPEC quintupled oil prices and the whole house began to fall apart.

True, it did not fall to pieces as totally and irretrievably as people feared. Financial mechanisms worked and were even able to recycle a sudden $80 thousand million oil debt. Social insurance and welfare payments gave the unemployed in market economies a margin of purchasing power. Indeed, strong wage bargaining protected the wage level so well that inflation continued even with five to six percent of the Western work force unemployed. Constant contact between governments and heads of central banks prevented panic actions. Floating rates protected weak countries against fatal runs on their currency. Compared with 1929, the position could have been worse. A curious muddled buoyancy kept some sort of system going. But one thing became increasingly clear. It was not the sort of muddle that half of humanity could live with, and it was not by any stretch of the imagination an "order" which could accommodate three thousand million more people in just thirty more years. Today, therefore, we confront a "moment of truth," an observation of the emperor's lack of clothes, or any other cliché available to describe a situation in which people stop, rub their eyes, and realize that what they have been imagining simply does not exist. And what is not there is precisely an economic order within which the majority of mankind in the world's settlements can hope to survive.

The core of this new perception is not the difficulty in developed societies of combining full employment with price stability—although that enters in. It is not the necessity, yet the difficulty, of drawing all partners in the industrial process into new forms of industrial democracy—although it is part of the problem. It is not the need for greater flexibility in planned societies or better sharing in market economies. It is not even, as yet, an intolerable strain on necessary resources and energy or any series of impending and irreversible ecological catastrophes. These are still over the hill. What is clear, immediate, unavoidable, and central is the fact that for at least one thousand million people now (and for two thousand million before long) in other words, for nearly a quarter of the planet with incomes of less than $200 a head, the gains, the growth, the expansion, the hope, the euphoria of the last two decades have simply swept by, leaving them in as great a misery as ever and with little hope of immediate improvement. According to World Bank estimates, the increase in income the poorest countries can expect in the Seventies is an average of three dollars—from $105 to $108. For the developed world, the forecast is for an average of $3,100 to $4,000, a gain of $900.

Nor is this comparison the end of the story. The world's poor increasingly know that their condition is not an act of God but the choice of man. The transistor radios have not been bought in vain. Ten percent of the poor world's wealthy elite have not built their villas or bought their cars unnoticed. The gap, the gulf between "the nation of the rich and the nation of the poor" is not only planet-wide. It is regional and local and wherever it exists it is becoming a profound and ineradicable part of planetary consciousness. One can even guess that in world terms, we have entered the equivalent of the nineteenth century's "Hungry Forties." The "Angry Eighties" lie ahead.

How could it be otherwise: What was hidden by the twenty years of postwar euphoria, by the political ending of colonialism, by the expanding trade figures, by world-wide increases in GNP, by the stages-of-growth theories which saw the rest of the world following America—or Russia—over the obstacles of early industrialization, was one bleak fact. For the poorest countries, there has been no decisive progress. The Indian subcontinent, equatorial Africa, parts of the Caribbean, and Andean South America are as poor as ever and the poorest among them are actually poorer still. In some other better endowed nations, notably in Latin America, change *has* occurred and average per capita GNP has increased sharply. But within the countries, once again, the poor have grown poorer. And the reason is as absolutely straightforward as it was from the earliest days of the burgeoning market economy when John Locke and Adam Smith missed its social significance. An uncorrected market does not help the poor. It is a mechanism for satisfying the demands of those who com-

mand resources and can enter the market as purchasers. Those who
lack the income stay out. It is also a system of power in which decisions about the distribution of the wealth that is created are made by
those with enough clout to command or bargain. If growth is pursued
without thought of distribution, there is a real risk that the early
gainers may become too entrenched in power and privilege to be ready
to change. In industrializing Britain, the entire surplus went to the men
of property for nearly a century—in fact, until the workers began to
learn strength through association, the franchise was extended to adult
males and the horrors of the new cities stirred even sluggish con-
sciences to directly corrective action by government. Ever since, these
three factors—strength through association, political power, and social
responsibility—have in various mixes determined the distribution of
rewards, both in market and in planned economies. But at the planetary level, these institutions, forces, and strategies barely exist: The
result follows with Euclidean precision. The poor lose out.

In fact, they are, as we have seen, at an even greater disadvantage
than the nineteenth-century poor. No open lands for migration and settlement await them. Forty million people crossing the Atlantic to the
Americas took considerable strains off nineteenth-century Europe.
Today, such a figure is less than three years of population growth in
India alone. Then, the whole productive apparatus was so new and relatively unsophisticated that iron masters and mill owners really desperately needed "hands"—manpower to do all the jobs the machines had
not yet been invented to do. Today, a modern workplace can cost
$50,000, a $12 million chemical complex provide forty jobs. In Venezuela's mineral-rich province of Guyana, each new work place—in
steel plants, aluminum smelters, and hydroelectric schemes—may
require $240,000. Meanwhile, population continues to grow by 3.4
percent a year. Yet who needs "hands" when an automated process,
does it all?

We should also remind ourselves that resources are not simply to
be measured in materials and energy. They include managerial skills,
accountancy, banking, insurance, research—perhaps, above all, research. All these costly inputs to an ever more sophisticated technological system are not available in sufficient scale in developing lands
or they are available in Western forms which can be wholly inappropriate to local conditions, climates, work habits, and availability of

labor (usually massive) and of capital (universally scarce). What the developing people do have—raw, unworked materials and raw, unskilled labor—are, so far, the least costly elements in any enterprise. So while what they have to sell is cheap, what they have to buy is dear. To give only one example, if we exclude oil, the export of twelve major raw materials accounts for about eighty percent of the export earnings of the developing countries. In 1974, they received $30 thousand million for these materials. By the time the goods derived from these exports were sold to the final consumers, they cost $200 thousand million. The bulk of the difference—$170 thousand million—was absorbed by wealthy processors and middlemen largely in the developed world. Under such conditions foreign trade growing by ten percent a year cleans out poor nations' resources all the more rapidly. The reefs go, the lodes are exhausted. Even for renewable resources, the strain is great. Competition from synthetics—man-made fibers, plastics, all the products of more sophisticated chemical breakthroughs—has profoundly depressed rubber and cotton and sisal markets for the poorer lands.

Yet all the while the unskilled labor force of the poorer countries goes on growing. To keep them alive, to secure some investment, the developing world has gone into debt to the tune of $130 thousand million. But out of the imbalance has come a steadily declining share in world trade for the poorest nations—from around thirty-five percent in 1950 to seventeen percent in 1970. The upswing of 1971/1972 has not lasted. Only oil and grain hold up. Virtually the whole "value added" has continued to drain off to the rich—the rich elite locally, the rich industrialized states in the world at large.

This was, of course, the classic pattern of transfer under colonialism. So far, the political change of ending colonial rule has changed economics relatively little. Indeed, the extraordinary postwar growth of Atlantic-based multinational corporations may have made economic dependence rather stronger. Since 1950, these giants have grown two to three times more rapidly than the industrialized economies as a whole. In 1972 the annual sales of the twelve largest manufacturing corporations equal $144 thousand million—a figure that exceeds the total annual national income of the world's thirty-five poorest states and of their thousand million inhabitants. The rationale of the multinationals' activity—to buy where labor and materials are cheapest, sell the product to the highest bidder, and keep the profits in lands of lowest taxation is a perfectly legitimate market operation. It maximizes returns and can easily be thought of as maximizing resource use. What it does not necessarily do is enhance the economic advantage of the countries on which its activities impinge. On the contrary, where such powerful engines of production come in, as complete operations, to undertake a manufacturing process, they often knock out local weaker enterprise or effectively, if unconsciously, insure that it never starts. This is especially the case where the multinational uses local loan capital for the operations but repatriates a good share of the profits. Once again, the uncorrected market works—but for the wealthy, not the poor.

The diagnosis of our disorderly "order" is clear enough. So is the needed antidote. It is, in simplest terms, to transfer to the world level the safeguards, bargaining powers, redistributive policies, and environmental concern which correct the market, guide its useful energies, and are now virtually a matter of course at the national level. This, surely, is what any "new economic order" is all about, to move from the powerful and capricious energies of the unalloyed market to the structures of cooperation and justice which have alone proved able to tame it and use it for the purposes of civilized existence. The change is fundamentally from basic "disorder" to what might begin to deserve the title of a community.

Part of the change is a matter of power. We have seen, in the action of OPEC, how effective such shifts of power can be. Since 1973, the most developed nations have had a little experience of what is the normal condition of poorer countries—the condition of not being in control of some of the basic decisions affecting their economic life. In fact, as we have seen, the whole vast accumulation of oil balances by the newly enriched oil states has not produced economic collapse, any more than the tripling of world food prices has irretrievably undermined European recovery. There is, we have learned, a good deal of "give" in our very disorderly economic order. But this is speaking only for the rich. The poorest lands are still hit by catastrophe. Higher oil costs mean higher energy costs, higher fertilizer costs, the risk of deepening agricultural inadequacy. The 1975 harvests have been good. But there are still no world grain reserves. What of the next decade? Unless some of the influence gained by the newly rich oil states can be used in the interests of the poorest—and this shift of emphasis accepted by the oil rich—we could still be only a year from famine on a massive scale.

The first step is, therefore, the acceptance at the planetary level of an "intended order" incorporating the institutional and social safeguards of domestic society. Only thus can catastrophe in men's settlements be fended off. A new bargain to stabilize commodity prices can be seen, if we will, as equivalent to the modern wage bargain which in market economies insures a higher flow of resources to the less well-off. Wider representation for Third World countries in such critical institutions as the World Bank and the International Monetary Fund corresponds, again if we seek an historical analogy, to the widening of the franchise and the slow but irreversible extension of universal suffrage. And the acceptance of a social ethic for the world as a whole, a determination to see that, as Dr. Henry Kissinger has put it, in ten years' time no child goes hungry to bed, is simply to take, once again, the established practices of the general welfare, now common to every civilized society, and give them a planetary dimension.

Its direct expression would be, as in domestic society, progressive taxation and the general welfare. At present, aid is barely a sketch of this. It is still charity, the patronage of choice, the selecting of client-states, not the automatic transfer of resources guided by objective universal criteria—so much percent of GNP on the side of the wealthy givers, so much poverty and need on the side of the receiving states. Other transfers guaranteeing the essential principle of automaticity could be the priority issuance of new, international credit—Special Drawing Rights—to the poorest countries, user-taxes on international waterways and air routes, commodity taxes paid by rich importers, revenues from whatever seabed resources are left after the 200-mile carve up by national coastal interests has, probably disastrously, gone ahead. There is neither doubt nor difficulty about constructing such an automatic system. What is lacking is political will.

In essence, when all the complications and arguments and confrontations and misunderstandings are overcome, the issue of political vision will decide the question of any new economic order. In physical fact, in instant communication, in increasing material interdependence, the globe is already one. Only we still lack the necessary social and moral solidarity to turn physical interconnections into a shared community.

The figures speak for themselves. There can be criticisms of the effectiveness and intentions of aid—mixing military clients with the genuinely needy, exporting inappropriate technologies, for years disastrously missing the crucial importance of the farm sector. But valid criticisms, generously attended to, would have improved the programs, not started to extinguish them. No, the fall in aid from the "old rich" from 0.6 percent of their GNP in 1960 to 0.3 percent in 1974, with the possibility of a further fall to 0.2 percent by 1980 is, above all, a retreat from justice, using specific failures as cover for the lapse of moral will. That the Scandinavian countries are near or at the one percent of GNP first proposed for aid in the Sixties, that virtually all the newly rich oil states have made commitments exceeding one percent of GNP—with Kuwait and Saudi Arabia at 15.8 and 13.4 percent respectively for 1974—are signs enough that choice, not necessity, has determined the falling away of Western aid. And the whole movement represents a retreat from the kind of global institutions of justice without which markets alone may go on creating wealth—but only for the minority. Until these institutions are in place, life for man on earth, life in his settlements, rich and poor, North and South, in village or megalopolis, must remain a haunted, danger-shadowed uncertain risk. However muddled the outlines may appear, a "new international economic order," aiming at justice and cooperation, is, quite literally, a matter of life and death.

27 THE COST OF JUSTICE

IF WE ACCEPT the goal of a world order specifically designed to secure a fairer distribution of the planet's resources and to put an end to concentrations of wealth, both within and between nations, that are profoundly incompatible with human justice, dignity, and self-respect, the next question is to determine the instruments, the scale, and the priorities of such an international strategy. In this process of budgeting, it is virtually impossible to separate the expenditures that can be specifically assigned to settlements. As we have seen, food, water, drainage, work, health, schooling, transport—all are critical elements in decent human communities, and the best investment for a city may well be a hybrid seed just as a market town may chiefly need a rapid bus or train link with a larger city. But the World Bank has made some tentative estimates of the basic investments required to overcome the fundamental obstacles to development over the next decade, and they provide a useful starting point.

In one sense, they are modest—food and nutrition, $42 thousand million; education, $25 thousand million; rural and urban water supply, $28 thousand million; urban housing, $16 thousand million; urban transport, $8 thousand million; population and health programs, $6 thousand million—in all, therefore, about $125 thousand million over ten years or $12.5 thousand million a year. This we can usefully compare with what the world will probably spend on armaments over the same period. At present, as we have seen, the sum is roughly $250 thousand million a year, more than the entire wealth (GNP) of all the world's poorer countries in 1972—with their one and three quarter thousand million people, with average per capita incomes of less than

$200 a year.* The cumulative ten-year figure for arms would therefore be $2,500 thousand million. If we take the World Bank's estimate of basic needs, we reach the remarkable conclusion that the entire proposed spending on the works of peace for an entire decade would amount to no more than half the world's *annual* bill for weapons. A yearly five percent transfer from arms spending to development would fund the entire World Bank program. Yet when, a couple of years ago, the Soviet Union proposed a ten percent cut in arms, the savings to be transferred to development aid, the response was a resounding silence. Even allowing for all the difficulties of verification and for the peculiar fact that, in terms of comparative GNP, the Soviet Union is itself probably the biggest spender on armaments among the larger powers, the proposal at least deserved examination and today, when the needs of the poorest nations are more desperate than ever, it should be revived. Quite a few children need not die of gastro-enteritis or live with the permanently maimed brains produced by protein deficiency if the world could lessen just a little its lunatic games of overkill and "first-strike capability" and "I'm the King of the castle" competitiveness, if it could set to work instead to counter the fundamental killers—deep-rooted, workless poverty, with the malnutrition it implies and the diseases that filth and lack of food make fatal—cholera, dysentery, measles, tuberculosis, and all the other scourges which send half the world to their graves before forty and give them, year in year out, the misery and weariness of griping intestines, confused minds, and aching heads. They ask for bread, so we give them a recoilless rifle. Or rather the developed nations appear neither to hear the plea nor to make any relevant comparisons. The total lack of proportion in the whole exercise gives it a weird atmosphere of unreality—as though one had strayed into a science fiction narrative and landed on a planet in which only fear and greed were institutionalized at a global level, a planet inhabited and ruled by anthropoids with only fossilized and vestigial intelligence and a hideous preoccupation with death.

Yet we must not despair of rationality. Perhaps the sheer vast scale of the wastage of materials, energy, and trained brain power involved in armaments can persuade humanity to come to see in such irrational and fantastic expenditures the most direct and easily divertible source

* China is included in this group.

of funds for peaceful development. And there is a further reason for hope. At some point, some statesman is going to discover the link between arms spending and inflation. If every tank were a tractor, better grain harvests in Russia might help to stabilize food prices. If some of the research funds and skills devoted to the next generation of missiles were available for critical breakthroughs in solar cell technology, energy costs could be falling, not rising. To transfer capital and skill from arms to development would not only help the poor, it could bring direct gains to the rich as well. If the nations insist on carrying such completely inflationary expenditures even at a time of gross inflation, how much more effectively might they not manage their own economies—as well as the world's—if resources and brain power were released from the arms programs in order to provide more food, more materials, more water, more trained minds, more skilled and healthy bodies—in short, more of all the basic inputs of productivity which because, unlike arms, they are *real* resources, would help to mop up purchasing power, lower the pressure on scarcity prices, and bring inflation under better control.

Let us then continue to hope that governments can be persuaded to consider something like a ten percent cut in arms and to decide to devote the savings to a steady flow of $25 thousand million a year for fundamental development. Such a flow would exceed by more than a quarter the aid provided in 1973—which amounted to $9.3 thousand million from the market economies, $1.5 thousand million from the planned economies (including $378 million from China, mainly to African countries) about $5.4 thousand million from the various international organizations (the World Bank group of agencies is in the lead with $2.6 thousand million) and, in 1974, $2.6 thousand million from OPEC (out of $8.2 thousand million committed to assistance). The additional ten percent released from arms spending and guided not by military strategy or client-seeking or political stratagems or any other form of "gross national self-interest," could set the world on a sounder path of development and provide the essential underpinning for growth in justice. And it would begin to institutionalize sharing, justice, and the common life, without which no community—planetary, national, or local—can hope to live in peace.

The achievement of justice would depend not simply on available resources but on the instruments of control and the priorities of policy.

Ideally, as we have noted, the instruments should become increasingly international with a steady increase in the representation of all interested parties—donors and recipients alike—just as, in a parliamentary state, all citizens are equally voters whether they are chairman of General Motors or a retired schoolteacher. In the last decade, the share of international organizations in world assistance programs has steadily increased—from little more than a thousand million in 1963 to the $5.39 thousand million figure in 1973. Some of the U.N. system's regional banks have shown an explosive growth of activity—the Asian Development Bank's investment, for instance, growing from $5 million in 1968 to over $360 million in 1973. Should the aim to institutionalize the whole giving of aid on a more truly multilateral basis gather momentum, some of the necessary institutions are already in place and some of them, notably the World Bank, have shown a steadily increasing scope and flexibility in their lending. Bilateral governmental assistance will no doubt continue. But if the concept of a genuine world community is to gather strength, international channels need to be used for continued and accelerating growth.

But all forms of governmental and multilateral assistance, with varying degrees of concessionary finance—from grants to low interest charges to long repayment periods—are still well short of the flow of private investment from the market economies into Latin America, Asia, and Africa. This has grown from $30 thousand million in 1967 to about $44 thousand million at the end of 1972, much of it supplied, particularly in Latin America, by multinational corporations. Here, too, institutional changes are required to turn an often exploitative relationship into a mutually beneficial arrangement.

One aspect of this readaptation is to encourage multinational management to reconsider the introduction of some forms of highly capital-intensive technology into economies chiefly characterized by abundance of labor. But this in turn implies local governments not completely hooked on automated car assembly plants and anxious instead to provide the mass of the people with the simpler goods of everyday life at a price which they can afford. Another possibility is a strategy of phasing out foreign ownership over a period of years, perhaps by the payment of local taxes in the form of equity shares. The nationalization of oil in Venezuela is an interesting exercise in mutual understanding and restraint, the oil companies continuing to provide world-wide links and services but the country securing control over its basic resource.

That there is need for a new framework of genuinely shared interests is now admitted. A formal code of practice has been worked out under the auspices of the UN and the OECD. Under it, companies agree, among other principles, to conform their policies to local national objectives, to avoid practices which impede competition from local or other enterprises, to avoid all forms of discrimination in employment, and to publish in much greater detail basic information about their financial operations. The code does not go as far as some governments would wish, particularly in making more explicit the relations between profits, capital movements, levels of remuneration, and the degree to which local affiliates of multinationals may be engaged in selling their products not on the open market but to their parent company and thus establishing an internalized monopoly. But national governments have probably more power than they are ready to use to keep a close check on the undesirable consequences of external investment. The member governments of the Andean Group in Latin America have, for instance, laid down their own code regulating the practices to which investors must conform. A more general adoption of such regulations would lessen the temptation for multinational companies to "shop around" to find the most compliant borrower to involve and possibly to exploit.

This brings us back to a central point. No aid, no change in the international rules, no greater readiness to give priority to the poorest countries will help people in their settlements if their own governments have no commitment to distributive justice. And many quite simply have not. It can only be repeated. Any kind of genuinely social and constructive development in the world's settlements—from village to metropolis—depends upon drawing *all* the people into the process, treating them as resources and not problems, and giving them a decisive part in the creation of their own future. Even under the incredibly favorable conditions of the nineteenth century, with free land to be opened up, with cheap food pouring in to prove Malthus wrong, with a slowly growing work force and a still labor-intensive industrial structure, a general advance toward modern standards of welfare occurred only after the ending of feudal relationships on the land and continued to expand only where a measure of political power and responsibility was secured by the whole citizen body. Where, as in whole regions of Latin America or in the constellations of villages across the face of the Indian subcontinent, eighty percent of the land belongs to less than ten percent of the people, the hopes of further development, under any conditions of external aid, are slim indeed. Similarly, in the vast cities, only a full involvement of the poorest citizens, the migrants, the "urban pioneers" in their own building and working and trading offers any hope of drawing the mass of people back from the margins of life and the margins of despair.

There is, therefore, some force—as well as daunting political difficulty—to the argument that multilateral aid as a matter of principle and all forms of aid as a question of practice should be concentrated not only on those areas which are in greatest need but on those where the full and active participation of the people is being sought and secured. The priority of priorities is to overcome inhuman poverty by investing in the productivity of the people themselves. Possible policies for achieving this participation have already been outlined—a new emphasis on the small farm sector; the building up of intermediate urban centers where public services, artisans, and workshops and small scale industry can attend to farmers' needs and also, as a result of adequate transport, sell to the bigger centers; the introduction of pure water and sewerage in both the small and the large settlements; the granting of secure tenure for city housing; encouragement of both entrepreneurial and self-help building; the creation of local centers for health and education (formal and informal); financial support for the "bazaar economy" and for small-scale industrial suppliers linked to larger manufacturing units—in short, all the variety of policies advocated in preceding chapters but brought together, underpinned by the needed capital and provided with that delicate balance of administrative and managerial assistance which encourages local initiative and self-confidence and does not take over from the people the responsibilities they can carry themselves.

Clearly such a program covers virtually every aspect of a developing economy. In the immediate future we cannot be sure either of a quick mobilization of the needed resources nor of the commitment of governments to priorities which often override the interests of their own elites. We need, therefore, graduated strategies, with phases prepared and actions that are possible short of a full-scale conversion of rich nations to the concept of sharing as a planetary obligation and of rich local leaders to the concept of social justice and citizen involvement as a condition of survival. At the general level, one such priority is to help the poorest nations first—those with annual average per capita incomes of less than $200. Another—examined in the next chapter—is to carry out the food strategy proposed at the World Food Conference in 1974. But to supplement it, reinforce it, and provide at least one essential part of it quickly, there is an area of action that could and should be undertaken at once. It does more of itself to build up people's own capacity than perhaps any other alternative. It represents a need so basic and human that not even the most indifferent or arrogant of ruling groups could block it. It avoids enormous human costs. By saving children's lives, it encourages the stabilization of family size. And—at $28 thousand million over ten years—it is only a small part not only of arms spending but of present flows of aid. This priority is quite simply to insure to every village and city safe drinking water and reasonable sewage disposal. If there can be an immediate commitment, let it be here. Free the people from the most crippling and degrading handicaps—of ill health, perpetually renewed and perpetually darkening every shack and hovel with the risk of an agonizing death. If we cannot accomplish this minimum, what hope is there for all the rest? But if we can, the consequent release of hope, energy, and resources might amaze the world. Wealthy societies and wealthy people have forgotten this particular human tragedy. London's or Moscow's cholera is over a century old. Only the occasional tourist picks up dysentery or hepatitis. But for the poor of the world, gastric troubles are the background of life itself. If they could be cleansed away, it would be a world reborn—not surely an extravagant achievement for less than $3 thousand million a year.

28 PLANETARY HOUSEKEEPING

THIS ISSUE of water and sewage brings us to the third of our contexts—using the world's resources with greater care and safeguarding the environment. And here, although—as with the goods of justice and cooperation—the major decisions rest with governments, local authorities, and the whole range of leadership in farming and industry, there are certain aspects of resource use and environmental protection that are beginning to involve wider regions and the globe itself. These demand new concepts and practices of shared sovereignty, new levels of responsibility, and, above all, a new readiness to see the world not as a simple uncorrected trading system but as the beginnings of a genuine and interdependent community.

Perhaps the most direct method of establishing the possible jurisdictions of this new interdependence is to study them not in abstraction but in two concrete case studies. One concerns a resource, the other a region. Both carry larger implications and principles for the world community. The resource is basic—food supplies—without which there can be no life, in or out of settlements. The region is the Mediterranean—an endangered, nearly enclosed sea but demonstrating risks relevant to the globe's wider oceans which, in the last analysis, are all inland seas enclosed within the frontiers of Planet Earth.

Let us begin this brief look at world food by recalling the shortcomings of the uncorrected market. First, the subsistence farmer does not enter the market at all. He provides for himself or starves. Next, any signs of scarcity begin to push up prices and as they rise, more and more of the poor and semi-poor find a minimum diet beyond their reach. Meanwhile, those with economic power—in this case, large farmers and merchants—are buying all the grain they can hoard in order to force up prices still further and enlarge their own returns. The cycle of deprivation extends to an ever wider group. Finally, at the peak of the shortage, between harvests, the majority are malnourished, a minority (or sometimes a majority) die and a small elite make large fortunes.

If, in the following years, there are a succession of excellent harvests and even gluts, these same farmers will be in the forefront of those demanding government intervention to keep prices up and to introduce public purchase and storage—on the lines of American policy in the 1950s and the 1960s. But if no such measures are introduced, the farm community will see the prices fall drastically and the smallest farmers will reach ruin by another route. In addition, if a country's absolute limits of food production have been reached—land entirely cultivated, water fully utilized, fertilizer at optimum levels of application—then the market can do nothing but insure the continuance of high scarcity prices, since they no longer perform their creative function in the market—that of encouraging the production of more supplies. The limits have already been reached.

In fact, farming is so subject to gluts and famines, so at the mercy of weather, so liable to insecurity and fluctuation, that few countries are foolhardy enough to leave its operation to the pure market. From 1950 to 1970, support prices, the withdrawal of land from cultivation, the transfer of food abroad on concessionary terms gave America stability in the price of grain. Similarly, although the gluts produced by European farming are not particularly beneficent, a glut is healthier than a deficit and under a wiser system of support, given not to prices but to farm incomes, Britain's long-neglected agriculture has become one of the world's most productive since World War II.

There have been disadvantages. In the longer run, shipping food to poor countries is less constructive than assisting the development of their own agriculture. But for two decades, there were no famines. Farming in developed lands went through a quite orderly reduction of its labor force. Steady food prices checked inflation. All in all, it was a time of stability. But it was not market stability. It was controlled by the community. At the national level, sole reliance on the market was modified by the stabilizing policies of national governments.

But we still have *no* such mechanisms at the world level and this in spite of the fact that in the next three decades, both the supply and the demand side of the food equation are likely to become more and more unbalanced. Demand will go up as the world approaches seven thousand million by the next century. True, not all these new nations will represent "effective demand" since most of the increase will be among those who already earn less than $200 a year and hence barely enter the market even now. Even so, they cannot simply be dismissed to starve, and the millions with a larger margin of wealth will begin to press in on food supplies and prices.

There will be comparable pressures on the side of world supply. Only North America has any hope of providing immediate food surpluses on any scale and today, with all its land brought back under cultivation and no reserves at present, even these surpluses are unsure. Add possible modifications in climate, cutting some days off the ripening season in the north. Add a fluctuating yet massive demand for grain by Russia as a result. Add the needs of the 400 million extra Chinese due to be born before the year 2000. And one conclusion alone is possible. Leave grain to an uncontrolled market and only the rich will eat. The archetype of this dreadful fatality is the British Government in 1847 exporting food from Ireland in the name of market principles while the potato blight plunged the whole people into starvation.

It is also necessary to repeat that at the moment the rich are actually overeating. North America increased its consumption between 1945 and 1970 from about 1,000 pounds of grain per capita to 1,900 pounds of grain. The Russians are catching up. The vast increase is due to consuming grain eaten and predigested by other animals in order to produce meat with something like an eighty percent loss of food values along the way. The Indian's 400 pounds—which is grossly inadequate—is largely eaten directly as grain. It is this increased pressure of affluent capitalists and communists stuffing themselves with high protein that has helped to push grain prices up to triple their 1971 level. Those who tend to blame world inflation entirely on OPEC's pricing of its major and often single resource, might perhaps ask the peoples of North America, Europe, and Russia whether the stomach, too, may not become an unconscious monopolist. The question is specially relevant when we recall that Norway has, for medical reasons, reduced high-protein imports, based on feed-lot meat production, and that a hardly radical organization, the American Medical Association, has recommended a third less meat consumption for sedentary America. To have obesity a widespread disease in a starving world is itself a perversion of right order. "Grain sheiks" we can all become, using our appetites to rig the market.

These trends, unchanged, point in only one direction—the near likelihood that by 1980 the world, considered purely as a market, will be condemning the world's poorer settlements to deepening deprivation and the risk of massive starvation. Then, as public order disintegrates and overall market demand declines, collapse may follow even for the rich, however confidently and profitably they market their oil and their grain meanwhile.

The answer to this fundamental problem facing the human city—for if people cannot eat, what else can they do?—is insoluble in purely local terms. Nations cannot invent food surpluses. Expanded production takes time. In some areas, it is not even possible. Nowhere is global interdependence more inescapable than in the basic area of man's daily bread. But if we accept the global dimension, there is an answer—the triple strategy of the Rome Food Conference which precisely meets the main weaknesses of the unmitigated market approach. The creation of a basic 10-million-ton grain reserve would prevent immediate short-term disasters and check the desperate cycle of hoarding and price increases which a food crisis, under market conditions, instantly precipitates. As yet, the 10 million tons fall a little short. America has increased its commitment of grain, OPEC of finance. Europe is, apparently, sitting on its hands.

The longer-term buffer stock plan is designed to insure that an agreed period of consumption—say, sixty days or some 200 million tons of grain—is always covered by carry-over stocks. Thus it insures stable prices, as in the Fifties and Sixties, and gives farmers security in production, food processors security in manufacture, and the consumer security of supply. So far, no clear response has emerged. But at least the debate is engaged.

But at the risk of repeating some earlier arguments, it must be emphasized that its starting point is the fact that the temperate grain reserve in North America will *not* be sufficient for the claims of the 1980s. The food gap by then could be as high as 80 million tons of grain a year and the Great Plains themselves can be subject to drought. The only security is a steady five percent annual increase in food production in the developing world with an annual investment of perhaps 25 thousand million dollars, possibly five thousand million of it coming from abroad.

The target is possible. The oil states are beginning to respond with promises of investment. So is its technical feasibility. Small-scale developing agriculture is desperately short of all the needed inputs—credit, fertilizer, improved seed, water, marketing systems, storage. The very poverty of present methods is the chief hope for such real and remarkable increases in productivity as have been achieved in China or Taiwan. But, as we have seen, all these improvements demand higher priority, more capital, land reform, sustained commitment, and new research. They stretch out into other areas of the world community—to energy for water pumps, tractors, and fertilizer, to biological transformations such as the development of nitrogen-fixing grain, to the export incomes of countries which can never be self-sufficient in food and must always depend upon what one can hope will become a social world market. And they also depend on a measure of direct restraint on the overeating carried on in the developed world's "protein sanctuary." Yet, whatever strand of the problem we follow, we come back to the same bedrock fact. If the world is to be no more than a trading system accommodating the special interests of groups of varying power, the poorest will starve. But, in a genuine community based upon planetary justice, obligation, and sharing, we can hope never again to hear the desperate cry raised by Thomas Hood in the Hungry Forties:

> Oh God that bread should be so dear
> And flesh and blood so cheap.

And if this is true of food, it is true of energy, of water, of every other fundamental yet potentially scarce resource. For all its immense value as an impersonal indicator of needs and wants in an abundant economy, the market's method of conservation of scarcity is simply to exclude the weak. In a true community, the solution is solidarity and sharing. There is no other choice.

The position is the same when we turn to the second issue of "planetary housekeeping"—conservation in the sense of cleanliness and environmental integrity. Once again, most decisions in this area are determined at the national and local level. But some of them transcend national frontiers and demand cooperation between states on a regional and a global scale. The interdependence is, inevitably, particularly inescapable when what has to be protected literally knows no frontiers and washes earth's "human shores" in total indifference to the line-drawers and makers of maps.

The more enclosed the waters, the more people living along the coasts, the greater the risks of pollution become and the greater, therefore, the need for regional management. The Mediterranean is just such a case. It is largely an inland sea, surrounded by eighteen countries, of which the northern ten are either highly developed or on the way there. The southern states, at an earlier stage of modernization, will nonetheless steadily increase the exploitation of their coastlines. In addition, the reopening of the Suez Canal is about to increase very rapidly the use of the Mediterranean for transit. So will the proposed linking of the Rhine and Rhone by a canal capable of carrying 3,000-ton barges.

But the load carried by the sea is already vast. Seventy-five percent of the people around the Mediterranean—27 million—live in Spain, France, Italy, Yugoslavia, Greece, and Turkey. All of them freely dump domestic sewage and industrial wastes into the Mediterranean. Indeed, the siting of power stations and heavy industry on the coastlines to take advantage of cost-free disposal has been a strong feature of postwar industrialization.

However, the intrusions of industry are as nothing compared with the impact of the tourist trade. In 1960, the number of visitors to the more developed countries was about 22 million. By 1973, it had all but reached 66 million, a trebling in little more than a decade. The other Mediterranean countries shared a rise from just under two to just over six million. For this inundation hotels and facilities were flung up all too often with minimum care and primitive sanitation. Collapsing hotel terraces and hepatitis on the beach are part of the price that has been paid.

The price to the sea itself may well be even more dangerous. The marine ecosystem exercises its function of cleaning up dirt by a chain of minute actions in which bacteria break down the wastes' organic compounds and put them back into the food chain. The little creatures need oxygen if they are to carry on their work. So, as we have noted, a usual measurement of the effects of waterborne waste is the amount of oxygen required to decompose it—the so-called biochemical oxygen demand (or BOD for short). The major polluters of the Mediterranean—Spain, France, Italy, Greece, and Turkey—dump into the sea industrial and municipal wastes which now require two million BOD units every year to decompose them. By way of comparison, Malta, Cyprus, Syria, Lebanon, and Israel together require only 87,350 units. In fact, the 27 million more developed peoples with their tourists and their cities and their industries are producing effluents equal to the wastes of 88 million humans and this is before all the other Mediterranean shore-dwellers have really got into the modernizing act.

Moreover, the sea they thus misuse is also hit by passing vessels. In addition to the oil refineries' share—about 20,000 tons of hydrocarbon wastes every year—oil tankers use so-called free zones to void their tanks and add another 300,000 tons of oil to the sea. Incidentally, this practice was outlawed in an agreement reached by the International Maritime Cooperative Organization (IMCO) in 1973. However, it has still, unhappily, to be ratified. Meanwhile the voiding continues. Loading and unloading at ports increases the pollution. Accidental spills can increase it again and offshore drilling, with all its potential accidents, is proposed for the future. One should also recall that surface oil spills of an intense, localized kind are particularly dangerous for the sea's small life—the phytoplankton which use photosynthesis to put oxygen back into the atmosphere, the bacteria which do the decomposing, the smallest, humblest servants of man smothered in oil for their pains.

All this raises the question whether, if present misuse continues, the sea's oxygen supply can be renewed. It is quite a lively sea. All its water is regenerated from the Atlantic every eighty years and the chill winds blowing down from the Alps make surface waters cold enough to plunge down and renew their oxygen in the sea's depths. But in areas around the coasts of Italy, where population has grown over six times more rapidly than in the interior and often without benefit of treatment plants, there are sections of the sea that are tending to lose their oxygen and a number of waterborne diseases—typhoid, hepatitis, even cholera—have surfaced in the last decade. The storm warnings are flying. Another twenty years of such treatment and the Mediterranean could lose all its oxygen, all its fish, all its organic life, and turn into a smelling swamp.

Clearly, no one country can reverse the risk. Even if Italy—at present, the worst offender—were to mend its ways, the sea could still deteriorate if Egypt, Tunisia, Algeria, and Morocco all plunged forward with the same kind of pollution. The only answer is a coalition of concerned nations and an agreed strategy for action in their settlements and in their industries—and indeed in their farm systems with the run-off of fertilizer—binding on them all.

Happily such a coalition is at least in sight. The governments have met. Under the aegis of the United Nations Environment Program they have agreed to set up monitoring posts and research stations. Much more careful measurement of pollution will be possible in the future and hence a more reliable diagnosis of where the offenses are being committed. At the same time, new maritime regulations could soon begin to control the voiding of passing oil tankers and one of the beneficent uses of sky satellites is to make sure that no vessel can now do a bit of voiding on the side in the hope of avoiding detection. For once, Big Brother watching is a blessing, not a curse.

But perhaps the most hopeful factor for a possibly effective Mediterranean coalition lies in the discovery that proper recycling of urban and industrial wastes can become an increasingly profitable business. The old plea—that the needed facilities were beyond the nation's purse or that to install them will expose it to the competition of more unsanitary neighbors—loses all validity when the treatment plants in fact turn in a profit. This fact, too, will permit the imposition of reasonably uniform standards. Otherwise, "sweating the environment," in this case the Mediterranean, becomes a very attractive option for poor developing countries who see no reason to burden their development with environmental costs the richer nations never had to pay. All in all, a certain modest optimism can be aroused by the Mediterranean prospect. Governments are, after all, not quite so incapable of constructive action, so unable to see beyond the next election as restless voters sometimes feel them to be.

It is difficult to feel the same confidence in the much larger and more critical area of man's increasing use of the world's oceans. We cannot leave them out of our consideration of the future of human settlements. Seventeen of the world's twenty-five largest cities are seaports. Water carries the bulk of the world's trade. Climate is largely determined by the watery seventy percent of our planet. Seventy percent of our oxygen comes from the oceans. All our wastes end there.

Above all, the oceans look like being the scene of the next great extension in the activities of urban, technological man. The manner in which this is done could even determine his survival.

We should understand what is happening. Land-based man, in his land-based settlements, could be on the point of "reinvading" the oceans from which life originally emerged. This invasion covers and intensifies every one of the old uses of the ocean—for transport, as a source of wealth, as an area for fixed installations (piers, lighthouses), for recreation, and, last and most formidably, as the ultimate dump of all human wastes. Every one of these activities is now taking a quantum leap forward, with entirely unpredictable results for man's settled life.

As recently as 1948, no cargo ship was larger than 26,000 deadweight tons. Now there are several tankers afloat nearing the 500,000 DWT mark (there is a million-ton tanker on the drawing board). Yet if one of these monsters collided and broke up, say twenty miles offshore, the damage could cost $3 thousand million (the equivalent of over a year's investment in clean water for poorer countries).

The catch from deep sea fishing increased, between 1950 and 1970, from 20 to 70 million metric tons. The equivalent of giant vacuum cleaners suck in shoals, located by sonar and helicopters, taking in young and old together and as a result risking the exhaustion of whole species. Japanese capitalists and Russian communists can reduce a whale on their factory ships from carcass to fat in half an hour. Since 1970, the overall fish catch has fallen. We have been warned. Happily, the Japanese have now announced their readiness to accept new quotas on whale fishing and the Russians are expected to follow suit. These quotas are fixed by geographical region and may get around overfishing in the waters of nonsignatory states. So perhaps we have been warned in time.

To this older exploitation we must now add deep-sea oil drilling and mining. By the year 2000, half the world's oil—some 35 thousand million barrels—may be coming from the sea, sometimes from depths of 5,000 meters, far beyond the continental shelves. This expansion may be accompanied by quite new methods of mining. We should recall the deep seabed resources of manganese nodules mixed with cobalt, nickel, and tungsten which, according to one World Bank estimate, could provide 400 million tons of ore a year *ad infinitum*.

All these activities are inevitably spreading man's settled activities out into the oceans. There are large underwater oil tanks in the Arabian Gulf and off Norway. A fourteen-mile oil pipe joins deep-water operations with the Nigerian Coast. Ships sailing in the Gulf of Mexico have to thread their way through oil rigs and platforms. The North Sea is going the same way. In the inventors' dreams are plans for mineral conversion plants in deep ocean with giant generators using atomic power to benificate ocean bed ore on the spot or produce hydrogen from salt water, all of the products ready for transshipment. No doubt, these installations will be surrounded by semipermanent homes for a growing number of workers. Building on the seas may also follow any further explosion of tourism. With all the world's beaches surrounded by wall-to-wall hotels (and most of the water polluted) what could a tour director think more desirable than a mid-ocean center complete with the Atlantis Hilton and every kind of aquatic sport?

And all this must add immeasurably to ocean wastes. Already we are quite ignorant of the cumulative effect of what we do now. Some scientists estimate the pollution of oil alone (including run-off from land-based motor traffic) at 100 million tons a year. Add DDT, plastic, heavy metals, radioactive wastes, raw sewage from coastal magalopolises growing by four to eight percent a year and it is not surprising that Thor Heyerdahl found an almost uninterrupted scum of filth right across the Southern Atlantic and the U.S. National Oceanographic and Atmospheric Administration reckons that from America's Eastern seaboard pollution, together with oil spills from passing tankers, has contaminated one million square miles of the North Atlantic as far south as the Yucatan Peninsula.

Of all these wastes it need hardly be said that the most potentially lethal are radioactive. Future plans may include a shuttle service of ships carrying waste nuclear fuel for reprocessing in regional centers. And if plans go forward to build nuclear reactors at sea—for cooling and to move them away from centers of population—it should be remembered that a 1,000-megawatt installation has an annual output of plutonium equivalent to a twenty-three-megaton bomb and we have no idea of what the spread effects of any accident would be amid the totally uncontrollable flows and movements of ocean tides.

If man is, as it were, to "occupy" the oceans, to turn them into extensions of his land-based activities—and it is hard to interpret the signs in any other way—he is embarking on a planetary sphere where everything interconnects with everything else in wholly unprecedented ways. As we have seen, the oceans largely determine climate and provide vast supplies of oxygen from vulnerable surface phytoplankton. If oil spills occur in Arctic waters, they are so long lasting that they may stain the base of the ice pack. As upper levels melt and the black ice rises, there is speculation whether the change might not change the whole balance of the sun's radiation. And, quite apart from these side effects, the oceans themselves are natural ecosystems and as such subject to the risk of degeneration. Given that they contain 1,349,929 million cubic kilometers of water, it may seem a bit stupid to worry about their ability to carry on. The trouble is, given the quantum jump proposed in man's activities on the oceans, we have no idea when a threshold of disaster may be reached. It could be the disappearance of a fish species. It could be a finally fouled ocean surface. It could be, especially in tropical waters, an irreversible accumulation of pathogens and poisons. And if the cradle of life itself is shattered, what happens to life?

These are pleas not for panic but for care. The worry is how little care seems available. It is true that IMCO (the international organization which deals with pollutions from ships) has declared the target of cleaning the oceans of oil pollution by the 1980s. There is a convention—not ratified, of course—on the Maritime Carriage of Nuclear Materials. But two sessions of the United Nations Law of the Sea Conference have produced little beyond a consensus to extend sovereign national rights to economic zones running 200 miles from the shore and the likelihood of a "free-for-all" struggle for resources everywhere else. Even if an authority were established to oversee the remaining oceans, it would probably have no more power than to license deep-sea mining on the basis of "first come, first served"—in other words, for countries and corporations rich enough and technologically adept enough to start at once—and just possibly diminish the export earnings of poor countries with land-based minerals such as copper or manganese. One dream—that this potentially vast wealth might be reserved for the poorest nations—seems to have faded amid the so-called realism of the negotiating sessions. Nor do the prospects look too hopeful for avoiding the extension, *via* cod wars and oil-drilling disputes, of man's millennial struggles for jurisdiction of the planet's watery sphere.

Once again, it is clear that only purposive cooperative action can prevent further extensions of competitive anarchy. Common rules for environmental protection and the protection of species must be maintained within 200-mile zones for, although the pretensions to sovereignty may remain static, the oceans will not and one nation's discard will roll on to become filth on another nation's shores. And beyond the 200-mile limit, a seabed authority, reserving deep-ocean resources for the poorest (and often landlocked countries) would at least make some contribution to redressing the world's deepening skew of wealth and poverty. Once again, the answers are the same—to create a community or risk losing a planet. In the nuclear age, it is, alas, no small thing to widen by all the breadth of the oceans the possibilities of escalating conflict. Having fought ourselves to the brink of Armageddon on land, are we now preparing for "the final solution" on the seas as well?

EPILOGUE

So, at the end of this long journey, where does the verdict stand—between hope and despair, between the technical fixers and the certain doom, between continuing détente or an ugly renewal of confrontation? It is hard to say. Our familiar trinity of power—the nation-state, the industrial economy, modern science reaching out to the limits of space and time—still fight their "mornings war" between constructive and destructive acts, still leave us with the possibility that arrogant nationalism linked to unslackened greed and powered by nuclear tools (for peace or war) could "fuse" in an explosion of destructiveness sufficient to bring to an end all man's settlements and all man's life within them. If the "doomsayers" point to such a risk, it is impossible simply to dismiss it. The Promethean fire has been stolen from the sun. We do not know whether the curse must follow.

But if we look at all the stirrings and changes at work in this last quarter of the twentieth century—of which only a minute proportion have been chronicled in this report—it is difficult to be a totally gloomy philosopher. Some of Dr. Johnson's cheerfulness will keep breaking in. In whichever of the three contexts of the human habitat that we have examined—the intended city, the just city, the healthy and beautiful city—the central point for hope is that virtually all the new ideas and experiments do *not* reflect the old national arrogance, the old greed, the old overconfidence in the "techno-fix." Mankind is always Janus-headed, turning to the past and the future. It just happens that today the face that looks to the future has a more human look.

The nation-state's pretensions are no longer taken for granted. Even if, at the highest level, world peace is maintained by the shifting equipoise of three major states, it is not a hopeless pattern. The empires of Rome, Persia, and China gave the civilized world a relatively long period of stability as the first millennium of the modern world began. This pause may give us time to look for more fundamental answers to the problems of order and law on our small and vulnerable planet. Beneath the patterns of power, a perception of the need to cooperate with neighboring states has brought into being the world's first network of truly international consultative bodies and the first modest examples of due process and an impartial police. The blue berets of the United Nations in Cyprus and Sinai may look as insignificant as the first protozoa within the vastness of the empty oceans. But nevertheless the secret of future life lies with them.

In the world's economic order, the old blind dependence upon market forces—and how violent the force could be!—is now somewhat modified by the readiness to consult and bargain and to admit that it is an international responsibility to care for the poorest first, and to take action to put an end to global risks of starvation. This was not the dialogue of 1914 or 1939. It is at least worth considering the possibility that what the market chiefly needs to correct its wayward energies—some concept of the general welfare—is beginning to enter the world's dialogue. In much the same way, the readiness of governments to discuss not the niceties of protocol or the defense of particular interests but the central issues of man's life on earth—the environment, population, food, employment, shelter (with water and energy to come?)—marks a consciousness of interdependence and of an inescapable intermixture of planetary needs and interests that, quite simply, has never existed before.

Perhaps we have not sufficiently remarked this dialogue, which adds an entirely new dimension to the political activity of mankind. In the Seventies, almost without being aware of it, the whole human family has started to discuss the humble necessary foundations of its daily life. The various international conferences may seem vast and unwieldy. There is a wariness of committees and a surfeit of rhetoric. But what is actually being discussed is the threatening growth in the world's numbers, the grain to feed them, the safe water to restore their health, work to end hopeless unemployment, the skews in income that are bitter with injustice, the energy—the safe energy—to carry on the whole human experiment. Never before has the world's housekeeping been thus discussed, and there is at least a chance that for each conference with all its preparations and explorations and with, it may be hoped, a rigorous mood to demand resulting action, the world can move from talking about its problems to beginning the forms of joint work and action which, in the long run, offer the only way of bringing into a single planetary community all the tribes and races and nations and ideologies, all the hopes and fears and energies of this fantastic human breed.

It is in this context that the discussion of human settlements, by bringing together all the dilemmas in their fateful and inevitable interconnectedness, can become not an instrument of confusion but of genuine learning and light. The United Nations Conference on Human Settlements—Habitat—taking place in Vancouver in 1976 is only a start. What is needed is some permanent instruments, not—heaven help us!—to undertake all the tasks in settlements but to keep men's minds alive to their urgency and interconnection. At the world level, a permanent Settlements Secretariat—directly under the Economic and Social Council or under the Governing Council of the United Nations Environment Program—could provide the focus of vision and innovation. At regional levels, perhaps linked to the U.N. Regional Commissions, task forces drawing on local expertise could help the governments themselves make the connections, learn from each other, and each contribute its experiences and successes to the common knowledge of the region and of the world community. Everything comes together in settlements. That is why they are the prime examples and signals for a world in which nothing any longer can be held apart.

The various bodies could also be insistent guides and goads to the needed range of international strategies in the decades ahead. A sustained determination to end hunger in the next ten years, a committed plan to provide every human being with clean water by the mid-Eighties, a strategy for decent shelter for every family as the new century dawns—none of these great hopes can be said to be beyond the means of humanity, and it is only by engaging ourselves actively, honorably, hopefully and *together* in the works of peace that we can learn, men and women alike, the nature of détente and coexistence, turn it from empty rhetoric into a positive search for community and begin to dispel the darkness of the nuclear shadow.

Within societies, too, the ideas that are genuinely new seem to break with some of the old and dangerous certainties. The concept of a purposive ordering of settlements, with the unearned benefits accruing to the community, is no longer the *avant-garde* idea of a few innovators. It is the settled practice of some of the oldest and most cultivated communities. A few conservatives in market economics may hanker for the deflating "disciplines" of the nineteenth-century economy. They would not last six months in office if they tried them out. The new ideas—of a more explicit sharing and partnership in the creation of national wealth and of new definitions of what true and less consumptive wealth can mean—are beginning to take shape. And they in turn are being given a jet-propelled development by such evidence of the effects of a possible future shortage as the quintupling of oil prices and the trebling of the price of grain.

Only a decade ago the voices urging conservation and careful use could hardly be heard above the gabble of market advertising or communist promises "to bury" capitalism under a larger load of wealth. Now they are central, listened to and respected. Looking back, we can even wonder what it was like to live in the early Sixties with all those unlimited bonanzas spreading ahead. Today we are in an altogether more serious world in which, even if prudence, thrift, and respect for life have not won all their battles, they are at least back in the lists and it is the advocates of unlimited consumption and careless growth who wear a defensive look.

And here, perhaps, we have the clue to what may well be the most critical change of all. In this time of reassessment, in this age of questioning as intense as any since the great debates of the millennium before the Birth of Christ, there is promise of an extraordinary and almost wholly unforeseen fusion of ideas which, separated and even hostile for many centuries, now seem capable of that mutual interpenetration which, in the nuclear as in the intellectual world, can release floods of new energy, new directions, new possibilities, new beings, new forms.

At the heart of the change is the new vision of reality which science has opened up to mankind in the last century. It is a bewildering balance of infinite power and infinite fragility. Our forefathers were perhaps more conscious of the power—of mathematics putting into man's hands the tool of mechanics, of the new ability to carve up and measure nature's continum the better to set it to work, of new forms of energy making possible the prodigies of the steam engine and the steel works, of control and plenty waiting to be wrested from the planet by those who were bold enough to invent and command and lead. Four centuries of a sense of increasingly intoxicating mastery lay behind the final unleashing of ultimate power in the nucleus of the atom. They were heady days of deepening confidence in human capacity and even arrogance about the certainty that "benefit" and "use" would be the result.

But all the while, other perceptions were beginning to gather strength. One was of the total interdependence of the natural systems men were trying to dominate. However much "discrete particulars" could be isolated for study and manipulation, they were still inextricably part of a wider context. Science began to recognize the connectedness by fusing fields of study—astrophysics, biochemistry, microbiology. This body of knowledge not of things in their separateness but in their inescapable interconnections has come increasingly to underlie the new insights of the environmental movement. The old images of power and use have left behind them mountains of waste, poisoned rivers, smog-ridden cities, unsanitary dumps, and polluted beaches. The new insight is that nothing is ever "used." It simply changes form and, without care and knowledge, that form can be pollutive and dangerous to life itself. Even fifteen years ago, this sense of nature's continuum was felt, in the main, by scientists in the relevant disciplines. Now it is beginning to be a new and general way of looking at the whole of man's settled, organized existence.

It is reinforced by another set of scientific insights. As scientists have pieced together the astonishing history of our cosmos—with the original explosion of hydrogen plasma accurately timed only in 1974 (some 10,000 million years after the event), what has emerged is the extraordinary delicacy and fragility of the systems through which organic life has been sustained on earth. Phytoplankton releasing oxygen, photosynthesis building up the planet's atmospheric shield, the billions of neurons in the human brain, the infinitely small structures of DNA, the double helix through which all the instructions are given to the cells of organic life—these mysteries of smallness are the gifts of science in the twentieth century. They emphasize not so much the vast and terrifying capacities of nature as the eggshell delicacy of the instruments which alone make the energies usable and safe. So here again the lesson for man is not selfish overconfidence and arrogance but the sense of interdependence and the need for most sober care.

As a result, scientists who were once the prophets of mastery and progress have tended in the postwar world to become more and more concerned with the consequences of mastery and progress. Some of the greatest among them rebut all myths of automatic advance and trouble-free "scenarios" and plead on the contrary for the utmost responsibility and concern in the use of the tools their knowledge has placed in human hands. It is almost as though we were seeing repeated in the language of exact experimental knowledge the conclusions which sages and philosophers drew from their historical experience of human behavior in the great reassessments of the first millennium B.C. Then and now, we are warned against the arrogant misuse of power. Then and now, we are reminded that to demand too much of our existence, whether in consumption or in power, risks the destruction of its physical and moral base. The old philosophers and the new scientists—for so long divided by the supposed incompatibility of man's ethical and religious traditions and the glorious new possibilities of human, rational, and material progress on earth—are beginning to speak the same language, plead for the same modesty and concern, warn of the moral dangers of overweening confidence, and ask for its opposite—respect for living things, especially the smallest, and cooperation, not exploitation, as the pattern of existence. Thus, to insure the survival of life itself, they advocate dedication to the constructive ways of joint work and common understanding and an equal rejection of blind assertion, whether of the community or of the self.

And it is just possible that this fusion of new knowledge and ancient wisdom could release a more potent explosion of moral energy than any earlier attempt to convert humanity from the false gods of greed and power. It is much easier to overlook words of wisdom, however eloquent, than to override the solid, incontrovertible evidence of material reality. What the sages once said is now what the nature of the planet exposes. Its fragile mechanisms cannot stand too much pressure. Violent misuse of its life-support system—in the great cities, in the fields and farms—destroys the life of rivers and soils and undermines the integrity of human existence. Violent consumption of its resources will leave nothing to consume. Above all, the resort to man's most destructive civic invention, war between the nations, will leave the whole city of man in the plight of his first demolished city, and it is for the planet itself that the cry of lament for Ur will be repeated:

> O my city which exists no longer,
> my city attacked without cause
> O my city attacked and destroyed

These overwhelming facts, if they are grasped in time, may give power and life to the new directions of our existence. If fear is the beginning of wisdom, then even the most fanatical ideologues or bloodthirsty nation-firsters may reflect that neither they, their cause, nor their enemies will survive the anihilation of an all-out nuclear conflict. And from this negative wisdom could grow the positive understanding that the risk of war, the ultimate risk to settlements, can be offset only by embarking, patiently, unswervingly, devotedly on the concrete and cooperative tasks of peace.

We cannot defeat something by nothing. Once it was said: "If you wish for peace, prepare for war." Now the aphorism is reversed: "If you wish to avoid war, you must *work* for peace." We have at least reached the point of talking together about the great common tasks of humanity—preserving our living environment, feeding the hungry, giving shelter to all our fellow creatures, treating with greater care and fraternal sharing the fundamental resources—of water, of minerals, of energy, upon which our common life depends. This dialogue could be the signal of a new but growing loyalty, not to our old divisive nationalisms but to shared tasks and common membership in the City of Man.

Too vast a dream? Too naive a hope? Perhaps—yet we can now talk to the ends of the earth as easily as villagers once conversed with each other. Our planetary interdependence is as great as that of earlier states. Our knowledge is world-wide. Our airs and oceans are equally shared. So are all the preconditions of material existence. If man has learned to be loyal to his nation as well as to his family and his town, do we have to argue that no further extension of loyalty is possible—to the planet itself which carriers our earthly life and all the means of sustaining it?

This is perhaps the ultimate implication of the underlying unity of scientific law first discerned by the Greeks, of the underlying law of moral brotherhood and obligation most passionately proclaimed by the Hebrew prophets. Today they come together in a new fusion of vision and energy to remind us of our inescapable unity even as we stand on the very verge of potential annihilation. The scientist and the sage, the man of learning and the poet, the mathematician and the saint repeat to the human city the same plea and the same warning: "We must love each other or we must die."

INDEX